Ancient Feet

Ancient Feet

Alan Nolan

Matador
9 De Montfort Mews
Leicester LE1 7FW, UK
Tel: (+44) 116 255 9311 / 9312
Email: books@troubador.co.uk
Web: www.troubador.co.uk/matador

ISBN 978-1906510-978

A Cataloguing-in-Publication (CIP) catalogue record for this book
is available from the British Library.

Mixed Sources
Product group from well-managed
forests and other controlled sources
www.fsc.org Cert no. TT-COC-2082
© 1996 Forest Stewardship Council

Typeset in 11pt Stempel Garamond by Troubador Publishing Ltd, Leicester, UK
Printed by The Cromwell Press Ltd, Trowbridge, Wilts, UK

Matador is an imprint of Troubador Publishing

And did those feet in ancient time
Walk upon England's mountains green
Jill Daniels

CONTENTS

CHAPTER ONE

BRING ME MY ARROWS OF DESIRE

'This will be the tenth time that I've done it, and it will definitely be the last,' said Tom.

'What does Pam have to say about that?' asked Andy.

'She's very happy with it. She thinks ten times is enough for any man.'

'Well, I've only done it once and I did it the other way round but I thoroughly enjoyed it, so I think you should try it that way before you pack it in altogether,' chipped in Don. Tom ignored him.

'Well, an old fogey like you couldn't manage it again either way round,' Andy muttered, trying to goad Tom into a reply.

As for me, I had never had any desire to do it even once, never mind ten times. Okay, I had always enjoyed fell-walking, but the idea of trekking almost two hundred miles across the country, in all weathers, and staying who knows where had never appealed to me. Not that I had given it much thought. I didn't need to. Give me a comfortable hotel bedroom with a nice en-suite bathroom, and I'll walk all day – as long as the weather's fine. So what was I doing here with these five elderly nutters, about to set out on the Coast to Coast Walk?

I had made an early start for the hour's drive from my home in North Staffordshire to Tom's house just outside Macclesfield in the beautiful countryside bordering the Peak District, looking forward to our great adventure with some trepidation. It was not yet seven o'clock as I walked through the door, but the others were already there.

'Hi, Andy,' I greeted the burly figure lounging at the kitchen table, 'long time, no see.'

'Hi, Al. I see you decided against the anti-ageing pills then?'

'Yes, I didn't want to have to carry my birth certificate around to prove I'm old enough to buy alcohol and drive a car, but it's obvious you haven't stopped taking the obnoxious pills.'

It must have been a couple of years since I had last seen Andy, but here we were exchanging insults as though we'd never been apart and I relaxed a little on the realisation that we were going to have a great couple of weeks, whether we completed our demanding escapade or not.

Don welcomed me with his usual firm handshake and broad smile, his eyes twinkling as always. Since his move from Essex to Norfolk a few years ago, he had been faced with an even longer drive to Tom's than me and, as he looked so fresh, I assumed he had driven over the previous day and spent the night at Tom's. Tall and slim, the grey beard enhancing the permanent sparkle in his eye, it is hard to believe that he can behave like the archetypal inventor, apparently living in his own world, oblivious to what is happening around him.

'Why didn't you call in and see us on your way to London, Tom?' he would ask.

'Because Norfolk is not on the way to London from Cheshire.'

'You could have called in on the way back.'

'Surprising as this may be to you, Don, but Norfolk is not on the way back to Cheshire from London either.'

'Well, perhaps you can call in next time,' he would say, as though arrangements were in hand to move Norfolk across the country.

Tom was busying himself with last minute preparations for our trip and barely had time to acknowledge my arrival, but I knew that he was preoccupied with ensuring that nothing was left to chance. For someone who seems to have a carefree attitude to life, he goes to great lengths to make sure everything goes smoothly and that everyone around him feels comfortable. Not that he could ever succeed with Andy, who seems to believe that his role in life is to needle everyone and Tom bears the brunt of his moans.

'I thought you said Trevor would be here with the minibus at seven. I could have had a lie-in,' he grumbled. As always, Tom ignored him. They had been pals for years and Tom loved the banter.

Paul greeted me with nothing more than a smile. He is the quiet one who is always on hand when you need him. He lives in the village just down the road from Tom's, so he had not had far to come. He is also a big pal of Andy's who had lived in the same village for many years until he moved the few miles to Glossop two or three years ago, where he had met the sixth and final member of our party, Joe, and they had become firm friends.

Trevor duly arrived and we piled into the minibus for the drive up to St Bees on the Cumbrian coast for the start of the Coast to Coast Walk. This would be Tom's tenth (and final) Coast to Coast Walk. He had done it for the ninth time in 2000 and his plan then was to do the walk again the following year for his final time at the age of sixty-five, when his intention was to invite all his companions from the previous nine walks to prove their endurance once again. The plan had been aborted because of the outbreak of foot and mouth disease in 2001 which closed most of the footpaths, and the idea of a tenth walk had been forgotten. Forgotten, that is, until one night in the pub when alcohol-induced bravado had prompted him to claim that nothing would stop him from completing the Coast to Coast Walk one more, definitely final, time. By next morning, he was regretting his stupidity but knew that he could not retract his declaration of intent if he wanted to retain any credibility. Over the next few months, he managed to enlist five companions to do the walk with him again. Strangely, of his previous Coast to Coast companions, only Andy had accepted Tom's invitation to go through the pain barrier one more time. I wonder why?

The pub seems to be the cause of a great many commitments in Tom's life although, more correctly, I think it is probably what the pub sells that is responsible for the repeated excursions between the Irish and North Seas. After a few pints, when bragging is at its most robust, he cannot resist recounting his experiences and falls into the trap of boasting about his stamina (usually hoping to impress any young ladies who may be listening) and utters the fateful words:

'Well, when I was doing the Coast to Coast Walk .....'

'Have you done the Coast to Coast? I want to do that,' someone equally uninhibited (a euphemism for stupidly drunk) interjects. Next morning, Tom wakes up and tries to recall at least some of the previous night's events, struggling to differentiate between his drunken dreams and what actually took place.

'Please tell me I didn't promise to do the Coast to Coast with someone this summer,' he groans.

'You enlisted half the pub and insisted that everyone sign their names as a commitment, so they can't back out,' says Pam, with a pitying sneer.

'Oh no. Where's the list?'

'I didn't say there's a list; I said you got them to sign.'

'All right; don't be so bloody pedantic. Where did they sign?' he asks, wondering why she seems to be so angry, when it isn't her who is going to have to think of an excuse.

'On the back of that new shirt I bought you last week.'

Sometimes, his boastful prospective companions come to their senses and find that 'work commitments' will not allow them to honour their pledge, although 'we'll do it next year' is their more usual way of avoiding the issue. Tom responds with a whispered 'thank God for that.' On this particular occasion, there was no backing out. Pam would be away with friends and he had thought it was an opportunity to complete his tenth (and did I say final?) trip.

I was in the bath when Tom phoned to ask whether I would join his party of intrepid walkers later in the year and my acceptance put me in Suzanne's bad books on two counts. She was out at the time but had told me that she was expecting an important call and that I must make a note of the phone number so that she could call back.

'Make sure you write it down; you know what your memory's like. You forget anything that happened more than two minutes ago', which I thought was an unwarranted slur on my message taking ability. I had been in the bath only a couple of minutes when the phone rang and I congratulated myself on having the foresight to take the phone in the bathroom with me. Suzy could not fail to be impressed with my efficiency.

'Suzanne's out but, if you give me your number, she'll phone you back when she comes in,' I said in my most competent telephone voice, 'oh shit, hold on a minute, I need a pen and paper!' Suddenly, I was in serious trouble again but, fortunately, the ingenuity of the mature male ensured that a satisfactory solution was at my fingertips. I could scratch the number on the bar of soap using the bottom of the toothpaste tube as the pen. Brilliant!

No sooner had I put the phone down than it rang again and it was Tom trying to enlist me for the Coast to Coast Walk. The dates he was talking about were just a couple of weeks after my sixtieth birthday and I had been wondering what I could do to celebrate the great event. I have to admit that the Coast to Coast Walk had not occurred to me but, what the heck, this was my opportunity to prove that there is life in the old dog yet. On my fiftieth birthday, I had walked up England's highest peak, Scafell Pike, and had promised myself that I would do it again on my sixtieth but, somehow, the intervening years had made me more, rather than less, ambitious and I was looking for something far more challenging. Indeed, I had been considering entering a team to take part in the 24 Peaks Challenge, a charity event organised by Care International, but had been having a little difficulty in recruiting a team, so the Coast to Coast would be a challenging alternative, despite the major drawbacks of having to carry on my back all my equipment for twelve days walking, and not having the comfort of a hotel bedroom at the end of each day. It must have been the relaxation brought on by the bath that lowered my defences and I allowed Tom to persuade me to join his Coast to Coast troop. At the time, he was anticipating about ten members in his indomitable band, but the numbers dwindled in the months leading up to the event itself. Having agreed to do the walk, I found that I was pleased I had something to look forward to and, preoccupied with thoughts of the twelve day walking challenge, I soaped myself down and completed my bathing experience just in time to hear Suzy return. Mustn't forget to give her that number. See, the memory isn't that bad at all.

'What do you mean, you wrote the number on the soap and then forgot and used the soap and washed it off? What sort of an excuse is that? And how could you agree to doing the Coast to Coast Walk in September; isn't that when you're planning to do that ridiculous 24 Peaks Challenge thing? The dementia is getting worse. How on earth you manage to run a business, I'll never know. And I suppose you expect me to cope with three dogs and running the house on my own for twelve days while you're off playing with your mates, do you?'

I excused her petulant comments on the grounds that she is at a funny age. She would not be able to understand my need to prove to myself that I am still capable of taking on new challenges. She was right though, about the 24 Peaks Challenge that is. This is a charity challenge, involving climbing 24 peaks above 24 hundred feet in 24 hours. Set in the Lake District, the event was scheduled for the Saturday and Sunday immediately following Tom's proposed Friday start for the Coast to Coast Walk. However, in view of the problems in getting a team together, I decided I would leave that until next year (or perhaps the year after that) as I would need to concentrate on preparing myself for twelve consecutive days of tough walking on the Coast to Coast. Although I had always enjoyed walking, I had never done anything like this before. Walking sixteen or seventeen miles a day for twelve days without a break sounded hard going. No problem though. After all, I had always kept reasonably fit. Mind you, none of that poncing about at the gym stuff. And none of that fitness training bollocks either. Taking the dogs for a walk most days and the occasional walking break in the Lake District had kept me unusually trim for a man of my age. My announcement that I would be retiring the following year had elicited many flattering comments from clients, who could not believe that I would want to retire at such a young age.

'Well, I will be nearly sixty-one by that time,' I pointed out.

'Oh, but you don't look it. I would have put you at no more than fifty-nine.'

'Thanks very much, but I *am* only fifty-nine *now*.'

The decision to retire had prompted me to look back at my life and I found it hard to believe that I had worked for other people for about twenty years before starting my own business as an Independent Financial Adviser. I was not suited to being an employee, so becoming my own boss was inevitable really and I ran the business on my own for fifteen years before taking on a couple of partners six years earlier. I had no definite plans about retirement at the time, but knew that I needed to provide an escape route for when the time came and the partnership put that in place. Oddly, the provision of the escape route pushed me towards retirement earlier than I would have anticipated. It's funny how things work out. Having built up a business over twenty-one years, it would be strange to give it all up, particularly as I knew my partners would want to make significant changes and I would be forgotten in no time at all. Nevertheless, I was looking forward to being released from the responsibility of being in my office by eight every morning, and to having the freedom to do different things. The one drawback was that I would miss my clients, many of whom I had come to regard as personal friends. That apart, I knew that I would be able to walk away without looking back.

Although I would not be retiring until the following year, I did not want to wait until then before launching myself into new projects so, when I read about the Care Three Peaks Cumbria Challenge, I just had to find out more. Care's website explained that this was a challenge to climb three of the highest peaks in the Lake District in under twelve hours, which included an allowance of one and a half hours driving time. Teams had to commit to raising at least £2,500 for Care International UK. Apart from the fundraising, I thought that sounded a reasonable challenge for a fit, youngish sort of bloke but then I spotted something far more interesting. The website showed that Care also organise the 24 Peaks Challenge which entails conquering 24 peaks above 2,400 feet in 24 hours (with no provision for driving time). Now that sounded more like a real challenge for someone with something to prove! There was just one little doubt, niggling away at the back of my mind. Something I couldn't talk to anyone about. Only a few weeks earlier, one of my clients had phoned and told me he had just come out of hospital after a quadruple heart by-pass operation. Stifling the urge to say I hadn't realised he had four hearts to by-pass, I encouraged him as well as I could, telling him that several of my clients had undergone similar operations and made a full recovery. As soon as I put down the phone, I checked his file and, to my horror, found that he was fifty-nine. The same age as me. Over the last couple of years, three other clients had either had heart attacks or by-pass operations (or both) and they were all fifty-nine at the time. It was obvious to me that a faulty batch of hearts had been issued, the lifetime guarantee being valid for only fifty-nine years. Hopefully, I was not one of the unlucky ones and, if I could just get through the next few months without mishap, I would be able to celebrate my sixtieth in style. Twenty-four hours of climbing up and down mountains would be ideal. The event was scheduled to take place just a couple of weeks after my birthday, so it seemed the ideal way to prove that reaching sixty does not mean that a man is past his best. It might knacker me for the rest of my life, but I could do it!

There were two problems. Firstly, the minimum fund raising requirement was £5,000 and, secondly, teams consist of four to seven people, so how to find enough mugs (sorry, like-minded people) to do it with me? Still, I didn't think that would be too much of a hurdle as I knew plenty of blokes who like to keep themselves fit and who would be just as eager to prove themselves as I was. I just needed to sift through all the possibles and invite those who I thought would be fit enough physically and who I thought would be able to raise at least £1,000 each. Also, it was important that I should ensure that everyone would be compatible, so I would not be inviting any whingers or any show-offs who might want to race ahead of the rest. I drew up a shortlist and planned what I would say to all those who did not make that list when they heard about it and complained that I had not invited them to be in my gang. With my list completed, I started phoning the elite squad. Bearing in mind that it was only March, I was surprised how many had already planned their holidays for September that year and how there seemed to be a spate of leg injuries (my friends were more stoic than I could have imagined as not one of them had brought their disabilities to my attention before then). I decided to spread the net to include the whingers and show-offs but still no luck, so I drew up a list of acquaintances who I knew had two legs and even started asking people in the pub whether they knew of anyone who could walk. It would have been easy to give up and forget the whole idea, but I was determined to achieve something to celebrate my sixtieth birthday. Mind you, my old pal Tom was as dependable as ever. When I phoned him, he volunteered immediately, even before I told him the full details. What a man! The only problem was that he volunteered to be the driver, to get us to the starting point on time and pick us up at the finish.

> *I got no team and it's breaking my heart*
> *But I've found a driver and that's a start*

Perhaps someone could make a song out of that!

By the time Tom phoned about the Coast to Coast, my team still consisted of me and one possible who had promised to take part if his hip replacement proved successful, but even Tom seemed to have forgotten his promise to drive. In the circumstances, I was happy to substitute the Coast to Coast for the 24 Peaks Challenge. Either way, Suzanne thought I was mad.

'What does Alan think about being sixty?' a friend asked, a day or two after the great day.

'I don't think he's noticed. He seems to believe all this guff about sixty being the new forty and, although there's no doubt that people are living longer and doing more adventurous things than previous generations, there is a limit. He's doing the Coast to Coast Walk in a couple of weeks and, whilst I'm sure there are plenty of sixty year olds who are capable of doing it, they must be a small minority, even in this day and age. All he seems concerned about is whether the others will be able to do it. I think he must feel a need to prove he's not completely past it. Mind you, the others are all as barking mad as he is. Tom, who's organised it, is sixty-nine would you believe? Mind you, he has done it nine times before, but I think he's forgotten that it's five years since he last did it and those five years will make a big difference at that age. I'll be surprised if they're not back after a couple of days.'

'It sounds a bit risky to me. Isn't this a bit out of character for Alan?'

'Well, you say that but, when he gets an idea in his mind, there's no stopping him. He doesn't seem to think about the consequences.'

'But he does come across as being quiet, doesn't he?'

'Quiet may be, but that's not because of any lack of confidence. And don't forget that he did set up his own business, which was a major risk at the time. He gave up a secure job with a company car, a subsidised mortgage and a pension of two thirds final salary at age sixty and he didn't have any clients and no promises of clients when he started. Come to think of it, he was thirty-nine at the time, so perhaps it's the approach of 'significant' birthdays that trigger these things.'

'You'd better watch out in twenty years time then!'

Suzanne may have been sceptical but at least my son in Italy was supportive of my efforts:

'I'll give £5,000 to charity myself if you manage to complete the course,' he said when I phoned. I didn't think he could afford it, but what a nice gesture!

As the minibus made its way up the M6, I tried to assess the fitness levels of my colleagues, wondering whether we were capable of achieving our ambition to walk the breadth of England. Although Tom had done it nine times before, he was now sixty-nine and, over the last year or two, had not been walking as frequently as in his younger days and had begun to have problems with his knees, so he could well struggle, I thought. Joe was a bit of a mystery. I had not met him before and all I knew was that he was a friend of Andy's and that he had been on a couple of expeditions with Andy, Paul and Tom in the last two years. As Paul and Andy are both strong walkers, I assumed he would be as fit as them, although I was surprised to see that he looked older than I had anticipated. Andy was the baby of the group at just fifty-one and I had assumed that Joe would be a similar age but, physically, he looked nearer Tom's age and did not give the impression of a man capable of completing a marathon walk across the country.

I had been amazed to learn that Paul was now sixty-one as I had always assumed he was younger than me, but he looked so fit that I had little doubt that he would have no trouble with twelve days walking, and he would have Andy to keep pace with him.

Don was a different matter. He is one of those people who is always coming up with some sort of madcap project that he cannot find anyone to undertake with him (well, who would want to do the Pennine Way by camel?). As a result, he never gets to fulfil his heroic adventures and I wondered what sort of shape he was in. I knew he had been travelling to America and Hong Kong on a regular basis in connection with work and would not have had much time for training and, after all, he was now sixty-two.

CHAPTER TWO

AMERICAN PIE AND PASTIES

'You know, I used to dream about being a roadie for The Spice Girls,' Trevor said, as we made rapid progress up the M6, 'and look at me now, my ambitions reduced to driving The Old Spice Boys to their final gig. Instead of having five gorgeous girls in the back of the van, I've got six old blokes, all past their sell-by date.'

'That's what I like about you, Trev,' I said 'you have a way of making people feel good. Anyway, even if we aren't quite as youthful as we used to be, I haven't noticed you clamouring to do the walk with us.'

'I'm too young to be an Old Spice Boy.'

'Too bloody lazy, more like,' Andy accused.

'I like the idea of The Old Spice Boys,' Tom piped up, 'I could be Sporty Spice. I used to play cricket for Liverpool Boys and the original Sporty Spice is from Liverpool.'

'Shorty Spice would be more appropriate,' I said 'seeing as you must have been off school the day the nurse came round with the height injections.'

'Hold on a minute, we are talking about Liverpool here,' Andy interrupted, 'it's more likely she was mugged and the serum was sold to the highest bidder. The HIGHEST bidder, get it?' We groaned at Andy's attempt at humour. Returning to the subject, I continued:

'As a financial adviser, I think I should be Dosh Spice,' to nods of approval.

'And Andy should definitely be Baby Spice,' Don added 'as he is so much younger than the rest of us.'

'Yeah, even though I am always being mistaken for his son,' quipped Tom.

'I can't think of any of us who would qualify as Scary Spice,' Don said.

'No, but you could be Hairy Spice,' Joe suggested, pointing at Don's beard.

'That leaves Joe and Paul and neither of you are Ginger, so we'll just have to think of something original.'

'Paul's easy,' said Tom 'he can be Sugar n' Spice, 'cos he's all things nice.'

'Trev, where d'you keep the sick bucket in here?' Andy asked, unable to resist the temptation to needle Tom. 'Anyway, I think Joe has to be Windy Spice.'

'Why Windy?' I asked.

'Haven't you noticed yet that he never stops farting?'

'Bugger off, Andy,' Joe intervened.

'It's true. And anyway, you should be proud of it. I don't know anyone else who can let Polly out of prison on command.' Turning to me, he continued, in serious vein 'he's very modest about it, and doesn't like to blow his own trumpet (except when he's competing, of course), but he actually won the All England Farting Championships a few years ago. His 'trump' card was his farted rendition of *Blowing in the Wind.*'

'Bugger off, Andy.'

St. Bees may be the ideal starting point for the Coast to Coast Walk, but it is the devil of a place to reach by road, particularly from the south. The Cumbrian Mountains form an effective barrier to travellers from the east, so it is necessary to skirt the mountains and approach from either the south or north. The northern route involves a further thirty-five miles on the M6, followed by about thirty miles on the A66 travelling west to Cockermouth, before turning south towards St. Bees. It seems odd to travel so far north only to have to drive south to the destination, but the roads are good and this is much the preferable route. Inevitably, Trevor chose the southern route which heads almost to Barrow-in-Furness before turning north, the road deteriorating the farther we travelled. A minibus is not the most comfortable mode of transport and the journey seemed interminable. I made a mental note to reduce Trevor's tip.

Even the short stop for breakfast along the way brought little relief from the tedium of being shaken about as the minibus bounced on the uneven road surface and slewed from side to side along the twisting highway. The one compensation was that, whilst the others were enjoying their full English breakfasts, I slipped to the pie shop next door to indulge in the secret training regime I had undertaken in preparation for the walk. Two Cornish pasties were much better for a serious athlete than bacon and eggs!

The long journey and the early start took its toll after a while and the banter subsided as we became lost in our own thoughts. Once again, I found myself wondering how we would all cope with the challenge ahead of us and whether there would be any personality clashes. Despite Andy's mission to irritate everybody to death, I knew that he was popular with all of us. His broad smile and ease with people draws them to him At fifty-one, he was the youngster of the group. Indeed, he was the only one under sixty. Tall and broad with a mop of fair hair, he has a winning way with the opposite sex, although a bachelor. Unfortunately, he suffers from both hypochondria and malapropitis:

'Trev, can't you drive more carefully, I've got a terrible pain in my neck,' he complained, massaging the area where his neck meets his shoulder, 'it's a stabbing pain, as though someone's sticking needles in my epitaph.'

'I think that should be called your effigy,' Paul corrected him in his quiet way.

'I don't know the medical term. It's just here between my shoulder and my neck.'

'Anyway, I thought you were concerned about blisters,' Paul added.

'Yeah, I am. I bought a new pair of boots for the walk and

tried them out on Kinder Scout last week and I've been struggling ever since.'

'No wonder everyone round Glossop calls you Andy Capp –
you're always suffering from one 'andicap or another,' said Joe, to
everyone's amusement.

> *A long long time ago*
> *I can still remember how that music used*
> *To make me smile*

'Oh, no,' we groaned, as Andy crooned. The original Don
McLean recording of American Pie ran to over eight and a half
minutes, but we knew Andy was quite capable of extending this to
an entire minibus journey to St Bees. It seems to be one of those
songs that doesn't have an ending, and it becomes more than a
little wearing after a while.

He spends some of his time helping out on a farm, which
gives him the look of a typical farmer – big, strong and with a
florid complexion. Whether it is this or his personality that makes
him attractive to women is a mystery to me, but he has a certain
confidence when in female company, which is a bonus when 'on
the pull'. On occasion, this self-confidence can be misplaced.
During a weekend in Amsterdam, he needed little persuading
when someone suggested a visit to the 'red light' district one
evening. The tour of the red light district is a must for all visitors to
Amsterdam, the majority of whom drink in the atmosphere with
no intention of participating in the activities on offer, so it was a
surprise when Andy was seen heading determinedly for the
entrance door of one of the properties.

'What are you doing?' Tom asked as he grabbed Andy's arm.

'Going in here. Have you seen that girl in the window? She's
gorgeous,' Andy replied.

'But you'll have to pay,' Tom explained.

'No, I won't,' Andy said confidently.

'It's a knocking shop. You don't get anything without paying,'
Tom insisted.

'No, I won't have to pay,' he said in an assured tone as he broke free of Tom's grip and headed for the door again.

'What makes you so sure?' Tom shouted after him.

'She fancies me.'

'How do you work that out?' asked Tom in desperation.

'She smiled at me and beckoned me in.'

'She smiles at everyone, you daft bastard, even the women. She's not particular, as long as they pay.'

Despite Tom's forthright appraisal of the situation, Andy still needed some convincing before he would move on and he had to be restrained on several more occasions whenever one of the 'ladies of the night' smiled at him.

Despite his naivety on that occasion, he is an intelligent man. His grammar school education means he has a wide vocabulary, although he does tend to use this with ingenuity:

'I'm having trouble with the crucial ligature in my right knee,' he complained on a previous trip.

'Shouldn't that be your cruciate ligament? And anyway, I thought you told me it was your left knee,' Paul said.

'No. That was last week and, anyway, it was the interior ligature in the left knee that was bothering me then.'

In his younger days, he shared a house with a rugby-playing pal and rumours started circulating around the village about the two rugby forwards living together. His housemate had a girlfriend who worked for Estee Lauder in the cosmetics department at Boots and she called at the house a couple of times each week on her way home from work, still wearing her white nylon outfit and carrying her leather bag full of cosmetics, so the word soon spread that the 'two gays' were suffering from AIDS and the District Nurse was visiting twice a week!

But February made me shiver
With every paper I'd deliver
Bad news on the doorstep

'The bad news must be Andy's going to sing.'

But something touched me deep inside

'Something will touch you deep inside if you don't stop that bloody caterwauling.'

'What's that you're reading, Paul?' asked Tom, noticing that Paul was even quieter than usual.

'It's the biography of Alfred Wainwright by Hunter Davies. As it was Wainwright who devised the Coast to Coast Walk, I thought I'd learn more about him. We all know that he wrote the guide-books to the Lake District and that he shunned publicity, but most people don't know much about him at all.'

'I think I have a lot in common with him,' I said.

'What, because you've got two legs and you're a grumpy old bugger, you mean?' Tom suggested, to unnecessary laughter.

'I was thinking more of the fact that we were both natives of Lancashire, except he was born and brought up in Blackburn whereas I come from Southport. And, like me, he had a love of the Lake District and he was six foot tall as well.'

'Now we know where those little scouse scallies sold the height serum they pinched from the nurse at Tom's school. It must have been Southport and Blackburn,' Andy said.

'So, you both love the Lakes and you're six foot tall,' Tom sneered, 'that must be true of about half a million Lancastrians. And don't forget that I'm a Lancastrian and love the Lakes.'

'Yes, but you're only a short arse little bastard,' Andy pointed out, eager to snatch at any opportunity to annoy Tom.

'But I have another thing in common with Wainwright,' Tom responded, resisting the urge to throw an insult back at Andy, 'I've written a walking guidebook as well.'

'Oh yes,' I said, grudgingly.

Now sixty-nine, it is nearly fifty years since Tom left his Liverpool home but he still retains that unmistakeable scouse accent. At a little over five foot seven, his lack of inches is more than compensated for by the sort of wit for which Liverpudlians are famous. Being the youngest of eight children, he was once asked why he had only had three children himself and, quick as a flash, he replied:

'I was going to have more until I read that every fourth child born in the world is Chinese.'

'Ah, the old ones are the best, Tom.'

'I most certainly am,' he responded, in all due immodesty.

He makes an excellent leader as he has an enviable knack of being able to judge personalities almost immediately and seems to know instinctively when to use the carrot and when to use the stick. This attribute was going to be put to the test over the next twelve days, leading a group of opinionated old farts across the country.

In addition to his leadership qualities, Tom is also a great organiser and had left little to chance in planning the trip. His original idea was that our overnight accommodation would be in youth hostels, wherever possible, and in Bed and Breakfast establishments otherwise. Those who enjoy hostelling seem to like conditions to be as uncomfortable as possible and hostels certainly try very hard to fulfil their requirements (and they are cheap as well!). However, there were two dissenters. Don had decided that modern hostels are not as disagreeable as they used to be, so he would be camping most nights. On the other hand, I had decided that they cater mainly for inverted snobs and vagrants and would spend at least some of my nights in the relative comfort of B & B's. Tom had decided that the walk should take twelve days and chose the overnight stops accordingly, then sent each of us a list of the places, in date order, with columns for us to tick showing whether we wanted to stay in hostels or B&B's (or camp), with asterisks indicating the nights when hostels would not be available. Very efficient. With the completed forms returned, he booked accommodation for each of us and sent us an itemised invoice for his services. No, he didn't really, although he could have done.

It was not only the accommodation that he organised, but also the equipment, based on his experience from nine previous trips. Each of us received a list of all the equipment and clothes we should take, bearing in mind that we would be away for twelve days but would have to carry everything on our backs. I found the list very helpful and very thoughtful of Tom. Of course, Don would be camping, so had far more to carry. Indeed, it had been quite a struggle for him to lift his pack into the back of the minibus.

'You do realise,' said Paul, looking up from Wainwright's biography, 'that Wainwright always travelled light. Although he spent all his spare time on the fells, he wore ordinary walking shoes and a tweed jacket and he didn't even own any waterproofs. I've just been reading about when he went on a fortnight's hike in 1938, on his own, and he says that his rucksack was virtually empty and that he could have done without it.'

'What, for a fortnight?'

'Yes. It says he couldn't understand how some hikers can enjoy themselves with huge, fifty pound packs on their backs,' he said, glancing over the back seat at Don's enormous pack. 'Apparently, he used to take a light raincoat or a cape, but *never a change of clothes.*'

'But what if it rained?'

'He said if they got wet, it was unfortunate as walking in wet clothes is unpleasant, but they always dried out afterwards.'

'Yeah, after he'd died of pneumonia as well.'

'On that particular fortnight's walk, he reckoned that his pack weighed less than two pounds.'

'Bloody hell, Tom, you put far too much on that list you sent us,' Andy said, 'we'd have been better asking Wainwright what to bring.'

'Maybe, but he's been dead for more than ten years, so you might have waited a long time for an answer,' Tom replied. 'Anyway, I wouldn't want to be sharing a room with you after twelve days in the same clothes.'

Eventually, we reached St Bees, a large village and the western-most point in the north of England, and Trevor drove down the narrow street to the beach half a mile away.

'Put a sock in it, Andy,' I said, as I hurled one of my two thousand mile socks, guaranteed to keep wearers blister-free, at his head.

> *Singin' this'll be the day that I die*
> *This'll be the day that I die*

'Too bloody right it will, if you keep that up much longer.'

CHAPTER THREE

THE BIRDS AND ST BEES

Having negotiated the narrow streets of St. Bees, we reached the seafront where there is an enormous car park next to the beach. Even though it is a lovely sandy beach, it is hard to believe that this remote spot is so popular that all three hundred or so parking spaces are ever full, although it is nice to discover that there are still some places in this crowded country where it is possible to park without having to spend half the day searching for a space. If the word gets out, it may become the biggest attraction in the North West for the multitudes who like a drive out in search of a lay-by where they can spend the afternoon drinking cups of tea from a flask. Just imagine three hundred cars lined up, each with a little foldaway table and two foldaway chairs set out alongside and three hundred primus stoves hissing away. Bliss for those who enjoy nothing more than sitting next to their cars and looking at tarmac. It could be the making of St Bees. Despite the fact that it was a beautiful day, only a handful of spaces were occupied (and I noticed only two primus stoves on the go) as we left the minibus, put on our boots, strapped our packs to our backs and walked on to the beach to dip our toes in the Irish Sea and collect the pebbles which we would carry to the North Sea coast, where we would dip our toes again in twelve days time and throw our pebbles out to sea.

I'd learnt a bit more about Joe during the journey and my suspicions about his age had proved to be justified. Not only did he look nearer Tom's age, he *was* the same age. To have two sixty-nine year olds in the group made me feel quite young, particularly as both Don and Paul were older than me as well. I had also established that Joe was a widower who lived in one of those mobile homes that are not mobile at all once they have been placed on site. He should have felt quite at home at St Bees as there is a vast area alongside the car park occupied by an untold number of these static homes. In fact, Joe is a remarkable man. Born in Sussex, he left school at an early age and went to sea as a young boy, serving in the Merchant Navy for a number of years before going into engineering. Politically, his views are very much left wing and he even toyed with Communism at one time. He was a shop steward for most of his working life but, now retired, he is doing an Open University degree in Roman History. He also sings in a choir. With his background as a trades union activist, he had locked horns with Tom when they first met, as Tom had been a Production Director of a company in which he was a major shareholder, so their views on workers rights could not be more different. After a heated debate, they had both been wise enough to steer clear of politics again and had developed a mutual respect. I had also been able to verify Andy's remarks about the frequency with which he passes wind. When holding a serious conversation with him, it is quite distracting to hear his comments accompanied by a sequence of farts.

Confirmation of his age heightened my doubts about his ability to complete such a strenuous walk. However, I have learnt not to judge people by appearances and, as I knew that he did a lot of walking with Andy and Paul who are both very strong walkers, I was not overly surprised when he and Paul immediately forged ahead as we set off to climb up to St. Bees Head. Neither was I surprised that Trevor didn't join us on the first part of the walk before setting off for home. He was well on his way to the M6 before we reached the headland.

Tom, Don and Andy were bringing up the rear and I found myself trying to keep in touch with both groups. Perhaps the fact that Andy was not attempting to walk with Paul and Joe was proof that he really was suffering with his blisters, and it soon became apparent that Don was suffering as well but, in his case, because of the weight of his backpack. Although a long-time friend of Tom's, the fact that he lives in Norfolk means that they do not spend a great deal of time together other than on adventures such as this. Typically, he had decided that he would be different and would camp, so was carrying his tent, sleeping bag and all the other paraphernalia needed for camping and, judging by the size of his pack, had brought everything including the kitchen sink! Clearly, he had not taken much notice of Tom's helpful list of minimum necessities. Because he had completed the Coast to Coast Walk once before and had camped on that occasion, he planned to do the same again, apparently forgetting that his earlier success had been over fifteen years ago when he was in his mid-forties and much fitter. Now in his sixties, he had not been camping for years, and had not even done any serious walking for quite a while. A mild-mannered man with a permanent sparkle in his eye, he can be very obstinate when he gets an idea in his mind, which is odd for a man who makes his living as a designer who has had to adapt to modern technology. This stubborn streak was apparent now as I looked at the golf umbrella strapped to the back of his heavy pack. He had always insisted that the best way of keeping dry when walking was to use a golf umbrella, and I had given up arguing that an umbrella would be useless on the high fells of the Lake District as the first gust of wind would blow it inside out. Telling him that holding a metal object above his head during a thunder-storm could be extremely dangerous was met with the same dismissive response. On one occasion, he had tried to convince me that his experience as a designer/inventor had enabled him to produce a wind-resistant, lightning-proof model but, much as I admired his ability in the designing world, the Legal and General banner on his brolly rather gave the game away.

Don's surname is Darby and, inevitably, he had suffered as a child when he was referred to as Donkey Darby. Having seen him struggle to lift his pack on to his back in the car park at St. Bees, we had quickly resurrected his childhood nickname.

The Coast to Coast route was devised by Alfred Wainwright and was first published in 1973. The route passes through three National Parks – The Lake District, the Yorkshire Dales and the North York Moors – and about three quarters of the one hundred and ninety miles of the route is within the boundaries of these National Parks. Wainwright preferred the west to east crossing mainly because the prevailing weather comes from the west on five days out of six, and it is better to have the wind and rain on the back rather than in the face. He gave another reason, perhaps less convincing, namely that the natural sequence is left to right as in writing or in listing the people in a photograph, and that going from right to left along a horizontal plane is abnormal and goes against the grain. When Don had done the Coast to Coast Walk all those years ago, typically, he had chosen to be abnormal and go against the grain and took the east to west route. Ever since then, he had sworn that east to west was the better way to do it and would argue all night to persuade anyone daft enough to listen that Wainwright was wrong. I was half-expecting to see a little pennant attached to the top of his pack proclaiming *EAST TO WEST IS BEST*.

Wainwright described the walk in fourteen stages saying *given reasonable weather, the walk can be done in two weeks, not rushing it nor trailing behind schedule*, but it can be completed in a longer or shorter period than fourteen days and we had chosen (that is, Tom had chosen on our behalf) to complete the task in twelve days. This is where campers have an advantage in that they do not have to plan their stops in advance, and they can vary their timescale depending on the weather and how they feel. On the other hand, walkers staying in B&Bs and youth hostels have to book their accommodation in advance, so that they must choose the number of days they will take, book the accommodation and make sure they reach that accommodation on the appropriate days, irrespective of the weather or any other consideration. This is serious walking rather than what Tom would call 'gratuitous' walking. He insists that if you can get up in the morning, check the weather, see how you feel, and still decide to go walking, that is gratuitous walking.

Released from the confines of the minibus to enjoy the sunshine on what was promising to be a glorious day, I felt exhilarated to be out in the open air as we made our way up to the headland. But, hold on a minute, weren't we supposed to be making for the east coast? We were heading in the wrong direction. This way led to the east coast of Ireland! Not to worry, the path soon turned to the north and would turn to the east after a couple of miles walking round the headland. The path followed the headland above the cliffs which towered over the sea, three hundred feet below. After the uncomfortable minibus journey, I was enjoying the exercise, as well as the views from the headland and, confident that my exercise regime had brought me to the pinnacle of fitness, I was really looking forward to the twelve days walking across the country with good pals to keep me company. Things couldn't be better.

However, it soon became apparent that Paul and Joe were not going to make any concessions about their pace, which was a great pity as this was a time to stroll, to enjoy the sunshine, the sea breeze, the calls of the gulls wheeling above and the scenery – the sea on one side and the green fields on the other. Rather than try to keep in touch with the pacesetters, I decided to wait on the headland for Tom, Don and Andy to catch up. Thousands of sea birds nest on the cliffs of St Bees Head and there is a RSPB viewpoint from which can be seen kittiwakes, herring gulls, fulmars, puffins, guillemots, black guillemots, cormorants and razorbills. By September, many of the birds had flown from the nesting grounds but there were still enough to satisfy the birdwatchers. As I waited, I was able to see how large areas of the red sandstone cliffs have been turned white by the defecatory activities of these sea birds.

I was standing in front of the RSPB sign when two young girls, aged about twelve, stopped for a moment and I heard one of them ask the other:

'What does RSPB stand for?'

The other, apparently far more knowledgeable girl, had to think about this for a few moments before replying:

'Royal Society for the Prevention of Birds,' she said, with some authority. The first girl accepted this quite happily and I have wondered ever since whether she is still under the delusion that there is actually a society, sponsored by Her Majesty, which is actively involved in the prevention of birds. In a few years from now, she will have children of her own and there could be a whole family brought up to believe that there is an active group of people dedicated to wiping out the entire bird population. Perhaps they will not only believe it, but establish their own splinter groups such as the SNP (Say No to Pipits) or CAMRA (Campaign Against Magpies and Rooks Association) or even the NAMBY (No Aviaries in My Backyard).

When the others caught up, we walked on together and we had not walked far before we met a group of five American women who hailed from various States, from Alaska to New Mexico and, on learning that Tom had completed the course nine times before, they were eager to hear all about the challenge that lay ahead of them. Tom enjoyed being in the spotlight and was happy to give them more information than they needed. Finally, they asked what arrangements had been put in place to enable walkers to get a drink or something to eat along the route. What did they expect – a food hall every few miles complete with Starbucks, Kentucky Fried Chicken and McDonalds? The Fell Top Food Hall has a nice ring to it, but I can't imagine the National Parks authorities granting planning permission, so Tom had to explain to them that on some days they would not pass any retail outlets or, indeed, any human habitation at all .

'Oh really,' one of them replied in that peculiarly American way. Have you noticed that? The 'oh' is said in a deep voice and extended to 'ohhh' and is followed by a much higher-pitched and speedy 'really' making it sound to English ears as though what they really mean is:

'What a load of shit; I don't believe a word of it but I'm going to look interested anyway.' The effect is exaggerated by a raising of the eyebrows in a look of feigned surprise.

'In fact, if you're walking from Ennerdale Bridge to Borrowdale tomorrow,' I said, 'you'll find that it's a very long way and there is absolutely nowhere to stop and buy a drink or food, so you'll have to carry enough for the whole day.'

'Oh, really,' one of them said again in that annoyingly questioning tone. At this point, there had been far too many 'oh reallys' for my liking and I felt I must explain that the American intonation can make 'oh really' sound quite offensive to us. Of course, I did this in my typically polite way, in order not to upset the 'special relationship', and concluded in friendly fashion:

'Most English people are fond of Americans generally and Elvis Presley in particular, so they will forgive the occasional 'oh really' but say it too often and you might get a slap'.

'Ohhh, really,' they chorused in unison.

Soon after noon we left the headland and turned inland, heading east for the first time and soon walked through the village of Sandwith, which Wainwright described as a village with more pubs than churches. The route passed only one pub, the Dog and Partridge, and it was closed! Come to think of it, I didn't notice a church either. Is it possible that there is no church, which would mean that the presence of the Dog and Partridge justifies Wainwright's statement? Was the old fellow having a bit of a laugh at our expense by inferring the village is blessed with an abundance of pubs? He was a bit of a wag, wasn't he? Bastard.

Before we left Sandwith, our attention was attracted by a *For Sale* sign on a disused yard: *Land For Sale with Outline Planning Permission for the Erection of Twenty Dwellings (Six Affordable).* Even with over two hundred and forty years of life experience between the four of us, we were baffled.

'Why would the Local Authority grant permission for twenty houses when fourteen of them will stand empty because they are unaffordable?' Don asked.

'Perhaps they can charge council tax on empty properties and it's a clever way of increasing income,' I suggested.

'But no sane builder would buy the land and build houses that nobody can afford,' Tom reasoned.

'I can't afford even an affordable house anyway,' said Andy.

'That's because of that Gordon Brown. Even if you find a house you think you can afford, you have to pay stamp duty of about five squillion pounds,' I added.

'And even if you can afford that, council tax at about ten thousand pounds a month will bankrupt you in jig time,' Tom asserted.

'It's not right,' Don objected, 'we're robbed by stamp duty, then we have to pay council tax and then, when we die, we're robbed again because we have to pay inheritance tax on the value.'

'That Gordon Brown's a fool,' said Tom. 'It's becoming impossible to buy a house now, so it's no wonder Local Authorities are granting planning permission for unaffordable houses. All houses will be unaffordable soon and then where will clever bastard Brown be?'

'He'll go back to Scotland. They probably don't have stamp duty there.'

'Or, if they do, he's probably arranged an exemption for former Chancellors of the Exchequer.'

'Or, he will have arranged for MPs pensions to include an allowance to cover stamp duty.'

'And council tax.'

'He thinks he knows it all just because he once read *The Well Off Nations* by Alan Smith,' Andy chipped in.

'It was actually called *The Wealth of Nations*.'

'And Alan Smith plays for Manchester United.'

'No wonder the book was crap.'

'Anyway,' Tom said, trying to bring the conversation back to his version of sanity, 'he's a fool. Unaffordable housing means people won't move, so he won't get any stamp duty and then prices will fall because no-one's buying, so he won't get any inheritance tax either.'

'Simple economics really,' I agreed. 'The man's a divvy.'

Having congratulated ourselves on our in-depth understanding of the principles of economics, we walked on in confused mood.

On this section of the walk, we found that the terrain was relatively flat, so made good progress and soon passed through the village of Moor Row, which is a place that has seen better days. The terraced houses once housed workers from the coal and iron ore mines which have long since closed. However, it is possible to obtain refreshments from Mrs Fee at the exotically named Jasmine House Tea Garden, a most inappropriate title for an establishment in a place like Moor Row. Perhaps the Earl Grey Tea Garden would be more apt (but without the 'Earl').

The tea garden turned out to be a paved area at the rear of the house with a couple of gazebos sheltering the picnic tables, alongside the conservatory where tea is served to those who prefer to be indoors. Mrs Fee chatted amiably as she swept the outside area around us and it became clear that she is a real entrepreneur. She had opened as a B&B only a couple of years ago and had opened up the tea garden a year later. Her website shows that she has five well-appointed bedrooms (all en-suite and with televisions and DVD players). She told us that she and her husband had just bought a hotel in St Bees, so they are obviously on the acquisition trail and on the way to becoming a major chain. If they open tea gardens in St Bees, I suggested they could call it Mrs Fee's St Bees Teas, but she didn't seem overly impressed, which I thought was a little ungracious on her part.

On the first day of the Coast to Coast Walk, the obvious destination is Ennerdale Bridge which is a distance of fourteen or fifteen miles from St. Bees. However, as accommodation in Ennerdale Bridge is limited, Mrs Fee takes advantage and by offering bed and breakfast in Moor Row, more and more people are walking as far as Ennerdale Bridge and getting a taxi back to Moor Row for the night, then being ferried back to Ennerdale Bridge the next morning. The hotel in St Bees is called the Manor House Hotel and Coast to Coast Bar (so no doubt about the target market then) and will offer accommodation to Coast to Coast walkers who travel up to St Bees and stay the night before setting off next morning. Her aim must be to capture walkers for the first two nights (and for tea along the way). Her entrepreneurial skills are not confined to the Coast to Coast market as she also attracts guests who are visiting or working at the nearby Sellafield nuclear plant. Having enjoyed our break, we asked for her (Mrs) Fee note, settled up and resumed our journey.

From Moor Row, we made for Cleator which is only a short distance but is through farmland and involves negotiating five kissing gates. This does not present a problem for most walkers, but it did for Don whose camper's pack was so large that he could not squeeze through without removing it. Typically, he was using a pack that looked as though it had been passed down the generations from his grandfather to his father and then to Don. There were four straps securing it to his body and they were of the old-fashioned buckle type, rather than the much more modern plastic clips which open at a touch, so it became a laborious and annoying process to undo the straps, take off the pack, lift it over each gate, risking a triple hernia each time, and then go through the reverse process of struggling to heave the pack on to his back again and re-fastening all the straps. He was carrying far more than the rest of us and was already struggling with the weight, and now he was falling behind because of the succession of kissing gates. I helped him at the first couple of gates but could sense that he was becoming angry, as well as frustrated, as even limpalong Andy was leaving us behind. Normally, he is a really nice bloke and it is unusual to hear him swear, but he was working himself up into a real paddy as we fell further behind at each gate. Eventually, I decided to leave him to it and walked on to catch up with Tom and Andy, rather than have my illusion of Don being a good-natured sort shattered by any further outbursts.

Of course, knowing what to take on an expedition like this is a major problem, particularly as the English weather is so unpredictable. We had to carry clothes for all weather conditions but, at the same time, take only the absolute minimum. After all, there is nothing more irksome than to find, at the end of a twelve day journey over a distance of one hundred and ninety miles, that you have carried something that you did not need. That never happened to Wainwright of course, even though he must have ponged by the end of his journeys. Amazingly for someone who spent so much time walking the fells, those who knew him described him as one of the clumsiest walkers they have ever seen and someone who would not attempt to use his hands for climbing or scrambling. Being the brave and athletic type myself, going arse over tit no more than five or six times a day on a walk like this, I had assumed that my hero would have had a similar iron will and supple limbs. Apparently, this was not the case. His son suggested that his favourite descent was on his backside and this method was confirmed in one or two of his books. Indeed, he recalled ripping the seat of his trousers on one such escapade and having to walk through the streets of Keswick with his underwear on show. It is very difficult to imagine what state he must have been in after a fortnight's walking without a change of clothes, particularly if he was as clumsy as suggested by others. I'm sure the answer for most walkers is to go for the happy medium of at least one change of clothes, without carrying the entire outfitter's shop.

Even for non-campers, the weight of the pack can be a strain, so how on earth campers manage with all the additional weight of their camping gear and supplies is a mystery to me. All the more important then to make sure that everything packed is really going to be used during the journey as any unnecessary weight could be crippling. As Don was an 'old hand' at the Coast to Coast, he should have been a master of the art of minimalist packing but I was beginning to have my doubts.

We soon reached Cleator, which is another small village, but with the benefit of a small shop and a pub. As we approached the shop for refreshments, Paul and Joe emerged from the Three Tuns looking very pleased with themselves, having made the most of their lead over the rest of us.

Paul is something of an enigma. We had been discussing him as we walked towards Cleator and had concluded that none of us knew much about him. Don't get me wrong here; he is very much one of the boys, although quiet at times. It's just that you never really get to know him. He is sixty-one, an architect and part-time National Park ranger but none of us knew very much more than that. He's always helpful and supportive but never seems to make a mistake or make a fool of himself. On a long distance walk like the Coast to Coast, the rest of us could expect either to fall down a hole or walk knee deep in a bog or say something stupid or perhaps all three, but not Paul. A good companion but not ideal if your intention is to write a book entitled *A Funny Thing Happened on the Coast to Coast Walk*.

Andy is the closest to him and he could recall only one occasion when Paul confided in him:

'He had a terrible health scare; *an' a full ' at trick shock.*'

'What, he was shocked by someone scoring a hat trick?'

'Must have been watching Everton then.'

'No, nothing to do with football,' Andy explained, 'he was stung three times by a wasp. Didn't you know that if you get stung three times – a hat trick of stings – you suffer a reaction? It's very serious. Some people die from it.'

'He should have got it to sting him a fourth time then, if it's only caused by three stings.'

'I think what Andy means is anaphylactic shock. It can be caused by just one sting if you're allergic to it,' Don said, bringing a sense of maturity to the conversation.

It seems that Paul was gardening when he was stung and, when he began to feel unwell a few minutes later, he went inside and sat down.

'Are you all right?' his wife asked.

'Actually, I feel a bit rough.'

'I think I'd better take you down to the doctor's,' she said, alarmed by his sickly appearance and his rare admission that all was not well. 'Come on.'

'I'll just go and wash my hands.'

'It doesn't matter about your hands. Let's go.'

'I've been gardening so I need to wash my hands.'

As he closed the bathroom door behind him, he felt dizzy and fell, cracking his head on the toilet cistern. He pulled himself up to the washbasin and saw himself in the mirror with blood gushing out of a cut above his eye.

'Are you all right in there?' Christine shouted.

'Yes, I'm OK. I just need to wash my hands and I'll be out.'

As he leant down to wipe some of the blood away, he fell again, this time smashing his nose on the edge of the basin. Once more, he pulled himself up, this time to find blood pumping from his nose.

'Are you sure you're all right in there?' Christine shouted again.

'Yes, I'll be out in a minute. I just need to wash my hands.'

When he emerged, she helped him to the car and set off on the short journey to the surgery. Unfortunately, he was sick before they got there. Paul was a sorry sight as they walked in, with blood trickling from both his eye and his nose and dripping on to his puke-encrusted shirt but, thank goodness, at least his hands were clean!

Moor Row and Cleator have nothing much to recommend them but, like all the villages in this area, there is a curious mix of small new developments and property which has seen better days. The contrast between the new houses, with the smart new cars parked outside, and the older properties could not be more marked. This area depends very heavily on the nuclear plant at Sellafield and, whatever people may think about the rights and wrongs of nuclear power, there is no doubt that the region would be economically devastated by the closure of the plant. Currently, it employs twelve thousand people, eight thousand directly and with four thousand contractors.

Reunited for the first time since we left St Bees, all six of us walked on together, now approaching the boundary of the first of the three National Parks through which we would travel, the mountains of the Lake District almost within touching distance.

'It's strange that it should be called the Lake District,' I said 'considering that there is only one lake.'

'But there are lots of lakes,' Andy responded, ready for an argument.

'No, there's only one. Bassenthwaite Lake is the only lake. All the others are either 'meres' such as Windermere, Thirlmere and

Buttermere or 'waters' such as Coniston Water, Ullswater, Derwentwater and Ennerdale Water. This is something you might want to remember for pub quizzes.'

It was clear that Andy wanted to argue and he was in deep thought for a while as he tried desperately to come up with another lake that didn't end with mere or water. After a short time, Tom, Don and I stopped near the almost derelict farmhouse of Black How for a drink and a sandwich. The other three walked on, entering Blackhow Wood for the ascent of Dent whilst we rested on a grassy bank. It was a relief to remove the heavy weight from our backs, if only for a few minutes, but Don had so much in his pack that he seemed to be having great difficulty in locating his provisions. After rooting in it for ages, he produced the largest box of Ryvita biscuits I had ever seen.

'Bloody hell, Don, couldn't you find a larger box than that?' asked Tom, sardonically.

'They don't weigh much,' answered Don.

'But they take up a lot of space,' I said.

A moment later, he produced the most enormous carton of cheese spread from his pack, as well as a table knife.

'Hell, Don, I didn't realise they made them that size,' I said. 'No wonder you're struggling with your pack if you've got the largest size of everything. Surely, you'd have been better buying those DairyLea slices and just bringing enough for a few days. You could buy some more somewhere along the way, if you run out.'

'Oh, I didn't want to think about having to stock up and, anyway, it's cheaper to buy in bulk.'

'But it's only cheaper if you eat it all, and you've got enough there for a month.'

'For three men,' added Tom.

He proceeded to apply the spread to his Ryvita biscuits and then, to our astonishment, delved into his pack again and produced the most humongous onion and a Swiss army knife, which he used to cut off a couple of slices of onion and added them to his Ryvita and cheese spread.

'You must be mental,' said Tom 'that onion must weigh over half a pound.'

'Yeah, even if cheese spread and sliced onion on Ryvita is your favourite snack, surely you could have done without the onion rather than carry the extra weight,' I added.

'Oh, it's not that much extra,' Don countered.

Tom wasn't finished. 'An extra pound here and half a pound there…..'

'and a golf umbrella over there,' I muttered.

'…..and you're soon up to an extra stone of weight that you'll have to carry for the next twelve days. Didn't you read that list I sent you?'

'But the weight will reduce as I eat the stuff,' he argued 'and that's another reason for walking east to west. The toughest days are through the Lake District and they are at the end if you walk east to west, and that's when your pack is lightest.'

'No, Don, your pack would be just as light at the beginning if you didn't have the entire fuckin' contents of your local super-market in there,' Tom reasoned.

With that, Don went off for a closer inspection of the derelict farm buildings and I took the opportunity to find out more about his obsession with walking east to west.

'Why does Don have such a bee in his bonnet about doing the walk the other way?' I asked Tom.

'Jealousy,' Tom replied firmly. 'The first time I did the Coast to Coast about fifteen years ago, I wanted to do it by myself. Although I'd done plenty of walking, I hadn't ever walked such long distances day after day, so wasn't sure how I'd go on and didn't want anyone else there if I couldn't manage it. And anyway, it was more of an adventure to do it on my own.'

'So you kept it a secret?'

'No, not exactly, but I didn't tell many people,' he continued. 'What happened with Don was that he happened to phone me on the Friday before I set off on the Saturday and it came out during the conversation and I couldn't get him off the phone. 'Why didn't you tell me before? It's been an ambition of mine to do the Coast to Coast for years. I would have come with you.' All that stuff. He went on and on.

Anyway, it must have festered away inside him all the next

week, thinking about me walking in the fresh air, doing the walk he wanted to do, while he was stuck in his office. By the Friday, he was so wound up that he decided to drop everything and do it himself, but he couldn't start until the Monday because they were going somewhere over the weekend. Of course, by that time, I was well over halfway and there was no way he could catch up, so he decided to start at Robin Hood's Bay. That way, at least he would see me as we passed and be able to thumb his nose at me. His idea was to surprise me but, after the first day, he realised how easy it would be to miss me, so he phoned home and asked Jane to phone Pam so she could tell me to look out for him on the Wednesday. We met on the Cleveland Hills and it was a good job I'd been warned because the weather was poor and we could easily have missed each other in the mist. It was a bit pointless really, because we only spent about half an hour together, having a sandwich and a natter.'

'That still doesn't explain why he thinks east to west is better,' I pointed out.

'He doesn't really,' Tom replied, 'he just won't forgive me for going without him and it's his way of needling me.'

Don returned from his inspection tour just as Tom chose to go and check whether anything needed watering, and I decided to hear his version of the History of Coast to Coast Walks.

'Don, you know you're always telling us that the east to west crossing is better? What made you decide to do it that way in the first place?'

'It was fortuitous really,' he replied. 'We have some friends in Yorkshire and we had a long standing commitment to go to their daughter's Christening. I'd always wanted to do the Coast to Coast Walk, so it was a good opportunity for me to combine the two things. We stayed at their house on the Sunday night and Jane drove me to Robin Hood's Bay the next morning. It was only about a twenty minute drive, so it was ideal.'

'But didn't you meet Tom along the way?' I asked.

'Oh, yes,' he said with a chuckle. 'That was funny. He phoned me about ten days before I was due to go and, when he heard what I was doing, he was so envious you wouldn't believe. He wanted to come with me but he was going away somewhere during the second week. Anyway, he must have been so irritated that he decided to do it on his own and set off that weekend. He only did it west to east so that he would bump into me towards the end and be able to say that he'd nearly finished.'

After Tom and Don had spent another twenty minutes indulging in their favourite pastime of discussing exactly how they would go about converting the farm buildings into the most desirable property in the North West or, alternatively, how they could transport all the stone to Cheshire or Norfolk and rebuild the farmhouse to their own design, we prepared to move on but Don had to repack all the belongings he had removed from his rucksack when searching for his food.

'That's a smart looking waterproof, Don,' Tom said as Don stuffed what was clearly a brand new jacket into his ancient pack.

'Yes, I thought it was time to treat myself and get a modern jacket. The fabrics they use now are much better and they look good too. Even though this is waterproof, it's really lightweight and has a super-soft feel; it's breathable and really comfortable. It's made from polyamide with a hydrophilic laminate liner.'

'You sound like a bleedin' advert, Don.'

By the time we were ready to move on, Tom and Don had decided that they would find a path round Dent, rather than go up and over, which made me wonder again about their fitness. It was obvious that Don was struggling, whether just because of the weight of his pack, it was impossible to say, although I was beginning to wonder about his general fitness. As for Tom, it was not like him to take the easy option. However, there was no point in asking whether he was suffering with his knees or had any other problem as he would see it as a sign of weakness to admit to any discomfort. I would have to wait and see whether his creaking limbs would last the distance.

As for myself, I was in my prime; at the pinnacle of fitness, having read with great interest Care International's tips on preparing for their Challenge, which I found very helpful, if not frightening. Although the Coast to Coast Walk was rather different to the 24 Peaks Challenge, I had convinced myself that, by following their preparation regime, I would be in perfect shape by the time we set off. Indeed, the first three or four days of the Coast to Coast are through the Lake District and involve scaling three of the 24 peaks on Care's route, so their literature was ideal. Mind you, some of the language could have deterred a lesser man.

A suitable level of fitness is crucial. It would be very dangerous to suddenly begin climbing a number of mountains, when your body is expecting a normal weekend as a couch potato (crucial, dangerous – this sounds serious stuff, I thought). *It will not be necessary to run* (thank goodness for that) *unless of course you wish to do so* (I don't think so). *A rhythmic pace, especially uphill,* (you mean resting every five paces then?) *will lead to much better progress than wildly charging at it* (don't worry, I'm not one for wildly charging). *We strongly recommend that you make use of our Exercise Programme and begin training at least ten weeks prior to the event* (ten weeks! They don't train that long for the Olympics, do they?) *The 24 Peaks event is physically more demanding than our other challenge events so participants should follow the adjusted exercise programme which includes an extra two weeks of activity.* (What? Another two weeks? One of the 24 Peaks must be Everest!) There were pages and pages of this stuff and I was tired out just reading it. And that was before I reached the Exercise Programme itself. *There is no point training for a sprint* (good, my sprinting days ended when they stopped making buses with open platforms and I looked rather foolish jumping against a closed door) *but at the same time you don't need to run any marathons* (not even one?). *The pace required is a steady walk* (I can cope with steady). *This is especially relevant to the 24 Peaks event* (oh, good). *The qualities required are firstly determination and commitment* (is that all?) *but you will also need a level of physical fitness* (any particular level?). *That is aerobic fitness, or to put it another way, a fit heart and lungs* (my heart and lungs do fit, especially since I filled out a bit).

By this time, I was worn out and I had only just reached the week by week programme. *Week 1. Try a brisk forty minute walk* (I should be able to manage that) *and, in this first week, you should be aiming to do between three and five sessions* (what, in a week?). *You should have enough breath to talk* (gee, thanks), *but not enough to sing or whistle* (that's all right – I had no ambition to sing or whistle for forty minutes three to five times a week).

I ploughed on and found that by *Week 5. You should be walking for one hour at least five to six times a week. Walk to work* (eleven miles wearing a suit? I don't think so. Anyway, I need the car for work – I sometimes do a bit of shopping on the way home).

Week 11. This week, slow down (that sounds more like it) *to 3-4 sessions of about forty minutes each* (that still sounds a lot).

Week 12. Exercise should be further reduced with only one or two light 20-30 minute sessions at the beginning of the week, followed by three to four days of complete rest and plenty of sleep prior to the event (complete rest and plenty of sleep. That sounds the ideal preparation for a sixty year old).

Remember to read the Nutritional Advice in the following section. By following this and resting in the days before the event (so it's all down to resting and nutrition then? That sounds better), *you will find that you are ready for the challenge* (after all that rest, I'm sure I will be).

Worn out, I turned to the Nutritional Advice, which talked about eating *the right kinds of foods* and referred to *a process called carbo-loading*. Apparently, this involves consuming enormous amounts of carbohydrates. *Eat plenty of bread, potatoes and pasta* (pasta? Bloody pasta? It doesn't seem to have given the Italians a reputation for staying power, now does it? Must be a misprint. Perhaps they mean pasty. Wonder whether that includes pies. This sounds much better – bread, potatoes, pasties and pies – I've lived on those for the last sixty years. No wonder I'm so naturally fit. Bloody hell, I was carbo-loading for over fifty years before they even invented the idea. Forget the exercise, I'll concentrate on loading the carbs).

Not having to bother with Care's exercise regime was a great relief and I decided that I would just drive up to the Lakes whenever I could and spend five or six hours on the fells each time. It seemed to make sense to practice under the exact conditions we would experience during the first few days of the Coast to Coast. The big drawback was that it was over a hundred and twenty miles to the Lakes, or over a two hour drive on a good day, so I visited the Long Mynd in Shropshire from time to time as that is only an hour's drive away. I took Tom along with me one day because he needed to get in trim for the Coast to Coast as well, and it was his first experience of walking there. He was clearly impressed:

'I didn't realise there was such good walking country round here.'

'Yes, I think it's very like the Lake District, but on a much smaller scale of course. It's ideal for practicing for walking up there.'

'I see what you mean, but there aren't any actual mountains, are there? Just hills,' he said, a bit churlishly, I thought.

'Well, yes.'

'And there are no lakes either, are there?'

'Well, if you want to be picky.'

'So, what you mean is it's just like the Lake District, but with no lakes and no proper mountains.'

'I suppose so.'

'In fact, it's nothing like the Lake District then.'

'If you have to put it like that, no.'

We completed our training that day with a couple of pints before making our way home, but the journey took rather longer than it should. We got a puncture. It had been years since either of us had changed a wheel, so I had to consult the manual even to find out where the spare was hidden. After emptying the boot, which turned out to have a false bottom beneath which the spare wheel had been buried by a mischievous car assembly worker, I was horrified by the extent of his mischief. The Jaguar S Type has enormous wheels, with tyres about twelve inches wide but he must have thought it would be great fun to substitute the proper spare with a wheel for a moped! We searched through the manual and found that, apparently, this was not a mistake but that Jaguar now provide a 'get you home' tyre for emergency use. To add insult to injury, the instructions added that speed must not exceed forty miles an hour with this wheel in place. By the time we had fitted the toy wheel, we were regretting the final part of our training regime as we both needed a pee, and it must have been the discomfort that put me in grumpy mood on the delayed journey home.

'This is bloody stupid. Firstly, I'm having to drive a car with three wheels and a stabiliser on the fourth corner. It's like a child learning to ride a bike. Secondly, I'm having to keep down to forty miles an hour. If I'd wanted to drive at forty miles an hour, I would have bought an entire bloody moped, not just one wheel. Thirdly, driving at forty miles an hour means that it will take us twice as long to get home, so there's twice as long for people to see me driving a Jaguar with a stabiliser. And fourthly ....'

'Yes, and fourthly?'

'And fourthly .... I'm sure there must be a fourthly but I can't just think of it at the moment.'

As for equipment, I had all that already. *Walking boots (above ankle), waterproof jacket, waterproof over-trousers* (they think it might rain), *hats and gloves* (they don't believe in global warming), *sun hat* (they do believe in global warming), *head torch* (they're expecting an eclipse), *clothing* (I thought I might need that) − *base layer (to wick away moisture), second layer (to trap the maximum amount of air), third layer* (sounds like a battery hen) − *to keep water out, keep the heat in and allow water vapour* (do they mean sweat?) *to escape, compass, high energy emergency food, note book and pencil* (why? Is this to allow us to write final messages to our loved ones in the same way as Captain Scott?), *maps, whistle* (there they go with that bloody whistling again), *spare batteries* (for the pace-maker?), *water bottle, compeed/plasters, first aid kit and a back pack to put it all in* (shouldn't I be wearing some of it?).

I said my goodbyes to Tom and Don and I would not see them again until the following evening as I was making for Ennerdale Bridge whereas the other five were staying that night at a camping barn at Kinniside, a mile or so short of Ennerdale Bridge. As there is no hostel in Ennerdale Bridge, Tom had chosen the camping barn as being the nearest uncomfortable alternative, but had taken the trouble to find a B&B for me. Because he knew we would not all be together the whole of the time, he had also provided directions for everyone for occasions like this and in case any of us wanted to walk at our own pace. Nothing was too much trouble for him.

I walked up through the forest and out on to the open fell and, although the summit of Dent is only 1131 feet, it was quite a stiff climb and it was not long before I began wishing that I had gone with the other two. Perhaps it wasn't just the condition of Tom's knees that had prompted him to choose an alternative route, after all. As I climbed, Joe soon came into view ahead of me and I was surprised to see that he was on his own but it was apparent that he had a problem as he was struggling up the hill, stopping every few paces. When I caught up with him, he explained that he was suffering from cramp (perhaps my first impression had not been wrong then) and that Andy was ahead of him somewhere, but Paul had missed a turning in the forest and had gone the wrong way. Unfortunately, he had been too far ahead to hear them calling him back. As our leader had told us that this was one of the easier days, the fact that Joe had cramp bothered me. How was he going to cope on the tougher days? I carried on up the incline and caught up with Andy as we reached the summit simultaneously and he explained that the pain from his blisters was so intense that he had felt unable to wait for Joe, as he needed to maintain what little momentum he had. It was becoming apparent that the blisters were more serious than his more usual (imaginary) complaints.

The view from the summit was magnificent and I had to remind myself that the elevation was only 1131 feet but, bearing in mind that our starting point that morning was actual sea level, we deserved the reward. The coastal plain was behind us now and the Lake District stretched out before us, three days of wonderful walking and it looked as though we were going to be lucky with the weather.

Andy decided to rest at the summit and wait for his pal, Joe, so I left him as I began my descent of Dent and I thought what a strange group we were. Things were not looking good. This was only the first day and Paul was already lost, Andy was suffering from blisters, Joe was suffering from cramp, Don was suffering from the weight of his pack (and a bad temper) and Tom was suffering from creaking knees. At that point, only Don and Tom were together and the rest of us were walking individually. This was not what I had anticipated at all and I wondered whether it was possible that we would all reach Robin Hood's Bay in twelve days time.

As I descended the steep grassy path from Dent under the burning sun, I noticed a sharp discomfort in my big toe and thought I might be developing a blister of my own. However, I knew this could not be possible, as I was wearing the pair of 2000 mile socks (guaranteed to keep wearers blister-free), which a friend had bought for my sixtieth birthday a couple of weeks earlier, so I dismissed the thought from my mind.

I wouldn't see the others until the following evening as I had the extra mile or so to walk to my B&B and because I hoped to take a slightly different route to them the next day. I wanted to take the more strenuous high route to Borrowdale, whereas the others had opted for the easier low route. What a good job I had been concentrating all my efforts on carbo-loading!

CHAPTER FOUR

THEY ALL TAKE THE LOW ROAD

I could feel the mid-afternoon sun burning my skin as I made rapid progress on the steep descent of Dent:

Helter skelter in a summer swelter

Bloody hell, he's got me at it now. That Andy's got a lot to answer for. Am I going to have another eleven days of American Pie swirling through my mind?

Mind you, Tom has a lot to answer for as well. Hadn't he told us that the first day was an 'easy' fourteen miles or so? In this heat and with this pack on my back, it doesn't seem that easy, I thought, and the steepness of the descent meant that I was travelling faster than I wanted. Tom had advised us to take our time on the first day, for two reasons. Firstly, to allow ourselves to become accustomed to the challenge of walking for six hours or more each day and, particularly, as the days which followed would be much tougher than the 'easy' first day's walk! Secondly, arriving at the destination too early would be a mistake, he said, as there is nothing to do when you get there. I could understand this, I thought, if you have been stupid enough to choose to stay at a camping barn in the middle of the countryside, but I had been led to believe that Ennerdale Bridge has two pubs, and a place that can support two pubs must have other attractions – maybe a nightclub or two?

Having completed the descent of Dent, I crossed the boundary into the National Park and was stopped in my tracks as my breath was taken away by the view ahead. The small, green, valley of Nannycatch Gate was something to savour and I followed Tom's advice (for once) and dawdled through this beautiful countryside. Unfortunately, however much I dawdled, it was not long before I was leaving Nannycatch behind and soon came to the road, alongside which I walked for the final mile or two to Ennerdale Bridge. As I approached the village, I began to understand Tom's warning about arriving too early as it was only half past four. The long drive to St Bees meant that we had not started from there until about ten thirty so, if we had set off immediately after breakfast (as we would each day from now on), I would have been here by early afternoon. Still, at least I could indulge myself and inspect the attractions on offer in this pretty village, whilst congratulating myself on my decision not to stay with the others in a crumby camping barn with nothing to do. I stopped for a drink at the Fox and Hounds, purely for re-hydration purposes in view of the hot weather, before resuming my inspection tour of the village. I passed what used to be the village Post Office cum store which, sadly, like so many village Post Offices, had closed and was falling into disrepair. This was a great pity as I prefer to patronise local businesses. Ah well, I'll just have to stock up at the supermarket, I thought. A few yards beyond the old Post Office was the Shepherd's Arms and I stopped for another drink, this time simply to avoid arriving at my B&B too early, you understand. Leaving the pub twenty minutes later, I was surprised to find that I seemed to be leaving the village as well. Where was the supermarket? At last the penny began to drop and I could understand Tom's concerns about reaching the day's destination too early. Apart from the two pubs, Ennerdale Bridge has no facilities.

A few more yards and I was at the front door of my digs for the night. Despite my two refreshment breaks, I was still 'glowing' after six hours strenuous walking under the relentless sun and to say my clothes were damp would be an understatement. As my landlady opened the door, I thought she might react in the same manner as women tend to do when they see Colin Firth as Mr

Darcy emerging, dripping wet, from the lake at Pemberley but her look of suppressed horror suggested that her recollection was more of the Monster from the Deep. Nevertheless, she invited me inside and I stepped over the threshold into a small, stone-floored sitting room and, immediately, she instructed me to remove my boots. Bearing in mind that we were in the middle of a mini-heat wave and I had not seen any running water since I had dipped my toes in the Irish Sea that morning, I was a little taken aback. Not that I had a problem about removing my boots. Indeed it would be a relief to my overworked and overheated feet and, in any event, I would have taken them off without being asked. No, it was more the fact that I was being asked to sit in a lounge chair whilst removing my boots and the landlady seemed more concerned about protecting her stone floor from my clean boots than protecting her upholstery from my damp (and possibly whiffy) clothes. It would have been more appropriate to take off my clothes rather than my boots, I reflected. Indeed, I was to arrive at the next few destinations in a similarly damp condition and yet not one landlady asked me to remove my clothes. Funny, that.

Whichever way you look at it, this was not the most friendly of welcomes at my first B&B of the trip.

'I'll just get some milk for your tray,' she said, as I started to unlace my boots, deducing that this was a euphemism for 'don't think I'm going to make you a pot of tea, you scruffy bastard. I'll give you some milk and you can make your own.' Things were going from bad to worse. I had managed to remove only one boot by the time she returned, milk jug in hand.

'Your room's up here,' she said as she disappeared upstairs. I found her waiting, impatiently, on the landing, ready to show me the bedroom which, inevitably, was at the front of the cottage with traffic passing immediately below the window, which would have to remain open all night in view of the unusually warm weather. Before leaving me to fend for myself with the kettle and teapot, she pointed to the bathroom across the landing, making a particular point of mentioning that the switches for both the light and the extractor fan were on the landing which, I was to discover, was important as there were no windows or natural light in the bathroom. Apparently, I was the only nuisance (I mean guest) that night so at least I would not have to queue for the bathroom.

'We lock the front door when we go to bed, and breakfast is at eight o'clock. I'll see you at breakfast then.' What? I had just arrived and it was only half past five. I was beginning to think I may have been better off at the camping barn. At least I would have had someone to talk to, even if there was even less to do.

I bathed and tidied myself up until I looked almost human again, before setting out to sample the delights on offer in Ennerdale Bridge. Although determined to stay out late and force my hosts to get out of bed to let me in, I was back at the B&B before eight thirty to find that they were entertaining friends to dinner. It was one of those Friday nights when there was a second helping of Coronation Street, presumably because something particularly exciting demanded an additional episode. I can't remember whether it was the time when Ken was roused from his stupor and was practicing darts on Deirdre, or whether it was Sally Webster planning to give 'the girls' something other than baked beans for tea. Whatever it was, I settled in the lounge and turned on the television to full volume. Well, their guests could have been Corrie fans.

My experience of B&B's generally has been very good, with most landladies making guests welcome and endeavouring to make them feel at home. They are very special people because, after all, there are not many who would allow strangers into their homes and let them have the run of a large portion of the place, even for money. Indeed, many of them give the impression that money is not the main reason for offering to share their homes for a night. They appear genuinely interested in their visitors and seem to enjoy their company and, I convinced myself, I was just unfortunate to be staying here on a night when the landlady was preoccupied with her dinner guests. At breakfast next morning, she seemed more cheery so I assumed I had simply arrived at an awkward time the day before (although it did pass through my mind that she was more cheerful because I would be paying and leaving soon but, perhaps, that was a bit uncharitable of me).

From Ennerdale Bridge, non-campers have no alternative on

the second day other than to walk to Borrowdale, as there are no B&B's along the way. Indeed, there is no habitation and no roads are crossed (so there is no opportunity to sneak a lift either). The day's walk would take me deep into the Lake District National Park, crossing much more difficult terrain than that encountered on the first day. In fact, Wainwright described two routes with the more direct route staying at lower levels and covering fourteen or fifteen miles. However, I had chosen the higher route, which he recommended for more energetic walkers as a fine weather alternative. Well, the weather was fine and I was energetic after all my pie-eating training, so I didn't need to give the matter much thought. Even though this option added several hours and some distance to the journey, it was the high route for me.

As I settled up with the landlady, it must have been the relief that prompted her to become more chatty and she enquired which route I would be taking.

'Oh, the high route,' I replied, confidently, knowing that she would be impressed by my stamina.

'They all say that,' she said, to my surprise and, I have to say, disappointment, 'but none of them do,' she added.

What? Well how would she know? This was the final humiliation. Unless all the landladies listed in Mrs Whitehead's Bed and Breakfast Accommodation Guide have regular conventions when they can exchange notes, how would she know? Of course, these days it's possible that they have an internet chat room, I thought, but it would be easier for her to ask where I was staying that evening and phone the next landlady.

'Have you got a tall Mr Darcy look-alike staying with you tonight? You have? Did he take the high route from Ennerdale Bridge?'

'Well, he said he did ..... but I didn't believe him.' I decided it wasn't worth wasting my breath trying to persuade her that my extreme training regime demanded that I should always take the tougher option and said my grumpy farewells.

CHAPTER FIVE

UPON ENGLAND'S MOUNTAINS GREEN

Even though it was only half past eight as I left the B&B, it was clear that it was going to be another hot day and I hoped that the two litres of fluid I had managed to buy from the pub the night before would be enough, as I knew I would not be passing any retail outlets throughout the day's journey. The trouble is that drinks weigh heavy and I could feel my pack pulling at my shoulders as I made fairly rapid progress before the sun really got to work. The first few miles were reasonably level and took me along the southern side of Ennerdale Water with magnificent views across and along the lake. I was in real Lake District country now, mountains rearing up to either side and ahead of me. There weren't many people out and about but, after three or four miles, I became aware of another walker coming up behind me:

'Good morning,' a familiar voice rang out and I would have recognised it as Paul without the unnecessary addition of 'you old bastard.'

'Less of the old,' I warned, as I turned to see him, looking sickeningly fresh despite having managed to catch up with me when I was on course for setting a record time for the day's journey.

He explained that he had set off on his own for a number of reasons, the first of which was that his usual walking companion, Andy, was not walking that day. Apparently, when they reached the camping barn on Friday afternoon, Andy had taken off his boots and socks to inspect his blisters and the others were horrified by the state of his feet. Four of them were staying in the camping barn itself but Don was camping outside, so they called him in for his opinion and he was equally appalled. Andy basked in the sympathy from his colleagues.

'You shouldn't have set such a *blistering* pace.'

'I bet you've been *bursting* to show us those.'

'Well, you'll just have to *rub along* as best you can.'

Although they were sleeping in the barn, the farmer's wife provided evening meals in the conservatory of the farmhouse and, when they went across for dinner, the subject of Andy's blisters was raised and he needed little persuasion to take off his sandals to display his ravaged feet. Indeed, he relished the attention which made the pain almost worthwhile. Fortunately, she was sensible enough to insist that he should visit the hospital and that he must not walk on Saturday. She told them that the Sherpa van would be calling in the morning to collect or drop off some bags and that Andy could go in the van to the hospital in Keswick.

The Sherpa Van Project is one of a number of organisations which provides support to Coast to Coast walkers and a minibus travels each day to all the B&Bs and YHAs along the route, moving bags from one destination to the next. For about £6, the van will take bags up to twenty kilos. There is no charge for passengers as long as they are paying for at least one bag and as long as there is enough room, so Andy was having a day off walking in order to sample the delights of Keswick.

Paul went on to explain that they had endured a disturbed night because Andy was in so much discomfort that he couldn't sleep and decided to watch the television in the barn in the middle of the night and because, although he was in a tent outside, Don decided to break the world record for the highest decibel level achieved by a snorer. Joe's farting was only a minor irritant compared to the other disturbances. In the circumstances, Paul had decided to make an early start although Don had set off even earlier as he wanted to establish a lead on the others because he had struggled so much the day before. The route Tom had mapped out for them avoided Ennerdale Bridge and went over a hill called Grike and, at one stage Paul caught sight of Don ahead of him but he had disappeared from view and Paul hadn't seen him since, so assumed he must have gone a different way.

As well as these other reasons for walking on his own, Paul explained that he was thinking of taking the high route but he was not sure of the way, despite some rough directions from Tom. In the circumstances, I agreed to let him walk with me but only on the strict understanding that he should walk at my pace.

We walked together as the lakeside path gave way to a forest track and the rising temperature caused us to contemplate the perils of dehydration as we wondered whether our drinks supply would see us through the day. Paul proved to be something of an expert, having suffered from it on a previous occasion. He was taking part in a charity event, walking from Birmingham to London along canal towpaths and, at first, he did not realise he had a problem. Now, most of us appreciate that canals and the accompanying towpaths are relatively flat, but what Paul saw ahead of him was the canal and path rising steeply as far as the eye could see. He found this confusing as his mind was still alert enough to tell him this was not possible, yet his eyes were telling him that it was. He was sensible enough to seek assistance before his condition became more serious but it was apparent that he had had a lucky escape from what could have been a very serious incident.

About five miles from Ennerdale Bridge, the high route branches off and ascends from the valley heading for the summit of Red Pike at 2479 feet. *Ordinary mortals should ignore the alternative and keep plodding along the road* Wainwright suggested, but Paul and I were no ordinary mortals and we needed no persuading to embark on the climb with gusto. Unfortunately, I found that the gusto didn't last very long and I was soon wondering whether I was an ordinary mortal after all. It must have been the heat sapping my normally abundant carbo-loaded energy levels and I began to think we should have postponed the high route option until a cooler day. The problem was that Paul was showing no signs of wilting, so I had to keep going somehow. This was a tough ascent of about 2000 feet which was to take us about two hours and it would be easy to become disheartened on this sort of long climb. On long ascents like this, I find it best not to look up as the distance to the top can discourage me (I know, it's hard to believe), so I put my head down and look at the ground immediately ahead and count my steps. The effect of counting seems to send me into a sort of reverie, casting all other thoughts from my mind so that my brain forgets to tell my body how much it hurts. This is a very effective means of maintaining progress because when I feel I must stop to catch my breath, I promise myself a break when I reach fifty and have to keep going until then and, when I reach the magic number, I tell myself I can keep going for another fifty, and so on. Well, it seems to work for me.

On this occasion, I found the ascent particularly taxing and began to fall behind. I resolved not to look up and ..... 1 ..... 2 ..... 3 ..... laboured up the slope ..... 22 ..... 23 ..... 24 .... and somehow kept going ..... 44 ..... 45 ..... 46 ..... bump, I had collided with Paul who had stopped to let me catch up. I took the opportunity to check whether we were nearly there and as I looked up, my heart sank at the sight of the steep incline stretching into the distance.

'Paul, you know when you suffered from dehydration and you thought the path went up forever..... I think I must have it.'

'Yeah, but the difference is that this *does* go up forever.'

Eventually, we reached the summit and, boy, was it worthwhile having taken the high route. The views were tremendous, with the lakes of Buttermere, Crummock Water and Loweswater all visible below. Paul allowed me to linger for at least thirty seconds or so, before we resumed our journey, walking along the ridge to the summit of High Stile, the highest point of the day at 2644 feet, and then on to the summit of High Crag before the long, steep descent of Gamlin End. The trouble with descents in the middle of the day is that, in my experience, they are always followed by ascents and this was to be no exception to that unwelcome rule. The summit of Haystacks may be no more than 1750 feet, but it is a steep and rocky climb for the weary walker on a hot day, particularly one who is trying to conceal his tiredness from his unnaturally vigorous companion and I was glad to reach the top.

'I'm knackered, and we've still got miles to go yet,' I gasped as we turned and took in the wonderful view stretching out over Buttermere and Crummock Water.

'You can do it,' Paul said encouragingly, 'and just think how all this is building up your muscles. You'll have calves like Mike Tyson by the time we get to Robin Hood's Bay.'

'What, black d'you mean?'

Although we still had several miles to cover before we reached our destination for the night, the youth hostel at Longthwaite in Borrowdale, the most arduous walking was behind us and I was happy to relax and enjoy the views for a while. On the other hand, Paul was restless and I released him from his obligation to walk at my pace as it seemed unlikely that he would lose his way now that the hard part had been completed.

Now on my own, I took my time as I worked my way across the fell tops to join the low route towards the Brandreth fence which Wainwright recommended as *the suggested rendezvous with any strong and experienced fell walkers in the party who may have preferred the High Stile alternative.* Strong and experienced – that must be me then. Funny he didn't mention knackered. *Sit down and wait for them: they will not be here for hours yet.* There was no sign of Don, Tom or Joe waiting for me, so I assumed they must have passed through here hours ago. I trudged on towards Honister, where I would see the first traces of habitation since I left Ennerdale Bridge that morning: that is, if you can call a slate quarry and a youth hostel habitation. At least I would be able to get a drink, having finished my own rations much earlier.

Just before I reached this haven of civilisation, hordes of fell runners began to hurtle past, almost mowing me down in their headlong rush. I am full of admiration for these barmy individuals who move at breakneck speed down impossibly steep terrain as well as managing to keep running when tackling the uphill stretches. Despite my admiration, they soon became a bloody nuisance as I felt compelled to stand aside every few seconds to let them pass. This was more out of self preservation than etiquette as they were moving at such a speed that I would have been flattened otherwise. There were bloody hundreds of them but, after a while, I came across one runner who had stopped as he was suffering from cramp. The only surprise here was that he was the only one. He told me that they were all taking part in the Borrowdale Fell Race and that he was just one of several hundred competitors. I found it quite staggering that so many entrants had travelled from all over the country to take part in such a demanding race. I imagined that local runners must have a distinct advantage in being able to train on the fells, whereas many of the runners were wearing vests indicating that they represented athletic clubs up and down the country and most of their training would have been on running tracks or roads.

I remembered that the Riverside Bar in Rosthwaite displays an honours board giving details of all the winners of the race over the years, with the incredibly fast winning times. There is also a map of the route, which takes in the summits of Scafell Pike, Great Gable and Dale Head so, although these runners had already been up two of the highest mountains in England, they still had another long climb to complete before the finishing line.

I decided to visit the Riverside Bar some months later and the winner that day was one Simon Booth and, incredibly, it was his eighth consecutive victory and his ninth in total. His time was recorded at an amazing two hours forty-six minutes. If that is impressive, then even more so is the record of Billy Bland, who won the race ten times between 1976 and 1988 and he holds the record time of two hours thirty-four minutes. The course distance is an estimated seventeen miles and involves about six thousand five hundred feet of ascent. The mind-boggling times put our own prospective achievements into perspective. I know absolutely nothing about either Billy Bland or Simon Booth but, clearly, they are the David Beckham and Wayne Rooney of the fell running world and isn't it unfair that they receive no real recognition or reward for their achievements? They have a talent which puts them at the very top of their sport but, because that sport is not easily televised and is a minority sport, their talent is unrewarded. Top footballers, pop stars and film stars are paid obscene amounts of money, not because their talent as footballers, pop singers and actors is any greater than Simon's and Billy's talent as fell runners, but because they are watched and heard by millions of people around the world. In other words, they provide enjoyment to millions, whereas a top fell runner can provide enjoyment for only a few.

It is an accident of birth. If the situations had been reversed and Simon and Billy had been born with the equivalent amount of football talent, they would be multi-millionaires. Whilst Wayne Rooney would be running up and down the fells, famous only within the fell running fraternity, wondering when he could upgrade his car to a second-hand Mondeo, Simon would be selling his golden metatarsals to the highest bidder, considering whether his advert for a full-time car cleaner for his fleet of high performance cars should include amongst the perks the free use of his fully-equipped gym and spa (including use of the state-of-the-art navel de-fluffing machine), and negotiating a publishing deal for his book, *Simon (How to make millions by getting a ghost-writer to write a few hundred pages of tosh and selling it to gullible fans by putting a photograph of me on the cover)*.

In the meantime, David Beckham would be living in a bothy in the Lake District, nursing knees shattered by the strain of all those miles running up and down mountains, hoping that a visitor to the Riverside Bar might buy him a drink for old times' sake and that Victoria wouldn't keep on about having a new bike. Billy would be receiving a fortune at L A Galaxy, having captained England more times than anyone (except John Motson) can remember, and would have to decide soon whether to accept the invitation to be Guest of Honour at the premiere of the new movie, *Bend it like Bland*.

The Borrowdale Fell Runners website gives full details of the race and, as I suspected, the local runners have a distinct advantage. Not only is Simon Booth a member of that club, but five of the first seven finishers were members. Simon finished five minutes ahead of his closest rival and only the first seven broke the three hour barrier. There were three hundred and eighty-three starters and only thirty of these failed to finish. The last four to finish just failed to beat the six hour mark. I mention the number of entrants and some of the other times as they emphasise the magnitude of the winners achievements. I am in awe of these people.

Despite the efforts of the fell runners to slow my relentless progress, I made it to the slate quarry in time to get a drink from the quarry shop. They leave tea, coffee and orange squash for thirsty walkers to help themselves, requiring only that they wash their cups or glasses and leave a small donation. A great example to others of kindness and consideration towards the fatigued hiker. I drank my fill and set off for the final three miles of the day's journey, crossing the road (yes, a road; the first I had seen in almost nine hours) and wending my way through gentler countryside to the beautiful Borrowdale valley, green fields nestling below the surrounding mountains. This is where Prince Charles stays on his visits to the area and it is easy to see what attracts him back on a regular basis. Having said that, I do know for a fact that he doesn't stop at the youth hostel, so at least we wouldn't have to put up with him snoring and farting in the dormitory all night.

It was about six by the time I arrived at the hostel, over nine hours after I had set out from my comfortable digs with my landlady's scepticism ringing in my ears. Well, I had proved her wrong; but how would she know?

CHAPTER SIX

AND THEN THERE WERE FIVE

Expecting to be the last of the Old Spice Boys to arrive, I was surprised to be greeted only by Paul and by Andy, who had both good and bad news to report. The good news was that he had enjoyed his morning with the Sherpa Van driver going round all the B&Bs in the Ennerdale Bridge area before moving on to all the B&B's in Borrowdale and then being dropped off at the hospital in Keswick. After his hospital visit, he had done some shopping in Keswick before catching one of the infrequent local buses that run from Keswick to Borrowdale. The bad news was that the hospital had told him that his blisters had become infected, put him on a course of antibiotics and told him that he must abandon any walking for the next week or two. This was a major disappointment not only for Andy, but also for the rest of us as he was the one who kept us amused. Tom would be particularly upset as there is nothing he likes more than a bit of confrontation and Andy provides that by the lorry load.

'You were wrong about there being only one lake in the Lake District, Al,' he said in a challenging tone.

'How do you work that out then, Andy?'

'There's a sign in Ennerdale Bridge that says *TO THE LAKE* and it doesn't mean Bassenthwaite,' he said triumphantly.

'But that's just a local sign directing people to Ennerdale Water.'

'It may be, but it refers to 'the lake' and the local people should know.'

'Well, no one is denying that it's a lake in the true sense that any inland stretch of water is a lake, but the point is that it's not *called* a lake, Andy.'

'But the sign says it's a lake, so when you told me there's only one lake in the Lake District it wasn't true.'

'Look Andy, the sign directs people to Ennerdale Water. What do you expect it to say – *TO THE WATER*? That wouldn't mean much to visitors, would it?' I said, attempting to remain calm, knowing that he was deliberately winding me up.

'I don't care. It's a lake,' he insisted.

'Look, the Ordnance Survey map doesn't give it the title of a lake. The map simply says Ennerdale Water. It doesn't say Ennerdale Water *Lake* and it doesn't say *Lake* Ennerdale Water. As far as the Ordnance Survey is concerned, it's not a lake.'

'What do they know?' he persisted. 'If the local people call it 'the lake' then it must be a lake.'

'Fair enough, Andy,' I said pleasantly ('irritating bastard' I thought).

Not long after this exchange, the other three arrived and Andy brought them up to date with his news, which they accepted with dismay, although Tom couldn't resist at least one dig:

'I might have known. The youngest member of the team; the only one under sixty and you can't stand the pace. You youngsters have no determination. Just leave it to the over-sixties and we'll tell you all about it when we get back.'

Their day had not been uneventful. Of course, Paul had told me already that they had decided to take the direct route from the camping barn to Ennerdale Water, avoiding the village of Ennerdale Bridge. This meant ascending the hill called Grike which is about 1,500 feet above sea level. The only problem was that this is not a well–known summit and is not walked regularly so that, although there is a public footpath shown on the map, there is no clear path on the ground. Having struggled with the weight of his pack on the first day, Don had decided to allow himself more time and had set off early, disappearing even before the others had eaten breakfast.

Joe and Tom walked together and they told me that they had found the descent from Grike very difficult because of the lack of a clear path and the steepness of the hillside but, eventually, they reached the path alongside Ennerdale Water and were able to make better progress. After they left Ennerdale Water behind and joined the Forestry Commission track, they had caught up with Don and found him in a foul mood. If they thought they had struggled coming down from Grike, they had had a comparative doddle according to Don. He had completely lost his way and struggled through the bracken and gorse and this, combined with the steepness of the fellside and the weight of his pack, had caused him to fall several times, so that he was scratched and bad-tempered. Apparently, the conversation had gone something like this:

'It was bloody ridiculous. I couldn't find the path, there was gorse growing everywhere, the bracken was up to my armpits, it was too hot ....'

'Don, we've just come over there as well, you know. We know what it's like,' Joe had said in a placatory way.

'Bloody ridiculous. I thought it was supposed to be a National Park. Why do we pay our taxes if they're just going to allow it to grow wild?'

'Don, the whole idea of a National Park is to retain it's natural beauty. If they chopped down the gorse and bracken and put in a paved pathway and put up signposts, nobody would want to come here.'

'Bloody ridiculous. I could have died in there. It was so steep I fell over, got torn to shreds by the gorse, landed on my front and couldn't get up because I was trapped by my pack. I was hidden from view by the bracken and could have been there for weeks without anyone knowing,' he said sullenly. 'It was pure luck that I managed to roll on to my side so I could release the straps on my pack and wriggle out.'

Joe and Tom had struggled to keep straight faces at the thought of Don writhing about in the bracken for days, trying to shoo away inquisitive sheep.

'Bloody ridiculous. And whose stupid idea was it to go that way, anyway?'

Paul now wondered whether he had overtaken Don whilst he was scrabbling about on the ground.

'Come to think of it,' he interjected, 'I did notice some grunting noises and bracken swishing about at one stage, but I got out of there as quick as I could in case there was a dangerous animal in there.'

'I've only known Don for twenty-four hours,' Joe confided in me, 'so I couldn't say any more, but I was surprised at Tom's reaction. I know he likes nothing better than a bit of confrontation and Don was giving him the perfect opportunity for a real ding-dong argument, particularly the comment about *whose stupid idea* it was, yet he let it all pass with barely a comment. Still, I thought, they've been pals for over thirty years and Tom must know how to handle him, and perhaps he thinks he's too sensitive to be taken to task. On the other hand, I've realised already that Don's the sort who gets himself so worked up about things that he'll ignore any advice and act completely irrationally rather than accept any advice, so I wondered whether Tom thought it just wasn't worth-while arguing.' I was beginning to realise that there was more to Joe than met the eye. Clearly, he was very aware of what was happening around him and assessing the strengths and weaknesses of his companions.

Taking the low route, the path passes the youth hostel known as Black Sail Hut after about ten miles. This is the most remote hostel in the land and, by the time they got there, Don had fallen behind. Joe and Tom stopped to refill their water bottles, before stretching out and relaxing on the grass. As Don approached a few minutes later, they recognised that, if anything, his mood was even darker and, as he un-strapped his pack and threw it to the ground, he well and truly gave vent to his feelings with a torrent of exple-tives, the like of which Joe had not heard before (well, not since they left Don an hour earlier).

'That's it. I've had enough. I'm going home,' he said at last. Tom's patience was at an end.

'Look Don, don't be so bloody stupid. You're in this mood because your pack's too heavy and that's because you're carrying all sorts of crap you'll never need and, if you'd had any sense, you'd never have brought. Why don't you just go inside the youth hostel and ask the warden for a bag and put all the things you're never going to use in the bag and ask the warden to send it home for you? Otherwise, you'll struggle for the next ten days and drive us mad the whole time with your fucking moaning.'

Joe was lying back on the grass, watching and listening.

'Tom, why don't you tell him what you really think?'

This seemed to do the trick and they had walked on from Black Sail together and, by the time they reached Longthwaite, Don was in much better spirits. After Andy's enforced retirement, I had listened to their story with growing concern that we would be down to only four after just two days of our journey, but his demeanour suggested that my anxiety was misplaced. For the moment, anyway.

Up-dated on the day's events, Don went off to pitch his tent:

'Make sure you don't pitch it within quarter of a mile of the hostel,' Andy shouted after him 'we want some sleep tonight.'

'Make that half a mile,' Paul added.

'Better make that a mile to be on the safe side,' Joe said.

When I had arrived at the B&B the evening before, I had so much on my mind that I had forgotten all about the discomfort I had noticed in my big toe earlier in the day and had not even bothered to check it out, but all the talk about Andy's infected feet reminded me that, during the long and arduous trek over the fells on Saturday, I had suffered more discomfort despite the 2000 mile socks guarantee to keep wearers blister-free. In the circumstances, before we went to our bunks, I asked Tom to check me out, which he did, albeit reluctantly. Give him his due, he conducted the most protracted and thorough inspection and, finally, announced that he could not see anything that could be causing any discomfort whatsoever. Knowing that I was not imagining the pain, I decided to take a second opinion but, after the most cursory look, Paul only confirmed Tom's diagnosis. I was not convinced, so performed contortions to see what I could find for myself (it is not easy for a sixty year old to inspect the underside of his big toe, particularly with muscles aching after a nine hour walk) and what I found was an enormous blister, covering the entire area of the bottom of the toe and which, consequently, I pointed out to Tom in my most polite manner:

'You can't see anything? What the bloody hell is this then?'

Putting on his glasses, which I have to admit I had not noticed he had removed prior to his earlier inspection, he prodded the affected area to see how much it made me jump, before agreeing to perform the appropriate pain-relieving operation. Even though his past experiences had prompted him to assemble the most advanced emergency first aid kit imaginable, what he had failed to include was a blister-popping implement. He searched through his bag for something that might be capable of making the appro-priate incision, and I looked on with some trepidation, if not terror, as he produced a pair of rubber gloves and then unwrapped a pair of sterilised scissors. Surely he didn't intend to cut the blister, did he? I need not have worried, as he very skilfully pierced the troublesome blister, releasing enough fluid to fill a milk bottle (all right, a jam jar then). Tom was looking very pleased with himself as he waited for some comment of appreciation.

'Tom, you may be the most eminent blister-popping specialist in the world but if you can't see a blister the size of a small tortoise, you won't be getting many referrals.'

Needless to say, my 2000 mile socks were consigned to the youth hostel bin, with about one thousand nine hundred and seventy miles outstanding on the clock.

'Anything interesting in there?' Tom asked Paul, who seemed

to be immersed in Wainwright's biography.

'Yes,' he replied, 'did you know that he didn't visit the Lake District until 1930 when he was twenty-three and he fell in love with it straight away? Amazingly, it was the first time he'd ever been away from Blackburn other than for day trips. Strange really, when you think what an easy journey it should have been because it couldn't have been more than fifty miles or so and trains and buses ran regularly in those days.'

'That's amazing,' said Tom 'for someone who explored the fells endlessly, usually on his own. You can't imagine that he would have been nervous about leaving home.'

That set me thinking, for a number of reasons. It had been a long day – nine hours walking over difficult terrain – and I had to admit that I had found it a strain in spite of my rigorous training regime. I knew that there would be no respite over the next three days, all of which promised to be just as tough. The following two days would be similarly arduous but would see us through the mountains but, the day after that, we would be faced with a twenty-two mile walk. Hopefully, that would be easier walking but the distance alone would make it tough, particularly after four days of walking without a break.

Although I had visited the Lake District regularly over the years, I did not know what to expect once we were out of the Lake District. Apart from a few days in the Yorkshire Dales, I had never been near the rest of the Coast to Coast route. I knew I could handle walking for nine hours at a time, but I found myself wondering whether I was capable of doing that day after day. Strangely, I hadn't given it a thought beforehand, but now I was beginning to count down the days until we could take it a little easier. If I could get through tomorrow, I would have only two more long days before a much shorter day came along. I shouldn't be thinking like this, I told myself. This isn't a chore. It is to be enjoyed, not endured. I kept my thoughts to myself, assuming that the others didn't share my fears. Anyway, apart from Paul, the others had taken a shorter and much easier route that day and had not pushed themselves to the extent that I had.

At least part of the problem for me was that I had not been as adventurous over the years as someone like Tom, for example, so I had not fully explored my capabilities. I needed someone like Tom to push me into doing something as challenging as the Coast to Coast Walk. Of course, things could have been very different if my life had taken a different course. Once again, I compared myself to Wainwright and convinced myself that there were similarities as young men, in that I had led a fairly sheltered early life, had been shy in female company and had not discovered the Lakes until I was a grown man. Growing up on a council estate in Southport with my parents and older sister, we had no money to spend. We were always clothed and fed and I cannot recall ever thinking that we were poor but the fact remained that treats were rare. We never went away on holiday (although that was not unusual as neither did any of the other people on the estate). Unfortunately, I was marked out as being different to the other boys I was growing up with at the age of eleven when I passed my eleven plus and went to the Grammar School. I stood out like a sore thumb because I had to wear the compulsory maroon and black striped blazer, whereas my pals were not compelled to wear a uniform to attend the Secondary Modern. Not only that, but I had to do homework before I could go out and play football in the street. Things got worse at fifteen when the Secondary Modern boys left school and started work on the building sites and suchlike. Now, they had money to spend and, instead of playing football in the street, they could afford the bus fare into town to go to the cinema and whatever else teenage boys did in those days. Of course, I had my pals at school but they lived all over the borough and, anyway, Southport is a pretty affluent town and most of the Grammar School boys had money in their pockets. I remember that some of my school pals used to go to a coffee bar in town after school where they would meet girls from the Girls Grammar School, but I couldn't go with them because I didn't have money for coffee (and, anyway, if you lived on a council estate, you didn't drink coffee). The result was that I had two distinct sets of friends and I found myself on the periphery of both.

Where I was fortunate was that nobody had any expectations of me. Not my parents, not my school. My sister was the golden girl, always top of her class, and head girl at primary school. I was proud of her, but grateful that it meant people didn't seem to notice me. It was a surprise to everyone when I passed my eleven plus the year after my sister. Indeed, I can remember my grandmother saying 'he's not as daft as he looks' which was not a flattering way of expressing her congratulations. A pleasant 'well done' would have gone down nicely. I did not enjoy school. All I wanted to do was to be outside chasing a football. The only periods I looked forward to were P.E. and Games (even though it was a rugby-playing school). When it came to 'O' Levels, again there were no expectations and my unexpected success drew another 'he's not as daft as he looks' from Grandma. In fact, I suspect there was disappointment in some quarters. Certainly, the schoolmasters must have groaned when they heard I was staying on to do my 'A' Levels, and I'm sure my father was hoping that I would be easing the burden by starting work. The truth is that I had no idea what I wanted to do and staying on at school deferred the day when I had to make a decision about my future. Although I hated school, I really had no idea what going to work entailed. So-called careers advisers always seemed to suggest banking or accountancy, but these sounded very boring to me, even though I had no idea what a banker or accountant did. My father was a driver/storekeeper and my uncles were labourers, postmen and railway porters. I didn't even know anyone who worked in an office. So, I put in another two years at school and, to universal surprise, my grandmother was saying 'he's not as daft as he looks' once again. My three 'A' Levels enabled me to land a job in an insurance office in Liverpool. I still had no idea what working for a living would be like and insurance sounded extremely boring to me. Mind you, all I knew about insurance was that a man from the Pru' called at our house once a week to collect some money that was referred to as 'premium' and every few years seemed to get very excited when there was talk of another 'policy' being taken out. I didn't know that people insured their houses (we didn't own ours) or their cars (we didn't have one) and I had never heard of 'public liability' or 'employers liability'.

I had to have a suit for work. I didn't know anyone who had a suit. My mother bought one from 'the catalogue' and I trotted off for my first day at work, having no idea what to expect. I loved it. After that first day, I couldn't wait to get to work each day. Perhaps the fact that it was 1963 and I was working in Liverpool had something to do with it but they were some of the happiest days of my life. Liverpool was the place to be – The Beatles had just hit the big time and all the other Mersey groups were following suit and both football teams were beginning to win trophies.

At eighteen, the world had opened up for me. Hard to believe now, but I had never been away on holiday or been inside a hotel or had a meal in a restaurant. They were for the future. In the meantime, I was happy. Going to work Monday to Friday (and every other Saturday morning) and playing football in the South-port and District League on Saturday afternoons. Then, one Saturday afternoon, talking to one of the old men in the team (he must have been at least twenty-one, but that seemed very old to an eighteen year old) we learnt that he had a static caravan on a site in Great Langdale in the Lake District. A friend who lived no more than a hundred yards from me played in the same team and we decided to rent the caravan for a few days and do some walking. Although the Lakes are no great distance from Southport, this was before the days of motorways and I had only ever had a couple of day trips to the Lakes with my parents who thought that the Lake District was Bowness. So, I was eighteen before I 'discovered' the Lakes, only a few years younger than Wainwright when he was captivated. If anything, his journey from Blackburn was even shorter but, it seems, neither he nor I had the wherewithal to explore what was virtually on our doorsteps until we were adults.

This was a great adventure for two young men, but particu-larly for me as I had only spent the odd night away from home before. Travelling was not easy in those days and we had to get a bus to Preston before catching the 'express' bus to Ambleside, where we got the local bus to Langdale. Fortunately, my pal seemed to have done some walking in the area before and knew what to do. On the first day, we set off in the pouring rain and walked up to Stickle Tarn. Never having been hiking before, I didn't have any of the accepted clothing or equipment and my 'waterproofs' consisted of a bright yellow bicycle cape, which made me look like a small mobile tent on legs and which failed to keep out the incessant rain that insisted on forming raging torrents of water on my face and head, which flooded down my neck. My footwear consisted of my most robust pair of shoes, the soles of which were soon flapping loosely, enjoying the freedom from the uppers granted by a short time walking in the great outdoors.

On the way down the mountain, I made the mistake of picking up too much speed and I hurtled down the slippery, rock-strewn mountainside, unable to stop. As I gathered pace, I saw vivid images of myself reaching the valley a thousand feet below in record time. My pal stepped aside as I zoomed past him at break-neck speed and, to this day, I can see his face turning white in horror and hear those mumbled words, reflecting his concern:

'You mad bugger!'

If I had stumbled, I could have killed myself but, from time to time, I did manage to inhibit my acceleration by landing on a rock which was at such an angle that it slowed my progress slightly and, eventually, I did come to a halt. We arrived back at the caravan cold and soaking wet and, in my case, lucky to be alive but I had learned a number of valuable lessons which have stood me in good stead ever since. We couldn't do any more walking on that first visit, partly because our clothes were soaked, but mainly because I didn't have anything to put on my feet!

Despite the rain and the near-death experience, I had loved every minute and it was not long before we were back again, this time equipped with boots and waterproofs. In fact, we had three or four breaks up there in the next couple of years. Sod's Law dictated that I need not have bothered with the expense of water-proofs as we had beautiful weather each time. We took risks, as young people do. I can't remember that we had maps or compasses – we would just set off in the morning with a particular objec-tive, such as the summit of Coniston Old Man, and when we achieved that, we would carry straight on, for no other reason than that we did not want to take the same route back. Sometimes, we would find ourselves miles from our base, absolutely knackered, and have to catch a bus back. Happy days.

Life changed again when I was twenty-one, when I got married. My first son arrived when I was twenty-two and my daughter when I was twenty-three, with my second son coming along ten years later. I loved my family and was content to devote my time to them and work. Twenty-odd years later, the older children were adults and the youngest was growing up rapidly and I found that my life consisted of working from Monday to Friday, with the weekends taken up by cleaning the cars, mowing the lawn and keeping the garden tidy. Going out or trying new experiences were things of the past. In short, I had become a real stick-in-the-mud. Worst of all, I realised that I didn't laugh any more. The separation and divorce were traumatic for everyone concerned, but a new life was opened up to me. I bought a newly-built mews house which required no maintenance and, for the first time in my life, I was living on my own. Suddenly, I could do whatever I wanted without having to consult anyone. At the weekends, I could get up in the morning and decide what I was going to do, without asking what anyone else had arranged, and knowing that I didn't have a lawn to mow or a garden to weed. Fell walking was something I could do on my own and so I would jump in the car and head off up the motorway. As a family, we had managed at least a long weekend in the Lakes each year and done some walking but most of that walking had been at quite low levels. Now, as a solitary walker, I could be more adventurous and I began to walk much longer distances, at higher altitude and in all weathers.

Apart from the walking, I began to enjoy going out again, meeting different people and trying new experiences. This was an entirely new way of life but, after all those years of routine, there were times when I needed someone to give me a bit of a push. So, even after nearly fifteen years of my 'new life', it is unlikely that I would have thought of doing the Coast to Coast Walk if Tom had not invited me and made all the arrangements. Although I was confident that I could complete the walk and, indeed, was absolutely determined to do so, all those years of avoiding anything new still seemed to hold me back sometimes. It was not exactly a fear of the unknown; it was as if I had lost the fearlessness of youth and, I realised, I still harboured a certain reluctance to tackle anything new.

During the evening, I had discovered more about Andy's day.

'There was a bit of a misunderstanding at the hospital when I asked about the rapist,' he said.

'What rapist?' Tom asked.

'Funnily enough, they asked me exactly the same question. So I told them. "Reginald Blain" I said.'

'Mr Blain isn't a rapist,' they said.

'Well why have you got him locked up in that room along the corridor?'

'Which room?'

'The one with the sign on the door saying Reginald Blain, the rapist.'

'That doesn't say the rapist,' one of them said, 'it says Reginald Blain, Therapist.'

'It was a pity really because one of the nurses fancied the pants off me but she seemed to go off me a bit after that.'

'I wonder why?' Tom reflected.

'Anyway, instead of spending the afternoon playing doctors and nurses, I ran a few errands for Joe in Keswick.' It transpired that Joe had been talking to Tom on Friday evening about his walking poles, his interest having been aroused by his attack of cramp that afternoon. Tom had been having problems with his knees for the last year or two and had taken to using walking poles and wearing a bandage on his right knee. Actually, he needed bandages on both knees but thought that wearing two would make him look even more of an old crock, so struggled to get by with one. Having observed his use of the walking poles, Joe asked him about them and Tom explained that he found that they helped him to relieve some of the pressure on his knees by taking some weight on his arms. He told Joe that they cost him £25 but what he omitted to tell him was that he had bought them at a discounted price. Knowing that Andy was going into Keswick, Joe asked him to buy him some poles (and a knee bandage) if he had time to do any shopping after his hospital visit. He was delighted when Andy presented them to him on the Saturday night.

'How much do I owe you?'

'£52.50,' Andy replied, with a big grin, obviously feeling very pleased with himself.

'Bugger off. How much were they really?'

'The poles were £25 each and the bandage was £2.50.'

'You were robbed, or rather I've been robbed. And £2.50 for a bandage? You've been to the hospital haven't you? You could have told them you've got a bad knee as well as blisters and they'd have given you a bandage for nothing. I won't be able to afford dinner tonight now. Don't think you're going to get a job as my personal shopper,' he grumbled.

CHAPTER SEVEN

THANKS FOR THE MEMORY

After breakfast on Sunday morning, we assembled outside the hostel and I had to do a double take as there seemed to be two Toms.

'Bloody hell, Joe, do you have to wear your bandage on the same knee as Tom?'

'I didn't know there was anything wrong with his knee,' Paul mumbled.

'And did he tell you to buy the same coloured poles as mine, Andy?' Tom asked.

Not only were they the same age and build, but now they had identical walking poles and bandages on their right knees.

'It's a good job Joe farts all the time or we wouldn't know them apart,' said Paul. 'I knew all his farting would come in handy sometime.'

'Bugger off,' was Joe's only response (apart from a fart).

'Did you learn any more about Wainwright last night?' Tom asked Paul as we waited for Joe to tie his laces.

'Yes, I told you that he came to the Lakes for the first time when he was twenty-three, and it was also the first time he had been away from Blackburn; well, the following year, in 1931, he passed his municipal accountants exams and won a prize for the second best results in the country and had to go to the annual conference in Brighton to collect it. Apparently, he had never been south of Manchester before and said he was glad to be on the next train back.'

'Perhaps it's a good job he didn't fall in love with Brighton then,' Tom said. 'Otherwise, he might not have written *The Coast to Coast Walk;* he might have written *The Road to Brighton Pier* instead.'

'I saw that in a bookshop a few weeks ago; I thought we could do that next year,' Andy said.

'Do what next year?' Paul asked, a puzzled look on his face.

'The road to Brighton Pier. Sounds a good challenge.'

'There isn't a book called *The Road to Brighton Pier,*' Paul explained, as patiently as he could, 'I think you're thinking about *The Road to Wigan Pier.*'

'There isn't a pier in Wigan,' Andy pointed out.

'I know that,' Paul said, a note of exasperation creeping into his voice.

'So why would Wainwright write a book about walking to Wigan Pier when there isn't one?' demanded Andy.

'It isn't a book about walking and Wainwright didn't write it. It was written by George Orwell,' Paul replied, raising his voice ever so slightly.

'Who's he?' Andy asked.

'He wrote *Animal Farm.*'

'Oh, he was a farmer, was he?'

'No, he wasn't a farmer; *Animal Farm* was nothing to do with farming,' Paul said, now beginning to lose his rag.

'Sounds a bit of a dickhead to me; he writes a book called *The Road to Wigan Pier* which has nothing to do with walking to a place that doesn't exist, and writes a book called *Animal Farm* which has nothing to do with farming! He won't sell many copies, I can tell you.'

'The point is,' Tom said, interrupting the debate about English literature in the twentieth century and giving no bonus points to Andy, 'we won't be walking to bloody Brighton or anywhere else in Sussex, thank God.'

'There's nothing wrong with Sussex,' Joe said, defending the county of his birth.

'I thought of moving to Sussex a few years ago,' Andy muttered. 'I saw a programme on television about four women who were single and all desperate to find a man, and what was really surprising was that they were all attractive, too. You'd be amazed at what they were prepared to do to get a man. I thought I could do with a bit of that.'

'And if you had moved to Sussex, how did you think you were going to find these four sex mad women?' asked Paul, seeing his chance to rile Andy in return.

'I'd have put myself out and about a bit and, anyway, I remembered that two of them were called Carrie and Samantha, so I could have asked if anyone knew them. There can't be too many Carries and Samanthas in Sussex.'

'Just a minute, Andy,' Tom said, in a knowing tone, 'did these women have American accents, by any chance?'

'I don't know. They did have accents but I assumed they were from Sussex; they speak funny down there anyway, don't they?'

'And were there a lot of skyscrapers?'

'I think there were a few. Why?'

'Can you remember what this programme was called?'

'I think it was something like *Sussex and the City*.'

We left Andy to wait for the Sherpa Van, and set off on what would be another long day's walk to Patterdale. Wainwright's original description spread the journey from Borrowdale to Patterdale over two days, the first of which is to Grasmere, a distance of nine and a quarter miles, followed by the trek from Grasmere to Patterdale, a distance of a further eight miles. Using the direct routes, each of these walks can be completed in four or five hours which leaves walkers with too much time on their hands, so we had decided (meaning Tom had decided on our behalf) to cover the distance in just one day. We had seen Don set off three quarters of an hour earlier whilst we were having breakfast, laden down by all his equipment, with pots and pans dangling from every available hitch and hook, moving uncomfortably and his profile reminding me of a one-man band:

'Seeing Don trudging along like that, doesn't he remind you of a London busker, carrying all his gear from one subway to the next?'

'You're right, Al, his pack could be his drum, protruding from his back,' Tom agreed 'and his pots and pans are the other instruments swinging from their fastenings.'

'The only things missing are the cymbals between his knees,' Joe added.

'But he's walking as though he's got the cymbals,' I laughed 'and the jangling of his pots adds to the effect.'

'Yeah, he looks like that fella who had a few hits in the late sixties. What was his name? Come on, Al, you've got a good memory for stuff like this,' Tom said.

'Funnily enough, his name was Don something, if I remember rightly. Now what was his surname? Pheasant? No, it wasn't Don Pheasant, but it was something like that. Some sort of gamebird.'

'Grouse?' suggested Joe 'Don Grouse sounds just about right for our Don.'

'Partridge. That was his name, Don Partridge. His big hit was called *Rosie*.'

Rosie, oh Rosie

'Bloody hell, you've started Andy off now,' Joe complained.

'Don't worry,' Andy reassured us, 'I can't remember any more.'

'Thank God for that.'

'He had another hit as well,' I recalled, 'that was called *Blue Eyes*.'

Blue eyes look my way
Make today my lucky day

'Fucking hell, will you stop giving him his cue?' Joe spluttered, 'he knows more than one line of that one.'

'Well remembered, Al,' Tom said 'I don't know how you remember all that stuff.'

'It's strange, isn't it,' I said 'I can recall things from years ago, but forget what happened last week. My theory is that the brain is just a massive computer, with an unlimited memory. When we're younger, there isn't much stored in there so we can remember everything but, as we get older, we use more and more storage space. It's like a giant filing cabinet and it can take ages to find the file that you want. You know it's in there somewhere, but you can't find the file you need. The older stuff can be more familiar because you've looked for it more times, so you know where it is, but you can't remember where you put the new stuff. Also, we probably have an in-built SAVE function. Again, when we're younger, we just save everything because there's so much capacity but, as we fill more and more of the storage capacity, we start to become more selective about what we save. If it's not essential, we don't bother to save it. That's why I can remember that Florian Albert played centre forward for Hungary in the 1966 World Cup matches, but I'd struggle to name England's centre forward in a game a coupe of weeks ago.'

'Well, that's good,' Tom said, a little scornfully it seemed, 'when Pam accuses me of forgetting something in future, I'll be able to say 'I didn't forget; I just didn't bother to press the SAVE button'.

It was another glorious day and, after spending about half of the first two days walking on my own, it was great to know that I would have company all day. The two legs of the day's walk are similar in that they involve long ascents followed by long descents to the destinations of Grasmere and Patterdale, so putting them together makes for a tough day and once again I wondered how many of us would reach Robin Hood's Bay, what with Andy having dropped out already and Don threatening to go home. Without Andy, we were down to five and I was not so sure about Don's capacity to keep going with all that weight and, of course, he had already threatened to go home. I didn't doubt Tom's determination, but it was clear that his knees were giving him more trouble than he would admit to us, and I knew that Joe had struggled on the first day resulting in his attack of cramp which had prompted him to send Andy on his shopping spree, spending an indecent amount of Joe's money. As for me, the pies and pasties had clearly done the trick from a physical point of view, although I would have been forced to admit, if pressed, that I had entertained some doubts on that long ascent of Red Pike the day before. Of course, I blamed Paul for failing to keep his promise to walk at my pace and forcing me to walk slightly faster than was comfortable. Paul himself seemed untroubled as I watched him disappearing into the distance as we climbed towards Greenup Edge. So, I was not concerned about Paul; it was the other three who were worrying me. Had they been eating enough pasties?

Mind you, Tom's leg would have to fall off before he would even begin to consider whether he should give up, so perhaps I should not have worried about him. He is a determined character who enjoys life to the full. He had an extremely stressful job which threatened to steer him towards setting a new record as the world's youngest ever grumpy old man. As Production Director, he was under immense pressure to deliver and was under fire from all sides. He arrived at work early and was immediately faced with the problems associated with employees arriving late, or not at all. Machinery would break down, halting production, suppliers would fail to deliver, the sales force would accept orders that were impossible to make, and customers and his Co-Directors would expect unrealistic production times. As a result, his days were spent arguing with employees, suppliers, customers and, worst of all, his fellow Directors. It was during this stressful period that he turned to fell walking as a means of relieving his tensions. He had done a little walking on the Lake District fells, although nothing very serious but, when he heard of someone who had climbed all two hundred and fourteen Lakeland peaks described in Wainwright's guides, he could not resist the challenge. He now had a motive for visiting the Lakes on a regular basis and he found that the beauty of the area, combined with the physical effort involved took his mind away from what was happening at work. Indeed, there were times when he had had enough of work by late morning and would drop everything and drive up to Cumbria and knock another of the two hundred and fourteen off his list.

He was about fifty-four when the business was sold, still

young enough to start again, but why subject himself to more stress? He was in a position to do what he wanted to do, when he wanted to do it, and he was determined to take advantage. He had re-married a couple of years earlier and Pam was still in her twenties and climbing the career ladder. She enjoyed going to work and was not about to give it up. Sure, she enjoyed holidays, but not all the time. This was a potential time bomb which ticked away for a number of years, threatening to explode and destroy the marriage. She was ambitious and wanted to climb to the top, whereas Tom had done all that and had come down again. It seemed they were travelling in opposite directions. But, as they say, love conquers all and they had worked things out over the years. Pam is now a Director of a household name company and still loves going to work each day, but can find time for several super holidays every year. As for Tom, as well as holidays with Pam, he visits relatives in Australia and the States on a regular basis and fits in lots of expeditions such as the Coast to Coast with his pals. Fortunately, he loves cooking and is happy enough to do some of the other household chores. As if that is not enough, he is always involved in some building project or another. If it's not a new bathroom or a new kitchen, it's an extension or knocking one room through into another. Whenever he runs out of ideas for knocking about (sorry, I mean improving) his own house, he'll be doing the same for one of his family or friends. He's probably busier than he wants to be but it works for both of them.

The first bewitching mile, every step a joy, is an idyllic journey Wainwright wrote and, in such beautiful weather, it certainly was. As we gained height, we were able to turn and look down and along the wonderfully green Borrowdale valley with its scattering of farmhouses. As the sun beat down, it was hard to believe that Seathwaite, only a few minutes away from where we stood, has the unwanted title as the wettest place in England. I remembered one of the handful of residents of Seathwaite trying to convince me that it doesn't rain any more frequently there than in many other places in England; it's just that, when it does rain, it really means it. As well as being a Mountain Rescue volunteer, he was a teacher at a school in Keswick and he reckoned that he could leave Keswick in torrential rain and arrive home fifteen minutes later in weather that made the downpour in Keswick seem like a few spits and spots.

It took us two hours of hard slog to reach Greenup Edge and, as we arrived at this pass, we caught up with Don who had stopped for a break. Paul had passed him ages ago, but Don now joined up with us as we began the descent towards Grasmere.

From Greenup Edge, the direct route to Grasmere is along Far Easedale but Wainwright described an alternative which keeps to higher ground and adds another mile to the journey and eventually leads to Helm Crag before descending to Grasmere. We decided (that is, Tom decided for us) that we would take the higher route. What he did not tell us at that stage was that there is another route (now known as neither the high route nor the low route, but as the Tomfool route) which avoids going into Grasmere and, he claimed when he sprang it on us, this would be easier as it involves less height loss. The Tomfool route follows the Wainwright higher route to begin with but, instead of continuing to Helm Crag and then to Grasmere, we turned and headed for Dead Pike and then more to the north along the ridge of Steel Fell. The objective was to descend to Dunmail Raise and cross the main A591 road at a much higher altitude than Grasmere. Tom told us that the map showed a path leading down from Steel Fell to Dunmail Raise, but he didn't bother to tell us that the contours are so close that, on the map, they look like a solid black mass. The descent was so steep that we had to shuffle down on our backsides for a considerable distance, which may have been one of Wainwright's favourite means of making downhill progress, but is not only very slow but also extremely uncomfortable, not to mention unseemly for respectable elderly gents. Fortunately, before we wore holes in the backsides of our shorts, we spotted an old wire fence away to our right and shuffled across to it in ungainly fashion and were able to hold on to the fence for the rest of the way down to the road.

Having crossed the road, we decided to stop on the other side to gather our breath and have a limited banquet. It was all very well avoiding the loss of height by steering clear of Grasmere, but the consequence was that we would not pass any shops or watering holes throughout the long journey that day. Fortunately, Don was still carrying enough to feed a sizeable army. As we recovered from the tortuous descent, Don, who had found the descent even more difficult as the weight of his pack threatened to cause him to topple over, gazed across at the almost perpendicular fellside opposite.

'It's impossible to come down there without ropes. There can't possibly be a footpath.'

'It's on the map,' Tom said irritably, and tossed it to him.

'Bloody hell, Tom,' he shouted after a moment's review of the map, 'it's a parish boundary. You've just brought us down a fuckin' parish boundary!'

CHAPTER EIGHT

WARDROBES AND POSH PASTIES

The ascent from Dunmail Raise to Grisedale Tarn proved laborious, in spite of Tom's assurances that we had saved several hundred feet of ascent by avoiding Grasmere. As the tarn came into sight, suddenly we had views of some of the highest peaks, enclosing the expanse of water in the foreground. As we made our way around the tarn, we passed the path which ascends to Dolly-waggon Pike which brought to mind some of Wainwright's comments on the alternatives to the main route, prompting me to make a thoughtful suggestion:

'We could go up Dollywaggon and then on to Helvellyn and make our way to Patterdale along Striding Edge. That would be much more exciting and it only adds two miles and two hours to the journey, according to Wainwright.'

I think it must have been the effect of the altitude which had brought on a temporary deafness in my colleagues, who trudged doggedly past the Dollywaggon path without deviating.

The outlet of the tarn is the place for contemplating the weather, the time of day and the state of the blisters. This is a crossroads where a choice has to be made between three alternative routes wrote Wainwright. Well, it seemed that one of the three choices had not even been considered, but then Wainwright had pointed out that the Helvellyn route, rising as it does to 3118 feet, *is for walkers who consider themselves to be supremely fit* and, looking at the state of my colleagues, I realised he may not have placed them in that category. However, I was still contemplating:

'We could still go up St Sunday Crag, which only adds an extra hour and it's only another one thousand feet of ascent as the summit is only 2756 feet,' I said.

'You can if you want,' Tom said, generously, 'but you'll be doing it on your own.'

I think he must have been hungry and wanted to get to Patterdale sooner rather than later. In the circumstances, I decided I should forego the pleasure of taking the higher route and accompany my friends on their more leisurely jaunt.

'Never mind,' I said, 'at least we'll have saved enough energy to take up Wainwright on his suggestion that before going to bed, we should walk across the valley to the path below Place Fell for a view of Ullswater that is *unsurpassed for loveliness.*'

'Fuck off, Al.'

We arrived in Patterdale after another nine hour walk and Don went off to find his campsite. I had decided not to spend consecutive nights in youth hostels and was booked into a B&B, so left the others to enjoy the home discomforts on offer at the hostel and arranged to meet up with them at the pub in a couple of hours time. As I approached my digs for the night, I pondered whether there is a regulation requiring all B&B's and youth hostels to allocate the room on the top floor and farthest away from the entrance to any walker who has walked more than fifteen miles and spent all day going up and down mountains. I came to the conclusion that this was a matter governed by one of the many directives issued by the EU, ignored by all members other than the British, most likely entitled the Directive on Regulations for Accommodation for Walkers En Route Standards (DRAWERS). Arriving at my digs, I rang the bell and, whilst waiting, removed my boots, as instructed, in the porch. It had been a long and tiring walk and I did not relish the thought of having to walk another step, let alone having to climb stairs and wondered whether my landlady complied with these regulations. She proved to be very businesslike and I was elated when, after only a few paces, she produced a key and opened the first door on the ground floor.

Clearly, DRAWERS were not mandatory in this establishment, I thought. It was quite a large room with a bath and a large shower cubicle. Just what I needed after a day of hard walking but, hold on a minute, where's the bed?

'This is your bathroom and here's the key,' she said, 'now follow me upstairs.' (I hadn't had such an invitation for a long time).

We went up a flight of stairs, turned right and walked along another corridor, past another flight of stairs (phew), but immediately came to another set of stairs. She turned left and led me up but, fortunately, there were only four stairs and we emerged into the lounge/dining area. It became apparent that this was more of a Guest House than a traditional B&B and run very much as a business, as she described the rules of the house and gave me a sheet of paper, listing what was available for breakfast and upon which I was obliged to indicate what I wanted next morning. I looked around and it was obvious that a great deal of money had been spent on redecoration and new furnishings, which made me more conscious of my sweat-stained clothes and damp appearance. Clearly, she had the same thought as she said:

'If you'd like to go and change, there'll be a pot of tea waiting here for you when you come down. I'll show you to your room.' I have to say that I didn't like the sound of those four words 'when you come down' because, if there's one thing I've learnt in life, it is that you can't 'come down' without having gone up first.

We went down the four steps and, inevitably, she turned right and up the flight of stairs situated immediately alongside the steps from the lounge. It was beginning to look as though she was a stickler for DRAWERS after all. This was an awkward manoeuvre, particularly as I was carrying a heavy rucksack in front of me.

'Mind your .....'

'Ow!'

' ..... head,' she warned, but too late.

The room was simple but comfortable and had the benefit of a small toilet cubicle built into a corner. That's good, I thought, I won't need to go down two flights of stairs if I need a pee during the night (you do have to consider these things when you are sixty, you know). I changed quickly and went down to the lounge, banging my head along the way, and found my landlady setting out the tea and biscuits. Whether it was my change of clothes or my refreshed appearance, I can't tell, but she was a changed woman. Her business demeanour had been packed away and she was all smiles, treating me like a long-lost friend. This was all very well, but didn't she realise I was tired after a long day on the fells? To be on the safe side, I decided I'd better push the wardrobe behind the door when I went to bed. Well, you can't be too careful.

After bathing and shaving, I felt nearly normal but couldn't risk my landlady seeing me at my most attractive, so had to creep down the stairs and make my escape to meet my mates at the Patterdale Hotel, as arranged. Andy had enjoyed his day with the Sherpa Van driver once again and now knows all the B&B's and youth hostels in Borrowdale, Grasmere and the Patterdale and Glenridding area. This educational programme was not entirely one-sided and the driver now knows one line of *Rosie* and two lines of *Blue Eyes* off by heart, and can hum the rest.

We took advantage of the buffet dinner option at the Patterdale Hotel and I was able to replenish my depleted carbs. I managed to consume five bread rolls with my soup (potato, of course), a mountain of potatoes with my vol-au-vents (a sort of posh pasty), followed by a large portion of pie (rhubarb, I think). This would be the last time we would all be together as Andy had decided to travel home on Monday morning, so we made the most of it and even put up with Andy's singing, without complaint. In fact, I thought I heard Joe join in at one point.

As I left the others to return to my digs, the boisterousness of the evening was replaced by a certain sadness at the thought of Andy's departure. The group wouldn't be quite the same without him and I was still wondering whether there would be any more drop-outs in the next few days, but these thoughts were replaced by another worry as I approached the B&B. How to reach my room without alerting my landlady to my return?

CHAPTER NINE

THE FLYING DUTCHMEN

I crept up the first flight of stairs without incident and, as I quietly approached the second flight, I was concentrating so hard on avoiding another crack on the head as I turned to commence the final ascent, that I failed to remember the creaking floorboard conveniently positioned to alert the landlady to returning revellers. My carelessness caused me to straighten up, banging my head again and, before I had finished swearing, she was on the landing with a bottle of wine in one hand and an empty glass in the other.

'Care to join me?' she asked, raising her eyebrows in what I interpreted as a suggestive expression. Suggestive of what, I was not sure. Resisting the temptation to reply with an 'I didn't realise you'd come apart,' I said:

'That's very kind, but I need to make an early start in the morning, so I think I'll go straight to my room.'

When I awoke next morning, I felt awful. Mind you, the en-suite toilet had proved a boon as I did not disturb the other residents by lugging the wardrobe about in the middle of the night. I had a shower and still didn't feel any better, but dragged myself to the dining room for breakfast. I was getting into the habit of not bothering with a packed lunch so as to save carrying the extra weight, so breakfast was an important meal and, of course

I had placed my order the previous evening when I had been feeling on top form and anticipating having the appetite of a particularly ravenous Sumo wrestler who had been fasting for a week. I struggled to eat anything much, which was a bit of a worry as this Monday would be the third consecutive day when we would not pass anywhere where we could purchase provisions en route. As I packed my gear and prepared to meet the others, I felt so ill that I wasn't sure I would be able to make it to the Youth Hostel, let alone the sixteen mile hike to Shap. Why did I feel so ill, I asked myself. Had I eaten too many posh pasties the night before? Was it the effect of walking in full sun for three long days? Or was it simply that I was not used to walking for so long, day after day? I was too fit for any of those explanations, after all my preparation, I told myself. The landlady must have slipped one of those date rape drugs in my tea the previous evening, I decided. Didn't she realise that she needed to administer a much stronger dose to subdue someone as fit as me?

I settled up and trudged slowly to the hostel. Even though it was only a few hundred yards of flat walking, I was exhausted by the time I arrived, with sweat dripping from me. Ahead lay a sixteen mile walk through remote country with nowhere at all to pick up refreshments. Not that I felt like refreshments at that moment. The day's journey would take us out of the Lake District, but not before going to the highest point on the whole Coast to Coast route, Kidsty Pike at 2,560 feet (except for those of us who had taken the high route on the second day). Just what I didn't need. It would be another tough day even if I had felt well.

I met the others outside the hostel and we said our farewells to Andy:

'It's such a pity you can't carry on ….'

I couldn't take one more step
I can't remember if I cried

'Let's go, quick, before he gets to the chorus.'

It would have been sad to leave him in any circumstances, but we had an extra worry because we knew that he can be prone to bouts of depression and the thought of him returning to an empty house, knowing that he should still be enjoying himself with us, might just trigger another dark period in his life. However, there was nothing we could do at that stage, but Tom would contact him as soon as we got home.

This was the fourth day of glorious sunny weather but, as we reached the open fell, I was not relishing the prospect of the initial ascent to Boredale Hause which is not difficult, but is at a gradient which makes it very tiring, even when not suffering from the effects of illegally administered drugs. My lassitude certainly wasn't caused by the vol-au-vents as I had seen Paul filling his face with them the night before and, once again, he was disappearing up the track. I had to force myself up the slope and, despite my determination, had to stop every few yards to rest and wipe the perspiration from my face. At least the frequent stops enabled me to take in the fabulous views of Ullswater and the Helvellyn range which were lost once we reached Boredale Hause and continued the ascent towards the beautiful Angle Tarn. Whether it was the beautiful scenery, or whether the drugs were wearing off, I don't know, but I began to feel a little better. Thank goodness. At one stage, I had been thinking that I might not be able to keep going.

It was apparent that there had been some significant changes since we started the walk on Friday. Then, the party had split so that we ended up walking individually but now it was noticeable that Joe was content to walk at Tom's pace. Clearly, he had paid the penalty for trying to keep up with Paul on Friday and his attack of cramp had brought him to his senses. Don seemed to be in better spirits, even though the size of his pack still made me wince. What I did notice was that the umbrella was no longer strapped to the back of his pack, so at least he had had the good sense to dispose of one useless item somewhere along the way. I never did find out what happened to it, but assumed that it had been damaged when he was scrabbling about in the bracken on Grike.

The fact that the four of us were walking together made it seem more like a joint venture and seemed more like what I had anticipated beforehand.

We took a break by the tarn and I took advantage of the stop to go behind a rock.

'Bloody hell, Al, that took a long time, didn't it?' Tom commented when I returned. 'Are you having problems with your flow?'

'Don't we all as we get older?' I replied, 'But it's okay. I've had a couple of health screenings over the last few years and all's well. I have a client who's a GP but he does some private work doing health screenings at a private clinic. He says it's hard work, but it's money for old rope, I'd say. The first time I went, I had to take out a second mortgage so that I could pay for the privilege of being told that I was fit and well, but at least I was reassured about the cost when they told me that there was no time limit for the assessment, so I could get my money's worth.'

'That makes a change from the five minute slots at the GP's surgery,' Don said, 'usually, you're just reaching the interesting symptoms when the printer prints out a prescription and you're slung out.'

'Anyway, the first three quarters of an hour of this assessment was spent with a nurse, who weighed and measured me, tested my sight and hearing, completed a detailed questionnaire, took blood and urine samples and explained in great detail how she left her first husband when, if I understood this correctly, she found him in bed with the neighbour's German Shepherd.'

'That's unusual,' Tom said, 'although I've heard of an Irish Wolfhound being cited.'

'All the time that I was with the nurse, Tim, that's the doctor's name, was in the next room working extremely hard doing the Telegraph crossword but, eventually, I was escorted to the inner sanctum and he swung into action. First, he had to lift some strips of coloured paper and carefully dip them in the urine sample and then he exerted himself by asking some questions, before telling me to strip off so he could watch the nurse shave patches of hair from my chest, arms and legs, before attaching electrodes. He must have been worn out by this time. When I was attached to the electro-cardiogram by about a dozen wires, he made me walk and then run on a treadmill for quarter of an hour. This must have been exhausting for him. At the end of all this, I was set free from the wires and he explained that the results of the ECG would be sent to an 'expert' for interpretation!'

'On the odd occasion that I have to visit a GP,' Joe said, 'I get the impression that the last thing he wants to do is examine me. It's as though he's thinking 'don't get too close or I might catch something from you. After all, you wouldn't be here if you weren't ill.' So he completes an ALD (that's an arm's length diagnosis), prints a prescription and sends me off, taking great care not to shake hands.'

'Yeah,' I said, 'but have you noticed that he'll make an exception to an ALD when he spots an opportunity to perform an internal examination. Never tell a doctor you are having a bit of tummy trouble. His eyes will light up and he'll be reaching for the rubber gloves before you have chance to mention any other symptoms that could lead to an ALD. Take my advice and describe other symptoms first, although even that doesn't always work. 'A headache? Are you sure your tummy's all right?' he'll ask. 'Let's just have a look at you' he'll say and, after shining a light in your eyes to lull you into thinking he's investigating your headache, he'll jab you in the belly with all four fingers and ask 'did that hurt? Yes? Get your pants off then.'

But, I must say that Tim is ideal for the job of health assessments because he has a very pleasant manner and a chatty way of putting people at ease. Even so, I became a bit suspicious when he started questioning me about urinary function. Being over fifty at the time, I knew about the possibility of changes 'down below' involving slow flow and more regular and urgent bladder emptying.'

'It's true,' Tom agreed, 'in fact, I find it very embarrassing now if I have to use a public urinal and a young man stands next to me and is zipping up before I've even half-finished, despite my best efforts to speed up the flow.'

'What I try to do,' Don said, 'is give the impression that it's taking so long because I'm absolutely bursting, so I make little semi-orgasmic noises of relief, hoping that my neighbour doesn't spot the feeble dribble in the drainage channel at our feet.'

'I aim at the plug hole,' added Joe, 'that makes a louder noise, as though you're peeing like a power jet.'

'It helps if there's a discarded crisp packet in the channel to aim at,' I said 'even a dribble sounds like a torrent when splashing off that. In fact, I know one bloke who won't go out without a crisp packet in his pocket (two if he's going to be out more than an hour).

Anyway, back to the health assessment; I realised that all Tim's questions about urinary flow were leading up to testing for prostate cancer to which, as you know, the over fifties are vulnerable. He told me that there's a test known as a PSI test, which I always thought meant pounds per square inch for measuring tyre pressure. I imagined that he was going to ask me to pee on a crisp packet to measure my own pressure.'

'It's a PSA test, not a PSI test, you pillock,' Tom pointed out in his subtle way.

'Yes, I know that now. I realised when he started to talk about prostate-specific antigens, or PSA. Apparently, it's a simple blood test but straight away he started telling me that it's not particularly reliable which made me wonder why he had raised the matter in the first place. 'Is there any alternative?' I asked in all innocence. 'Digital rectal examination' he beamed, and reached for the gloves.'

'So that was why you looked so worried when I got out the rubber gloves the other night,' Tom laughed.

'Too bloody right,' I said, 'so I told him I'd have the blood test, but he wouldn't give up. 'Well, it's up to you but the DRE is much more reliable,' he said, 'I recommend all my male patients over fifty to have one each year as a matter of routine. Quite recently, I was able to refer a patient to a consultant when I found an abnormality during a routine check and he received treatment at a much earlier stage than normal.'

'How many patients have you examined?' I asked.

'About two thousand,' he said.

'I'll have the blood test,' I told him.'

'Good for you,' Tom agreed.

'Yes, but he never gives up. A few months ago, I decided I'd saved up enough to afford another health check and he tried to convince me again.'

'And what did you say?'

'Told him I'd do my own test: 'I'll stick to pissing on a crisp packet,' I said.'

From Angle Tarn, the ascent continued but the gradient was such that the walking seemed relatively easy and, after a while, we were overtaken by two Dutchmen who seemed to be setting a cracking pace. The others had seen them at the Patterdale Youth Hostel the night before and, although greetings were exchanged, I sensed that there was no warmth on either side. This seemed odd as most Dutch people seem very friendly but these two must have been the exception. As they raced on, the question I wanted to ask was how do Dutch people practice for walking in the mountains of the Lake District?

One of the noticeable changes since the start of the walk on Friday was that Joe had not only become Tom's twin, but also his constant companion, almost as if he felt protected from Paul's cramp-inducing company by attaching himself like a limpet. Earlier, the fact that I had been struggling and had to keep stopping meant that I had fallen some way behind the others from time to time but, now that I was beginning to feel better, I found that I was feeling surprisingly fit, despite my extra exertions during the first two days, not to mention my wardrobe removal activities overnight. In spite of that, I had felt so ill for the first few hours of the day that I didn't want to push my luck now. I was still more than happy to tag along, freed from any compulsion to take more strenuous alternative routes, so I fell in immediately behind Joe, who was in his now customary position one pace behind Tom. Feeling very content in this role, I was taken by surprise when Tom stepped aside and signalled for me to pass.

'No, I'm quite happy to saunter along at the back,' I said, amiably.

'You may be, but I don't want you behind me. Piss off.'

Genuinely, I was delighted to walk at Tom's pace, but he was clearly unhappy about me bringing up the rear, even though it was Joe who was immediately behind him, so what had caused him to dismiss me from his troop? I recalled my own feelings a couple of days earlier when Paul was following me up Red Pike when, even though I had made him promise to walk at my pace and he had agreed quite happily, I felt under pressure to walk that little bit faster than I wanted. What is it that makes us feel this way? Is it polite concern or foolish pride? Probably a bit of both, I decided. When Paul was behind me, I know that I was bothered about holding him up, in spite of his assurances that he was happy to walk at my pace, so I was concerned for his sake yet, at the same time, my own pride forced me to show him that I could still make good time. This was very foolish of me as walking faster than you want to do is extremely tiring, as Joe had found out on Friday. I could only assume that Tom felt under pressure to walk faster when I was behind him. Clearly, he didn't feel the same way about Joe being a pace behind him all the time because they seemed to be attached by an invisible umbilical cord, as they trudged along, right knees bandaged and walking poles clinking in harmony.

Of course, if I was not behind him, I had to be in front which poses another problem when companions walk at different speeds and, as we made our way towards Kidsty Pike, we passed a young couple illustrating this very point as I overheard the sort of exchange that is not uncommon on the fells:

'But I do keep stopping for you,' he said, as she approached him in a state of near collapse.

'Yes, but that gives you time to get your breath back and, by the time I catch up with you, you start off again. If you'd just walk *with* me, you wouldn't have to keep waiting for me.'

Whenever I see a young woman trailing behind her man like this, I feel like going up to her and asking 'Do you still love him?' If only I had the nerve, I could compile a survey of responses and maybe write a book!

It was clearly a day for young men to be demonstrating their prowess as walkers and navigators, as we had not gone much farther before we came across a young man attempting to teach his girlfriend the principles of navigation and we watched as he became increasingly frustrated at her apparent inability to relate what was on the map to what she saw in front of her, and at her lack of a sense of direction. Whilst he was building up to a state of apoplexy, her demeanour indicated a complete lack of interest and I was sure it was only a matter of time until she said:

'I do not *want* to know how to navigate, I do not *need* to know how to navigate. I'm only here because of you and, as long as *you* know where we are, *I* don't need to know. Doesn't it occur to you that I would never be on the stupid fells on my own, you tosser.'

That young man was typical of the breed of Lake District know-alls who are compelled to try to impress all around them with their knowledge. During a short break at a hotel in Great Langdale a few years ago, the guests included two men who were probably in their thirties, and who were in the habit of talking very loudly in the dining room each evening, recounting their exploits of the day so that everyone could hear and, no doubt, would be impressed. I am always a little suspicious of those walkers who seem to know the names of every peak and every little tarn and beck as though they have swallowed the Ordnance Survey map of the area, and these two talked very knowledgably about exactly where they had been and what they had achieved. They were the Chris Boningtons of the New Dungeon Ghyll Hotel who, apparently, covered distances unachievable by ordinary mortals and ascended some of the toughest peaks in the Lake District before breakfast each day. They seemed to be capable not only of doing more in a given day than any other hotel resident, but also of talking about it non-stop throughout the evening to the annoyance of all the other guests. They really were the most irritating bastards. On the final day of my stay, I walked to the top of Coniston Old Man and bumped into one of the two at the summit and was a little surprised to see him on his own.

'Where's your friend?' I asked.

'Oh, he's doing a bit of shopping. He doesn't like heights.' Well, what a giveaway! Pity I would not be returning to the hotel to spill the beans to the other residents.

Before reaching the summit of Kidsty Pike, we joined the Roman road along the ridge and which leads to the summit of High Street, so named because, well, it is a *high* street. This was the highest road built in England by the Romans and travels for several continuous miles at a height above 2000 feet. What an incredible achievement! And what about those legionnaires? If they wore those skirts they're always portrayed in when they marched up here in the winter, the privates must have found it a bit nippy. With the summit of High Street ahead of us, we left the Roman road and branched east towards our immediate goal, Kidsty Pike, with wonderful views of the fells all around, but now with our first sight of Haweswater below. After about two and a half hours walking from Patterdale, we reached the summit, the highest point on Wainwright's main route and the final opportunity to enjoy the beauty of the Lake District fells stretching out westwards. Once the descent to Haweswater begins, it is the beginning of the end for lovers of the Lakes.

From Kidsty Pike, the Wainwright route continues eastwards and drops sharply towards the southern end of Haweswater, following which there is a four mile walk up the west side of the reservoir. At first, this is quite pleasant with views across and along the lake but, after a while, the route becomes quite tiresome as the view is obstructed for some distance by trees between the path and the lake and also because the bracken grows to head height on either side of the path for long stretches. Indeed, Wainwright suggested that a man with a scythe should be sent annually in August. It would be more appropriate for a hundred men with machetes to do the job these days! We decided not to follow the Wainwright route from Kidsty Pike because we had forgotten to pack our machetes (apart from Don, of course), and so we headed due north from Kidsty Pike to High Raise, which is slightly higher at 2,634 feet, and then followed the ridge north eastwards to Low Raise and continued in the same direction before dropping down to join Wainwright's route along the lake at Measand Forces, where we stopped for a break.

This was the fourth day of perfect walking weather and we were enjoying our rest when the two Flying Dutchmen came along. They were taken aback to see us there as, hadn't they overtaken us a couple of hours earlier? They asked how we had managed to get ahead of them, but were in too much of a hurry to wait for a reply.

'You must have taken a short cut,' they said, in what was an unmistakably accusatory tone, as they disappeared along the track. I could see now why my companions had not taken to our Dutch visitors who seemed to be excessively serious. Saying that we had taken a short cut was almost like accusing us of cheating. How dare they? It is our Coast to Coast and we can do what we like with it. In any event, I thought Dutch people are supposed to be liberal about everything and, as long as we walk from one coast to the other, who cares what route we take?

As it happened, they stayed at the same B&B as us that night in Shap where they were as serious as ever but, fortuitously, we did not come across them again after that.

The walk from High Raise had its advantages. Firstly, the descent was not as steep as the descent from Kidsty Pike to Haweswater and, secondly, it avoided walking three of the four miles alongside Haweswater. Interestingly, almost all the Coast to Coast walkers we met during the following days commented that the descent from Kidsty Pike and the walk through the bracken was the section they remembered as the least enjoyable. So, despite the disapproval of our Dutch visitors, we were very happy with our choice of route.

We walked on alongside the lake and had not travelled far along this section before we caught up with a Geordie, who was carrying an enormous pack, and he explained that he was camping and hoping to complete the Coast to Coast Walk in a total time of ten to fourteen days. We joked with him about the size of his pack and he mentioned that he had been slimming for a few months.

'I've lost a load of weight over the last three months like, and I weighed meself with me pack on before I set off an' I weighed less than I did three month ago. Being so used to carrying weight, I thought I'd have no trouble carrying me pack, but I'm really struggling.'

As we walked on, we puzzled over the Geordie's weight issue.

Having lost weight, presumably from all over his body, why would he have problems carrying a smaller amount of weight concentrated in a small area, namely his back, when we would have expected it to be the other way round? No doubt when the Department of Health hear of this, they will want to appoint a research group to investigate and report, in no less than ten years, at great expense (ours, of course) but before they do, I can give them a clue. Walking up and down mountains is bloody hard, however the weight is distributed.

Passing the dam at the end of the lake, the path reached a gate upon which there was a sign, reading:

DANGER
DEEP FAST FLOWING WATER
DEEP CHAMBERS
HIGH VOLTAGE
MOVING MACHINERY
DANGEROUS CHEMICALS
RAMPAGING ELEPHANTS

Well, I admit the last one was my imagination, but why would anyone (in this case, presumably United Utilities) place such a sign on a gate leading into woodland where none of those dangers were present?

This path used to lead into the almost derelict community of Burnbanks but something has been happening in recent years. The decaying buildings are being replaced by new houses and there is an instructive sign at the other end of the development which reads:

REBIRTH OF MODEL VILLAGE

The Manchester Corporation Act 1919 authorised the construction of water works at Haweswater. The construction of the dam was finally completed in 1940. The remoteness of the site, severe weather and unyielding rock tested stamina to the limit. The workforce could not be supplied locally so from the late 1920s hundreds of unemployed workers were recruited from Manchester

*and West Cumberland using grants from the Ministry of Labour.
Labourers were the first to arrive digging foundations and
constructing roads to transport building materials. In the first place
the workers sought lodgings in scattered farmhouses but
Manchester set up a model village close to the dam and provided
sixty-six self contained bungalows of a sturdy cast iron construction with electricity, hot and cold running water and modern
kitchens and bathrooms which were the envy of many a local
farmer. Community life flourished and Manchester provided a
Mission, recreation hall, dispensary and shop and paid for a
policeman, nurse and a shopkeeper as well as financing the
expansion of Bampton School. In the 1960s and 70s, the
population of Burnbanks began to dwindle and some of the
houses were dismantled and re-erected elsewhere. Later when local
government was reorganised and the Lake District National Park
was established responsibility for Haweswater and Burnbanks
passed out of Manchester's hands. Much of Burnbanks became
hidden under self-seeded trees and shrubs. The uncertainty over its
future was resolved when planning permission was given for the
rebuilding of eighteen surviving bungalows and the creation of
the new village green.*

The new houses are mostly semi-detached but with one or
two detached and it really is an attractive little development in a
very pleasant woodland setting and is an area where red squirrels
survive. We were fortunate to spot one scurrying along a
drystone wall just before we reached Burnbanks. However, the
place is so remote that most of the properties will serve as
holiday homes.

Leaving Burnbanks through a wood, we entered open
farmland and we were now out of the mountains of the Lake
District into completely different countryside. This was limestone
country; farmland of fields, pasture and rolling hills and this
pleasant countryside stretched out ahead of us all the way to Shap.
Although Tom might claim that I don't have much in common
with Wainwright other than a love of the Lake District, I do have
to agree with the great man's sentiments when he said, *farewells to*

Lakeland are always sad and what follows is an anti-climax. Anti-climactic it may have been, but there was still plenty to look forward to over the next eight days.

The absence of shops along the way meant we had to carry an adequate supply of fluid. Of course, this added to the weight of our packs but I try to keep the weight down to a minimum by buying half-litre plastic bottles of water and sports (or energy) drinks. Not only are these relatively light, but also the half-litre bottles fit nicely in the side pockets of the backpack, so that it is not necessary to go rummaging through the main pack every time a drink is needed. I started drinking sports drinks a few years ago after being impressed with the marketing of the product. I picked up a bottle in a supermarket and read the label .... *Orange Body Fuel.* Body fuel – I like that. Whoever came up with that earned his fee. Their advertising claimed – *keeps top athletes going thirty-three per cent longer.* I had to have some of that, even though I was supremely fit already. Not surprising really after all the football I had watched over the years. Anyway, what's wrong with a little supplement to keep us in top condition?

'Those sports drinks don't work,' I told Tom a few weeks later, 'I drank a bottle last week and I can't keep going thirty-three per cent longer.'

'Two things, Al,' he said, 'first, I don't think one bottle's enough. Second, they claim it keeps top athletes going thirty-three per cent longer and I don't think they were thinking of you when they came up with that catchphrase.'

Despite Tom's disparaging comments about my athletic prowess, I continue to buy the product because the bottles do fit snugly into the side pockets of my rucksack. And anyway, more recently I've noticed that they have dropped the 'keeps top athletes ...' crap from their advertising, so they must have had complaints from other top athletes!

During the afternoon, we found a nice spot and stopped for a break and I got out my sports drink and watched Don trying to find his drinks bottle in his pack. He took out his waterproofs, his trowel (yes campers really do carry trowels so that they can bury their 'doings'), his box of Ryvita, his monster tub of cheese spread, his machete (only joking), his camera and his map before he started struggling with a large metal object. After going a full fifteen rounds with his pack, he managed to extricate what appeared to be a small torpedo and, with some satisfaction, began to unscrew the top. When he began pouring water from the torpedo into the unscrewed top, I realised that this must have been the sort of flask that would have been standard issue to the army in World War One, capable of withstanding a direct hit from a German shell. It seemed to be made of cast iron, but with a stainless steel inner which was so much narrower than the outer casing that I could only assume that there was an asbestos lining between the two layers and which left only enough room for a couple of swigs of water.

'Bloody hell, Donkey, that must weigh a ton,' I suggested.

'This is the best flask I've ever had,' he said. 'I've had it since I was a lad and it keeps water as cold as ice.'

'Yes, but it can't be worth carrying all that weight for such a small amount of water. I carry four of these half litre plastic bottles which seem bloody heavy when I set off in the morning but the great thing is that when they're empty, they weigh nothing. Your torpedo doesn't hold anything like two litres and will weigh almost as much empty as when it's full.'

'But, plastic bottles don't keep the water cold.'

I decided to adopt a more subtle approach:

'You should try these sports drinks – they're much better than water, as well as being much lighter to carry,' I said, waving my body fuel (I do like that) at him. His expression suggested that he was unconvinced, so I read from the label.

'*You need to tackle the two key factors that affect performance* – do you know what they are?'

'I'm sure you're going to tell me.'

'*Energy loss and dehydration.*'

'But I'm drinking water so I won't be dehydrated.'

'It's not the same. Listen … *Sporto has been scientifically formulated to deliver essential carbohydrate, fluid and electrolytes to help fuel your performance and maintain hydration – giving you an edge when it matters most.* You must be impressed by all those long words.'

'What a load of bullshit.'

'Scientifically formulated to deliver essential … thingies.'

'And why would I need electric lights?'

'I didn't say electric lights, I said electrolytes. They're good for you.'

'Why, what do they do?'

'Erm … they're like carbohydrates,' I stammered.

'In what way are they like carbohydrates?' he demanded.

'Well … erm … they've got four syllables.'

I never did find out what happened to his golf umbrella but it was clear that I would not be able to persuade him to discard his torpedo.

We arrived in Shap late in the afternoon and arranged to meet Don later as he was camping behind the Bulls Head. There is no YHA in Shap so the rest of us were staying at New Ing Farm where Paul was already waiting for us in the large guest lounge. New Ing Farm is no longer a working farm and the farmhouse is on the main A6 at the north end of the village. This is a real B&B. Although there was a bench in the porch where walkers could sit and remove their boots and leave them there, the landlady didn't seem concerned whether we removed them or not. She offered us tea in the lounge, but showed us to our room first. As there were four of us, we were surprised when she told us that we were all in the same bedroom and, as we climbed the stairs to the second floor, we were wondering what awaited us, preparing to give Tom a bollocking if we were expected to share double beds. And, I pondered once again, why are we always given rooms on the top floor in every B&B and Youth Hostel? Do they think we look as though we need more practice for going up and down hills? No, I decided, it must be because we look so fit compared to all the other guests. After several rest breaks along the way, we reached the second floor and found the bedroom was enormous, with three single beds and one double. Despite the four beds, there was still plenty of room for a couple of armchairs and a washbasin in the corner.

Tom allocated the double bed to me and I have to acknowledge that he always seems to be concerned about my comfort. At least part of this must be because the rest of the group were happy to stay in youth hostels and, of course, Tom knows that I am not a fan of YHAs. In the absence of a youth hostel in Shap, he had been forced to book a B&B and now he could not bring himself to allocate the extra comfort of a double bed to himself or the other YHA lovers.

Also, I think this has something to do with his upbringing. Being the youngest of eight, he was used to making do and sharing (including beds) from an early age. Also, he is old enough to have done National Service and army barracks must have been akin to youth hostel dormitories. The result is that he seems to be able to sleep anywhere – in a chair, on a plane, in a car (hopefully not whilst driving) or on a train. With that sort of background, he doesn't feel the need for the comfort of a double bed.

Shap is a sad place whose fortunes changed dramatically in 1970. The village is little more than a ribbon development along the A6, being the main route to Scotland on the west side of the country, and the traffic used to be heavy and constant. In my younger days, Shap was regularly in the news during the winters as the A6 was closed on a regular basis as a result of the heavy winter snowfalls (whatever happened to them?). Although the traffic was the bane of the lives of Shap's residents, it provided a livelihood for many of them. This changed overnight when the M6 was opened and the village became quiet. At least it still has two or three pubs and there is a small Co-op where walkers can stock up on food and drinks.

After smartening ourselves up, we met Don at the Bulls Head and had a relaxing couple of hours. The pub allows campers to pitch their tents on the lawn at the back of the pub and lets them use the toilet facilities. Don was very pleased with the arrangements and insisted on taking us out to the garden to show us how comfortable he was, claiming that this was all far superior to our

B&B. After failing to convince us, we went inside and sat down for our meal. Whether the food was good or bad is impossible to say as we were having such a good time, recounting everything that had happened during those first four days. Don was in excellent spirits, but that didn't stop us reminding him about all his grumbling which prompted us to re-name him Whinger Spice and, whenever he showed his grumpy side, Tom was told he'd become Old Bastard Spice. After a great evening and a good laugh at our own expense, we left Don to enjoy his cosy facilities, agreeing to meet him outside the Co-op at half past eight next morning, not that he needed to stock up on his food supplies!

CHAPTER TEN

THE OLD MAN AND THE TOWEL

When we drew back the curtains on Tuesday morning we were astonished at what we saw. Or, rather, we were astonished at what we could not see. There was a thick mist which prevented us from seeing even the traffic on the A6 a few yards away. After four days of almost perfect walking weather, it looked as though a change could be in the air.

Fortunately, I seemed to have recovered fully from whatever had afflicted me the day before and I was able to enjoy a hearty breakfast, before we returned to our room to prepare ourselves for the day's walk to Kirkby Stephen. I packed my things and was ready to go when I noticed a bit of a kerfuffle and a great deal of swearing coming from Tom's direction. He was cursing at his rucksack as he struggled to fit everything in, as though it was the rucksack's fault!

This was Tom's tenth Coast to Coast Walk and he claims to have mastered the art of travelling light. Indeed, he tells everyone the story about how, when he did the walk for the very first time, he took far too much with him and that by the time he reached Shap, he was so shattered that he asked his landlady for a box, into which he put everything he had decided he would not need and gave the landlady enough money to post the box home for him. Next day, Pam was delighted to receive the parcel, thinking that her loving husband had not forgotten her after all and had sent her a token of his affection to show her how much he was missing her. She tore the box open in great excitement, only to find Tom's dirty washing.

This experience (and the tongue lashing from Pam) prompted Tom to think carefully about what he took on his subsequent jaunts. After completing the course nine times, he was such an expert that he had been able to give each of us his very helpful list of what we would need, keeping things to the absolute necessities, for which I for one was very grateful and I had little difficulty. What he didn't know was that Pam had confided in me that despite all his experience and his helpful list, he had not yet failed to send home a parcel from Shap. Indeed, it had become such a regular occurrence that she no longer opened the parcels, but chucked them in the garage and left them to fester until he got home.

I wondered what it is about Shap that causes so much difficulty for Tom and his rucksack as I watched him battling to fit in all his belongings. He was using both hands to press everything down and trying desperately to fit in his towel on the top. In the end, Paul had to help him, holding the rucksack still whilst Tom pressed everything down.

'I seem to have more than I started with, which is bloody impossible,' he grumbled. 'I'll make sure I don't pack as much next year.'

'Why, what's happening next year, Tom?'

'Did I say next year? It must have been a slip of the tongue. This is definitely the tenth and last time I do anything as stupid as this.'

Eventually, we were on our way and met Hairy Spice outside the Co-op as planned. He had been so buoyant about his comfy arrangements the previous evening that we prepared to be bored to tears by his self-congratulatory boasting. However, he was not in a good mood and we soon wished we had stuck with Whinger Spice.

'Did you sleep well, Don?'

'No. I thought there wasn't supposed to be much traffic on the A6 these days. Well, I can tell you there are bloody heavy lorries thundering along at regular intervals all night and when the lorries weren't waking me, the pub's air conditioning would kick in and wake me,' he complained. The air conditioning unit was situated on the wall at the back of the pub, expertly positioned to keep campers awake. 'I've hardly had a wink of sleep.'

'Well, at least now you know what it's like for the rest of us trying to sleep when you're snoring nearby,' Joe said in his usual sympathetic way.

The direct route to Kirkby Stephen is approximately twenty miles but Wainwright gave an alternative route through the village of Orton which must add a couple of miles to the journey. It is well worth taking the longer route as, otherwise, it is yet another long day with nowhere to stock up along the way. On the other hand, Orton has a wonderful tea shop as well as a Post Office cum store where walkers can purchase extra supplies (and people like Don can fill up their torpedoes).

By the time we set off, the mist was lifting and it was beginning to look as though we might be lucky with the weather again, after all. Leaving Shap, the path took us across the mainline west coast railway and passed through a number of fields before a footbridge took us over the busy M6. Crossing the M6, I could not help thinking that here we were walking a hundred and ninety miles from one coast of England to the other, mostly through open country, and yet there are people who can't even navigate to the end of their roads. Southport, where I was born and brought up, is about twenty miles north of Liverpool and, some years ago, a cousin of mine set out with her husband on the road journey from Southport to London to visit some of his relatives. Driving inland from Southport, the M6 is joined after about fifteen miles and it should then be an easy journey on the M6 and M1 to London. Unfortunately, they reached Carlisle before they realised they were travelling in the wrong direction. Not just in the wrong direction. About a hundred bloody miles in the wrong direction. I have never been able to work out how two adults could travel along a motorway for a hundred miles, passing regular signs for 'Carlisle and The North', without realising that 'Carlisle and The North' are not on the route to 'London and The South'.

My cousin is not the only dunce when it comes to geography. Some years ago, when I still had cause to visit the hairdresser's, the young girl assigned to cutting and styling (I think they called it that) chirped away happily in the way that hairdressers seem trained to do, asking questions as if from a clipboard questionnaire:

'Have you been on holiday yet?'

'Yes, I've just had a few days in the Lake District.'

'Ooh lovely. That's where I want to go – Scotland.'

What do you say to that? Do you point out as politely as possible that the Lake District is not in Scotland and risk causing embarrassment, or do you say nothing and hope that she does not discover her error within the next few days and feel very foolish? Fortunately, this is not too much of a dilemma when the person involved is not someone you know well, but it becomes potentially very awkward when it involves a friend. When Suzanne told a friend we were going to Tuscany, she was taken aback by his response:

'Lucky devil. I wish I was going ….. I love France.'

She decided not to embarrass him and hoped that he would not watch any travel programmes over the following few weeks which might alert him to his faux pas. Unfortunately, he went straight home and told his wife.

'Alan and Suzanne are going to Tuscany. We should go ….. it's ages since we went to France.'

'Tuscany's in Italy, you divvy.'

'Is it? Oh shit, I've just made myself look a complete dickhead.'

Luckily, he was big enough to admit his mistake and we had a good laugh about it.

From the M6, the walk continued with the traffic in view for some time and the noise for longer. Having passed through

Hardendale Quarry, the wonderful walk to Orton ensued. The limestone countryside was entirely different to what had gone before, lacking the rugged grandeur of the Lake District, but wonderful in a contrasting way and great walking country. As usual, Paul had forged ahead but, this time, I was pleased to see that Don was keeping pace with him. Now that we were out of the Lake District, the walking was much easier (although the distances longer) and perhaps Don was stronger now after four days of strenuous walking, not to mention four days of reducing the size of his onion! However, not much more than an hour later, we caught up with Don who was now on his own and looking the worse for wear, having been unable to sustain Paul's pace, so we stopped for a drinks break. When we got up to leave, Tom was again fumbling with his pack and battling to fit his towel on top of all his other belongings.

'I'm sure I didn't have as much as this before. I managed to get everything in yesterday.' Eventually, he completed his packing and the four of us walked together towards Orton. Tom decided he would divert from the Wainwright route as he had seen another, more direct, footpath shown on the OS map, but I walked on the 'official' route, agreeing to meet the others in Orton.

As I walked down a field towards Broad Fell Farm, within striking distance of the village, I noticed a buzzard overhead, making those ridiculous squeaking noises which sound so absurd for such a powerful bird. I was walking downhill with a drystone wall to my right and with a copse ahead on the other side of the wall. As I drew level with the copse, the buzzard swooped down at about head height no more than ten yards in front of me and flew into the copse. I was surprised at just how large the buzzard is at such close quarters and after a few more paces, I stopped and saw the bird no more than twenty yards or so away sitting on a branch in the copse and looking straight at me. This was a wonderful moment and I stood for a short time taking in the view of this magnificent bird. I thought that its behaviour was slightly unusual but continued down the path. I had not walked far before I felt a rush of air above my head and heard a 'whoosh' as the buzzard swooped from behind and must have missed the top of my head by no more than a whisker. It wheeled away to the right and back into the copse. What amazed me was that I had not heard a thing until it was over my head and it made me realise that its prey has no warning whatsoever. This event made me wary (I could have been Wary Spice or even Scaredy Spice) and I kept looking over my shoulder every few seconds. However, without warning, there was another rush of air above my head and another 'whoosh' as it made another swoop from behind and again wheeled away into the copse. At that moment, I would have gladly joined the Royal Society for the Prevention of Birds. For a second time, I had had no warning of its approach but I was now extremely wary and looked over my shoulder every other second. It wasn't long before it made another attempt but, this time, I was prepared for the assault and waved my arms and shouted 'buzz off you blooming buzzard.' All right, those weren't the exact words but I did use a similar alliterative phrase involving the letter B. Come to think of it, it was the exact same phrase I use whenever I see Tony Blair or Gordon Brown on the news, simply substituting 'buzzard' for 'Blair' or 'Brown' but at least it caused it to abort its attack. It must have realised that I could do serious damage with an Ordnance Survey map in my hand. I was now past the copse and, although I kept looking over my shoulder, there were no further attempts to 'buzz' me. Perhaps this is the derivation of the word buzzard.

A few moments later, I reached the gate into the farmyard at Broad Fell Farm and, before I could open the gate, an old farmer emerged into the yard. I shouted to him to check that the path did, indeed, pass through the farmyard and he pointed to a gate on the other side of the yard and mumbled, somewhat reluctantly it seemed, that the path went through the yard to the other gate. As I entered the yard, I said that I had just been buzzed by the buzzard and enquired whether there had been any other similar incidents. He replied that he had not heard of anything but that his eyesight is not so good these days so that he could not tell whether birds circling the copse were buzzards or crows but, after thinking about it for a short time, he remembered a previous incident:

'There were a chap who came through here, now let me think, it must have been thirty-five years back and t'buzzard had

had a go at him, and he had blood on his head.' He considered this for a few moments and then added 'mind you, he were ginger.' Well, this explained everything.

I reached Orton at the same time as my buddies and, having taken about three hours to walk from Shap, we were ready for a proper break and sat outside the New Village Tea Room enjoying a pot of tea and home-made scones and cakes. Whilst we were enjoying our break, I related my buzzard encounter to them, culminating with the old farmer's comments.

'What is it about ginger hair that provokes hostility?' Tom asked. 'I was browsing through Paul's book last night, and did you know that Wainwright had ginger hair and suffered for it? When he was a boy, he used to wear a cap all the time to cover it up, according to his biography.'

'You never would have thought Wainwright would have been ginger,' Don said.

'No,' I added, 'by the time he agreed to allowing photographs and being interviewed on television, his hair was white. Just a minute,' I exclaimed, 'the farmer said about thirty-five years ago; that would have been just about the time Wainwright was devising the Coast to Coast route.'

'It could have been him,' Tom agreed.

'I told you I had a lot in common with him. Me and Wainwright; the only two people in recorded history to have been buzzed by a buzzard,' I said excitedly.

Having described my experiences on the route to Orton, it was now time for me to hear about theirs. Apparently, the paths shown on the map were not well used and they had found it difficult to find their way but they were alarmed when they came to a padlocked field-gate displaying a sign *Bull in Field,* even though the map showed that the footpath went through the field. They had no alternative other than to climb over the gate and skirt around the edge of the field, on the opposite side to the bull, and then had to climb another padlocked gate into a farmyard. There was an old farmer in the yard and it was clear he had no time for walkers.

'There's a bull in that field,' observed Tom.

'I knows there's a bull in t' field and it's to keep you fuckin' walkers out.'

'But there's a public footpath through the field.'

'Fuckin' public footpaths. It's my fuckin' field an' I'll decide whether the fuckin' public can walk through it.'

In the absence of his old adversary, Andy, Tom's appetite for confrontation was at its peak and he was ready for this. The argument which ensued degenerated into a battle of how many swear words could be fitted into one sentence.

'Just tell me where the fuckin' footpath is,' Tom said at last.

'The fuckin' road's just down there.'

'If I'd wanted to use the fuckin' road, I'd have come in a fuckin' car,' said Tom, at which the farmer reluctantly pointed to a gate which led to a cart track down the hill and into Orton. Invigorated by his altercation with the farmer, the others found it difficult to keep up with Tom as he made rapid progress to the village. The proprietress of the tea shop overheard some of the story and had to add to the excitement:

'Oh, you had a lucky escape there then. That must have been farmer Snitch and he hates walkers. He was up in court only last week for discharging a shotgun at some ramblers and when the police were called out, he shot at them as well. He was fined and banned from holding firearms. Otherwise, you might have been shot.'

It was well worth the diversion to Orton and, after trading stories, we relaxed for a few minutes to enjoy the sunshine and observe the villagers and visitors coming and going. It is unusual these days for sugar to be available in sugar pots and amazing how we accept change without really thinking about it, but the presence of proper sugar on the table brought this to mind. Changes pass some people by and can make them look foolish when placed in a different environment, and I recalled watching an old man faced for the first time with an alien method of serving tea. Or, rather, having to serve himself at a motorway service area (shouldn't they be called *non*-service areas or motorway *self*-service areas?). He was completely perplexed by the equipment in front of him, but was sensible enough to stand and watch other people until, suitably embold-ened, he collected a mug, took the tie off a tea bag, hung the tea bag over the lip of the mug, placed it under the nozzle of the hot water machine, removed the tea bag when the colour of the tea suited him and went to the till. The cashier took his money, threw a couple of sachets of sugar on his tray and he went off to find a table. This was a new experience for him, but he now knew that tea is served in bags at these establishments, rather than as the more traditional loose tea leaves. He had cracked this new-fangled stuff. Elated, he picked up one of the sachets of sugar and dropped that in his mug, wondering why there was no string attached to that to allow him to pull it out when his tea was sweet enough. Well, you can't fault his logic and, at least, he had not developed that annoying habit of shaking the sachet before opening it. Have you noticed that? Most of the world's population seem to think it necessary to harass the packet into submission before opening it. They pick up the sachet between forefinger and thumb and give it a good old shake, almost as though it is too hot to handle, and then shake it next to their ear as if to check that whatever's inside is dead. Some go even further and bash the sachet against the palm of their other hand, whilst some go further still and batter the innocent sachet against the edge of the table. Why do they do this? Who was the first person to do it, and how did he recruit his devotees? Do they think that it contains a sugar lump that must be pounded into granule form? Answers, please, to the *Guinness Book of Weird Rituals*.

After enjoying our break in Orton, we travelled on towards Kirkby Stephen. This stretch involved some road walking as well as some easy walking through pleasant pasture and moorland. By afternoon, there was little conversation and, as the four of us tramped silently along the road, I looked round to see Tom and Joe walking as always in perfect time, heads down, eyes on the tarmac immediately in front of them, Joe one pace behind Tom with matching bandages on their right knees, walking poles moving in unison, looking like twin Compo Simonites from *Last of the Summer Wine.* I was just thinking how glad I was that I was unlikely to bump into anyone I knew who would wonder what I was doing with two scruffy old buggers like that, when it dawned on me that their reaction might be that I was one of four scruffy old buggers! I consoled myself that I must look at least a tad more distinguished. At least I wasn't wearing an unwashed knee bandage. Then I had a brainwave. As we would be in Kirkby Stephen that night, I could buy three more knee bandages and three sets of walking poles and then Don, Paul and I could surprise Tom and Joe next morning by setting off behind them wearing the bandages (on our right knees, of course) and tagging on to them in a line, poles moving in time with theirs and clinking on the tarmac. We would make them look even more like a family of elephants walking with trunks wrapped round the tails of the ones ahead. On reflection, I thought better of it, deciding that £150 was too much to spend for a minute or two's hilarity.

Of course, Tom was troubled by both knees but refused to wear bandages on both. I did try to persuade him to wear the bandage on his left knee one day in an attempt to confuse Joe, but he refused to co-operate.

As we walked on, I continued to think about how walkers are generally perceived and my own perceptions were confirmed as we passed a party of walkers, which seemed to consist of more women than men, going in the opposite direction. After exchanging greetings as we passed, Don was the first to comment:

'What a bunch of scruffs,' he said.

'Funny, that,' I said 'I have yet to see a group of walkers with whom I'd want to be associated. They all look so weird.'

'It's because of the way they dress,' Tom surmised, 'it's impossible to look smart in walking gear.'

'Yes,' Joe agreed, 'in the winter, they're all muffled up in fleeces and waterproofs and wearing a silly hat.'

'And even in the summer, the combination of shorts and hiking boots doesn't make them look exactly sexy,' Tom added.

'Well,' I said, modestly 'if I can manage it, I don't see why other people can't.'

'And,' Tom continued, ignoring my contribution, 'there's no point in wearing make-up, which is only going to run if it rains or if it's hot.'

'You do realise,' Joe said, 'that they're probably having exactly the same conversation about us right now.'

'Don't be daft, none of us wear make-up,' Don pointed out, sensibly. 'Do we?'

By mid-afternoon, we were ready for another break and a bite to eat and, as we sat on a bench at the roadside enjoying the sunshine, I watched Don as he produced his Ryvitas, cheese spread and onion from his bag.

'Anyone for Ryvita and cheese spread?' he asked.

'Yes please, Don,' replied Joe, with a fart, 'I've taken a liking to them.'

As Don cut more slices of onion, I could see that there was still almost half of it left even after several days slicing, but he had been cunning enough to enlist Joe's assistance in reducing the weight on his back.

It was still warm enough for us to be walking in shorts and teeshirts and Don decided it was time for him to sing the praises of his outfit once again.

'Do you know that this teeshirt is polyester with dynamic moisture control? It keeps you cool in summer and warm in winter and it's highly breathable, wicks moisture away and is incredibly lightweight as well as being very quick drying. These modern fabrics are really good, you know.'

'Is that right?' Joe's question was delivered in a tone perfectly pitched between admiration and mockery (as well as between farts).

Don's monotonous tributes to the efficiency of modern fabrics were getting to Tom, who could hold his tongue no longer:

'Don, do you remember when you, me and Al went up the Old Man of Coniston about three years ago?'

'Yes, I remember. It was bloody cold.'

'It was indeed, but that was because it was February. And, do you remember that by the time we reached the top of Dow Crag, we had to stop and put on another layer of clothes?'

'Yes, and it was still cold, despite global warming.'

'And do you remember that when we reached the top of the Old Man you were shivering and didn't have anything else to put on, but me and Al both still had another layer in our bags and, because we were a bit worried about you, I gave you my extra layer?'

'Did you?'

'And, do you know why you were cold, even though you had put on all your layers and why we still had a layer each which we didn't need to put on because we were warm enough?'

'No.'

'Well, I'll tell you why. It was because you were wearing a cotton base layer and a cotton shirt, which are not breathable or wickable or anything fuckin' elseable. And, do you know how bloody irritating it is to listen to you prattling on about how great your new gear is when we were the ones who introduced you to the bastard stuff?'

If Don saw the point, he did not acknowledge it.

'Were you really worried about me?' he asked.

'Yes. We were worried that you might be suffering from hypothermia and that we'd have to call out the Mountain Rescue, and we'd freeze our balls off hanging around for them,' Tom responded, in vehement tone.

'Actually, Don, I wasn't too concerned,' I interjected 'I was going to volunteer to go down and raise the alarm and then I could've waited in the pub in Coniston.'

Our refreshment break was only occasionally disturbed by a passing car but, at one point, a veritable convoy of six cars passed, driving almost nose to tail.

'There goes one of those pillocks driving far too slowly and irritating the shit out of those behind,' I said.

'There can't be many safe places to overtake along here,' Don pointed out.

'What's really annoying about those drivers is that they tootle along in their own little worlds and when they get home, their wives say 'Hello darling, how was the traffic?' and they reply 'No problem. I hardly saw another car.' Well, try looking in your rear view mirror, you annoying prat,' I whinged.

'I hadn't thought of that, but you're right, they'll always have a clear road ahead, driving at that speed,' agreed Don.

'Have you noticed that the car at the front of these convoys is always red and is usually either a red Mini Metro or a red Nissan Micra?'

'And the driver always wears a hat,' added Don.

'I wonder whether they wear their hats when they shag,' Joe pondered in a distracted way.

'They never shag,' Tom said, knowledgeably 'that would be far too exciting for them.'

'Talking about exciting,' Don said, 'I was on the motorway the other day and I was overtaken by a Porsche and it was one of those sections where they have those chevrons on the road and signs saying Keep Apart Two Chevrons'.

'Yeah, it's almost impossible to keep two chevrons apart, isn't it?' I said.

'Isn't it just?' Don said. 'He must have been doing a hundred and twenty and I never got closer than three chevrons.'

'Last time I was on the motorway,' Joe commented, 'I had to come off early because of roadworks.'

'Why? Was the motorway completely closed?'

'No, but there was a sign saying Roadworks After Next Junction. Delays Possible Until October. Well, I couldn't afford to be stuck on the motorway until October. I was bursting for a pee!'

After our few minutes of relaxation and enlightened conversation, we gathered our belongings together and once again Tom was engaged in a battle with his rucksack.

'I'm sure I couldn't have had this much before,' he mumbled, as he tried to hold down the towel with one hand whilst pulling the bag up with the other and getting more and more annoyed.

'This is bloody ridiculous. I didn't have this much trouble yesterday. Why can't I get ..... hold on, this is not my ..... oh, shit.

This is not my towel. I must have taken this from the B&B.'

It took us some time to recover from fits of laughter before we could make one or two helpful suggestions.

'If Mrs Kirkby's noticed by now, she's probably been on to the police to report a theft. In fact, she's probably being interviewed right now and she'll be saying 'I don't know why anyone would want to steal a towel, but he was a little scouse bastard and they steal anything, don't they?' The scuffers will be waiting for us in Kirkby Stephen and you'll have to spend the night in the cells. But, look on the bright side, it should be more comfortable than the YHA.'

Thinking about it, the abduction of the towel was understandable. We were carrying our own towels as they are not supplied at YHAs and Tom had become accustomed to using his own for the first three nights. Forgetting that he was in a B&B in Shap and that B&B's provide rather more than a bunk and a combined sheet/pillow, he had simply pushed the towel in his rucksack that morning as if it was his own.

When we reached Kirkby Stephen, he telephoned Mrs Kirkby and explained that he had taken the towel by mistake and promised to post it back to her in a week's time when he arrived home. She mentioned that she had noticed that a towel was missing (but, presumably, had not reported the matter to the police).

A week later, when we were on our way home after completing the walk, I thought I should let Tom know that the episode had not been forgotten:

'Tom, you know that towel. You know you've been carrying it around the north of England for the last week and, when you get home, you'll have to go to the trouble of parcelling it up, and then you'll have to go down to the Post Office and pay to post it back to Shap and, almost certainly, the postage will be more than the towel is worth. I didn't like to say this before, but wouldn't it have been more sensible to throw the towel away and send Mrs Kirkby a fiver when you get home?'

'Shit. Why didn't I think of that?'

We walked on and, as Kirkby Stephen drew nearer, Don and I were some distance ahead of Tom and Joe. On the few occasions that I'd tried to walk at the back of the group, I found that my presence there was unacceptable. I might get away with it for a few minutes but it would not be long before Tom would step aside and tell me to 'Piss off. You can walk in front.' By the Tuesday afternoon I was beginning to get the message and so walked on with Don who seemed to be growing stronger by the day.

Don has been self employed for most of his life and is one of those unfortunate people who has seen his livelihood eroded by new technology. At a time in his life when he should be at the peak of his earning power and looking forward to a comfortable retirement, he was struggling to find work. Indeed, on occasion, he has had to turn his hand to doing odd jobs for friends and neighbours in order to keep a bit of money coming in. Most of the British companies which had kept him busy for many years have either been driven out of business by cheap foreign imports or have sold out to larger American companies. He is left with just one client – a large American company which calls on him sporadically when it encounters a problem which can only be solved by a human brain. When he is called upon, he has to spend time away from home in the States or the Far East, which is another thing that he had not anticipated at his time in life.

'How are things at home, Don?' I asked in a conversational way.

'Okay,' he mumbled in what I thought sounded a less than convincing tone.

'Well, not that okay, actually,' he added after a moment's thought. 'That's one of the reasons I'm doing this. Jane and I decided it would be a good idea if we spent a bit of time apart; thinking time, if you like. Things haven't been great between us for a couple of years; ever since she had to go back to work a couple of years ago. She only works part-time, but she didn't expect to have to go back to work in her sixties.'

'What, do you think she blames you? That seems unfair. After all, it's not your fault that work's dried up,' I said, making a mental note not to ask anyone how things are at home, ever again. Also, I couldn't help thinking about a story related to me by a divorced lady, a few years earlier, when she told me about the breakdown of her marriage. Apparently, she lived a very affluent life by courtesy of her husband's successful company but, she learned later, business had been poor for a couple of years and their luxury lifestyle had been sustained by loans and a mortgage on their very desirable home. When she discovered that not only was their life of affluence at an end, but also they were likely to lose their beautiful home as well, she could not bear him even to touch her any more. Whether her feelings for him changed because she saw him as a failure or whether it was because he had put their entire way of life at risk without her knowledge, I never did find out. Whichever it was, I thought it best not to relate the story to Don at this moment.

'I don't really know what she thinks any more. If we try to discuss anything, we just end up arguing, so it drives us further apart.'

'Well, the last thing you want at your age is to split up, so you need to sort out your differences. It's not too late, is it?' I asked.

'I think it might be,' he sighed, 'I think she's having an affair.'

Oh, no, I thought. Never, ever ask anyone how things are at home, ever again:

'What on earth makes you think that?' I asked calmly.

'It's just little things really. She seems to look forward to me going away on business and she encouraged me to come on this trip. She's gone to stay with a friend. At least, that's what she says,' he said, glumly.

'But, that sounds reasonable, Don. Perhaps she thinks it will do both of you good to spend some time apart and be with your own friends. I'm sure everything will be fine when you get home,' I said, hopefully.

'Oh, I don't know,' he said in a dejected tone. 'I don't even know what I want now.'

'You do still love her, don't you?' I asked, feeling alarmed at his apparent defeatism.

'I'm not sure,' he said slowly, as though he had not thought about it for a lifetime. 'I really don't know,' he said, looking me directly in the eyes, realisation dawning as he spoke.

'Listen, Don,' I said, reaching the limit of my marriage guidance ability, 'you'd better make up your bloody mind, sharpish. When did you last tell her you love her?'

'I can't remember,' he said.

'Well, get on the phone and tell her. It'll make all the difference,' I said, sounding far more confident than I felt, 'and if you can't bring yourself to say it, then send her some flowers with a note saying you love her. She'll find that dead romantic.'

'I'll have to think about it. Anyway, she won't be home until the weekend and we agreed not to phone each other before then. That was something else that made me think she isn't visiting her friend.'

I couldn't think of anything else to say, so left it at that but it made me realise that there are a lot of very troubled people around us and we have no idea what's going on in their minds. Also, I thought, perhaps this is why Don's been so tetchy, poor bloke.

The plan was that we would go our separate ways in Kirkby Stephen with Don camping, Paul, Tom and Joe staying at the YHA and I would be at the Jolly Farmers Guest House. On the approach to Kirkby Stephen, the track becomes a road which serves the backs of the houses on the main A685 road which runs through the centre of the town. I knew that my B&B was on this main road and Don was going to camp at the campsite he had used fifteen years earlier on his previous Coast to Coast adventure. This was just out of the town on the A685 and he took the first opportunity to cut through to the main road to make his way back to the campsite. I walked on a little further and, after only a short distance, I passed the backyard of the Jolly Farmers which seemed to be in a row of terraced houses. I took the next opportunity to cut through to the main road and turned back only to see Don walking towards me.

'The campsite's farther than I remembered,' he said. 'I'm going to stay at the YHA with the others.' I could see that Don's enthusiasm for camping was waning after his disturbed night behind the pub in Shap. It was obvious that he had not had time to measure the distance to the campsite (which I later discovered was not very far) and he had an easy alternative with the youth hostel because Andy's pre-booked bunk was available. I checked in at the guest house which was neither Jolly nor a Farmers but had to be better than a youth hostel.

Kirkby Stephen was the largest centre of population we had encountered on the walk so far. It is a very pleasant market town where all the main banks are represented. This was important to us as it was the first time we could use a cash machine without being charged for access to our own money. It is a veritable shopping centre with plenty of pubs and restaurants as well as an array of shops, although none of the usual high street stores, and there are plenty of hotels and B&Bs. Unfortunately, we chose to eat at the Black Bull where we had an unmemorable meal before I made my way back to the Glum Terrace (sorry Jolly Farmers), a part of me wishing I had opted for the youth hostel.

CHAPTER ELEVEN

BLACK SAIL IN THE SUNSET

My own initiation into youth hostelling had taken place only a few years ago, when I was well past my youth. Until then, I had refused to submit to the temptations offered by the YHA as my preference is for a certain amount of comfort, particularly after a hard day's walking. Whilst acknowledging that they served a very useful purpose, I found that I could resist their charms without much difficulty. Over the years, the Youth Hostel Association has been updating its image and improving the accommodation as well as relaxing some of the old restrictive rules but the idea still did not appeal to me. Regular hostellers can't understand this as they think hostels are the most wonderful places and yearn for the old days when the conditions were truly basic.

I succumbed finally a few years ago when Paul, Andy and Tom announced that they were planning an eight day tour of the Lake District, taking in as many peaks above 2,500 feet as they could manage but with the major drawback, for me, that they would be staying at youth hostels. This was another of Tom's escapades which resulted from a late night at the pub. The three of them were reminiscing drunkenly about their youth hostelling days of many years ago, when one of them suggested recapturing the sense of adventure (and discomfort) of hostelling in the Lake District. What started as the prospect of a day or two of leisurely hostelling became an eight day epic taking in some of the highest peaks in the country. At the time, a number of other revellers had enlisted and, no doubt, were responsible for proposing the idea of climbing these high peaks but, by the time they had sobered up, they found that they could not fit it in. As a result, Tom decided that he needed to invite me. Otherwise, he would be faced with the daunting prospect of trying to keep pace with Paul and Andy. Tom was offering me the opportunity of spending eight days in the Lake District, but with the serious downside of staying in YHAs. In the end, I decided I could not miss the chance to spend more time in the Lake District.

On the first night, we were to stay in Grasmere but, as Paul would be returning a day early because of business commitments, we drove first to Great Langdale, where we were due to spend our final night, so that he could leave his car there. There are two hostels in Grasmere and we were to stay at the Thorny How Hostel and it did not take long for me to realise that my worst fears were justified. We entered a scruffy reception area where we booked in and where I faced the humiliation of having to pay a fee to become a member of the YHA after resisting for so many years. As I looked round the gloomy reception area, I noticed that members were given the opportunity of purchasing provisions to sustain them on their tiring journeys. This was a big bonus if you liked Mars bars as the choice seemed to be Mars bars or more Mars bars.

The dormitory to which we were directed was in an annex to the main building and was reached by a covered walkway. There were more than twenty bunks in the dormitory and the place was full. My inclination is always to go for a bottom bunk on the basis that younger men should take the top bunks as they are less likely to have to get up during the night. It was apparent that the dormitory had been three rooms originally but doors had been removed and doorways widened to make it into one, but the odd shape made for plenty of wall space against which bunks could be pushed. The washrooms were situated in the main building but I noticed that, fortunately, it would not be necessary to go back to the main building if taken short during the night, as the dormitory had its own single toilet, the door to which was opposite my bunk. I had difficulty in falling asleep in such a strange atmosphere and found myself lying stock still, afraid to move as every movement seemed to cause the bunk to creak, quite apart from the rustling of the bedclothes. Although I was doing my best to make no noise, the other 'inmates' had no such inhibitions and there was a tumult of coughing, sneezing, farting, and snoring. This was were I learnt the unwritten rule of the Youth Hostel Association, namely that snorers must fall asleep before non-snorers.

After a couple of hours, I was finally dropping off to sleep when I heard a rustle of bedclothes and a creaking bunk, followed by the sound of bare feet on the hard floor, a light switch being pressed and the turn of the handle on the toilet door. There was a flash of light as the door opened, the sounds of the door closing, of someone having a pee, followed by the flushing of the toilet, reaching a crescendo as the door opened again with the flash of light, the click of the light switch, the closing of the door, the padding across the room, the creaking of the bunk and the rustle of bedclothes. Five minutes later, this procedure was repeated and then seemed to go on throughout the night as the occupants of the dormitory formed a convoy of visitors to the facilities.

Not having had much sleep, I rose and visited the washrooms but, having to stand shoulder to shoulder with half a dozen other men whilst having a wash and shave is not my idea of enjoyment.

My companions tried to lift my spirits by reassuring me that this was one of the worst hostels they had visited and that it was unfortunate that my first experience was in such a place. We were to spend the next night in Patterdale and, fortunately, Tom had been unable to book us in the youth hostel there (what a stroke of luck), so I was able to look forward to the comparative luxury of staying in a B&B, for one night at least.

We set off after breakfast and Andy and Paul soon left us behind and we did not see them again until we reached the B&B, where we had a much quieter and more comfortable night.

However, the third night was to be spent at the Thirlmere Youth Hostel and, after the day on the fells, Tom and I began making our way down from our final peak of Watson Dodd towards the hostel. Once again, Paul and Andy had disappeared into the distance soon after we set out in the morning. As we made our way down the fellside, Tom decided to offer me the benefit of his experience of staying in a great many hostels over the years:

'Now, I do have to tell you that the YHA guide describes the Thirlmere hostel as basic ..... but, don't worry, sometimes the ones described as basic are the best.'

Brrrrr. Alarm bells sounded in my head. This was a classic piece of what I call Tomatalk which can be as dangerous as the Red Indian weapon of similar name. I knew from bitter experience that this was Tom's euphemism for 'now, this place is going to be absolute crap and if you thought Thorny How was bad, wait till you see this place. I'm telling you now because I don't want you fuckin' moaning about it when we get there.'

An hour or so later, my worst fears were confirmed once again as we approached the hostel. I could see a wooden hut with a corrugated roof and with a YHA sign outside. There was a single dormitory for men and another for women. There were sixteen bunks in the men's dormitory and we could see that Paul and Andy had claimed theirs already. Most of the other bunks had rucksacks on them so it was clear that the place was going to be full that night. The men's 'facilities' consisted of just one cubicle and two washbasins (we have more than that at home and there are only two of us) but the good news was that at least the hostel had a shower. Unfortunately, the bad news was that to reach the shower it was necessary to run the gauntlet of the drying room which was simply a room with a stone floor and with washing lines hung from wall to wall. After battling through other people's (men's and women's) wet clothes, a sliding door (with no lock) provided access to the shower.

After another uncomfortable night as my second experience of youth hostels, we set off in the morning to conquer the high peak of Blencathra. It was an unpleasant day with steady rain and mist and we faced a long walk along St John's in the Vale to Threlkeld before starting our climb.

'I think we should keep together today lads.'

Alarm bells and sirens sounded as Tom said this. I knew well enough that this was another piece of Tomatalk which I translated as 'this is going to be fuckin' dangerous today but if we keep together there's a chance that one of us might survive, because the last one to fall off the mountain should have the impact cushioned by landing on the other three.'

We approached Blencathra from the east which meant we had to negotiate the notorious Sharp Edge which would be difficult enough in dry, calm weather with good visibility, but which was extremely hazardous in the wet conditions and with visibility down to no more than a few yards. Perhaps we should have been grateful that we could not see how far we would fall if we lost our footing. We were lucky to have Paul with us as he is as sure-footed as a mountain goat and he was able to move about nimbly and point out to us the safest route. We had to concentrate as though our lives depended on it (which they did) and Tom commented afterwards that it was the longest that he has known Andy to keep quiet.

We reached the top safely and Tom discharged Paul and Andy from their obligation to stay with us and, as they disappeared into the mist, he revealed his innermost thoughts about the rest of us.

'I wouldn't do that with anyone I love,' he confided. Well thanks for that, Tom.

This was not the first time that he had done this to me. On a visit to Snowdonia one November, we decided to climb Tryfan from Llyn Ogwen, which is more of a climb than a walk. There had been a hard frost the night before and as we ascended, we found that it was more and more icy underfoot and the climb became ever more hazardous. That really was an occasion when we took our lives in our hands and the relief at reaching the summit safely was diminished somewhat by his comment that he would not want to do it with anyone he loved. This suggested that I was expendable, whereas he could not cope with being responsible for the death or serious injury of his wife, children or grandchildren. I could sort of understand what he meant even though it didn't make me feel that great.

We walked on through the rain to Keswick and there was quite a pleasant surprise awaiting me as the youth hostel there was a big improvement on my first two hostelling experiences. We had our own dormitory with just the four bunk beds, and the bathroom facilities were much better, with plenty of shower cubicles. Also, the drying room was well set out and we mingled with all the other hostellers filling the drying room with wet clothes. At least they would be dry by morning.

After a much more comfortable night, we were preparing for breakfast when Andy came in complaining that our clothes were still wet as the heating had not been switched on in the drying room. He had already raised the matter with one of the assistant wardens at the reception desk whose response had been that he had not realised that anyone had wet clothes.

'As it rained all fuckin' day yesterday, it should have been fuckin' obvious that everyone would have wet clothes,' Andy had pointed out in his polite, understated way.

'Right,' said Tom, who had not been enjoying anything like as much confrontation as he would have wished, as he set off for the stairs. Unfortunately for him, by the time he reached reception, a senior warden was on duty and he was extremely sympathetic and apologetic so Tom felt that he could not give him the bollocking that he had intended for the assistant warden.

From Keswick, we were walking to Buttermere and would take in Causey Pike, Sail, Crag Hill, Grasmoor, Wandope and Whiteless Pike along the way.

'We could divert and take in Grisedale Pike after Crag Hill and before we go on to Grasmoor,' Tom suggested 'but that would make it a very long day and I think we should leave it for another time.'

'Well I don't agree,' Andy demurred 'I think we should do them all in one foul sweep.'

'I think the expression is one fell swoop,' Paul murmured.

'Whatever, in the final analogy, the proof's in the pudding.'

'I think you'll find the correct saying is the proof of the

pudding is in the eating,' Paul said despairingly, not bothering to mention Andy's other misuse of the English language.

We spent that night at the Buttermere Youth Hostel where we also had a dormitory to ourselves and the facilities were good. After the two nights at the Keswick and Buttermere hostels, I was beginning to warm to the idea of hostelling (well, almost). Perhaps it was just the relief after the abject misery of my first two nights in hostels.

The next two nights were to be spent at Black Sail Hut and my colleagues were really looking forward to what they regarded as the highlight of the tour. The very fact that this was the only hostel where we were to spend two nights is testimony to their regard for the place. Black Sail Hut is a hostel which is talked of with great affection by youth hostellers who seem to have a great need to suffer deprivation and hardship, and they are available in bucketloads at Black Sail. Apart from the fact that it is little more than a remote hut out on the fells, several miles from the nearest road, with absolutely no home comforts, there is no alcohol either which, for Tom and Andy, seemed to be the only drawback.

'Last time I was over there, I hid two cans of beer in a drystone wall behind the hostel and I'm going to sell one of them to the highest bidder,' said Tom, when the subject of the absence of alcohol was raised, 'I should get at least £10.'

'That's alright,' said Andy 'I'll have the other.'

After walking from Buttermere over Red Pike, High Stile and High Crag, Tom and I reached Black Sail at about four o'clock and we were just in time as it began to rain just at that time. Paul was there already, having walked on his own that day. Whilst we were having breakfast that morning, he had announced that he was suffering from terrible pain in his shin and, indeed, he could barely walk. As a consequence, he said he would take the shortest and lowest route to Black Sail in the hope that he would be fit for the following day. Andy was still out on the fells somewhere, now getting very wet as the rain teemed down.

If I had thought that the Thirlmere hostel was basic, I soon learned my mistake. Black Sail is a stone-built refuge on the open fell, admittedly in a beautiful setting, but miles from anywhere. Viewed from the front, there are three doors, those on the right and left being to the men's and women's dormitories respectively. The middle door is to the common room (some might say so common that it should be known as the 'fuckin' common room') which also serves as the dining room. There are no connecting doors so it follows that access from the dormitories to the dining room involves going outside. The single toilet is situated on the left side of the building so, again, use of this facility involves going outside and round the side of the building. Apparently, there is a shower but this is at the back of the building and entails an even longer expedition round the building and, with a full house of twenty people at the hostel, it is hardly worth the effort of repeated journeys to check whether it is free. Until relatively recently, there was no electricity supply at Black Sail but, to the chagrin of traditional hostellers who reject any form of comfort, it does now have its own power generator. However, the power supply does not extend to the men's dormitory which is illuminated by gas light and the washing facilities consist of a large bowl and a ewer of cold water.

To cap it all, there are understandable problems about emptying the septic tank, what with the hostel being so inaccessible. As a result, there is a sign in the toilet requesting prudent flushing with guidelines in verse (not attributable to the great Lakes poet, William Wordsworth):

If it's brown, flush it down
If it's yellow, leave it to mellow.

Now do you begin to understand my dislike of hostelling? Of course, I realise that all the regular hostellers who have not yet visited Black Sail will be salivating after reading this and rushing to their phones and computers to make a booking.

The men's dormitory houses eight bunks and both the men's and women's dormitories were full that night. Although Paul was in obvious discomfort and had endured a very long limp from Buttermere that day, he was not one to complain. However, Andy was a different matter. When he arrived, soaking wet, it became clear that any pain Paul could endure was nothing more than a flea bite in comparison to his suffering. His problem on this occasion was that his back was giving him gyp, although he hoped that he would be able to sleep through the pain.

'Can someone pull my boots off for me?' he asked, as he sat on the edge of his bunk with one leg raised, waiting for assistance.

'Piss off, Andy.'

Having claimed our bunks, we made our way to the common room, getting a good soaking en route as the rain continued to pelt down. The common room was not only full of people, but of drying clothes which hung from rails which were hauled down using a pulley system every time a new arrival appeared, allowing more wet clothes to be hauled up towards the ceiling. Wet boots made full use of the ceiling beams, looking like a coconut shy at a fairground. At least there was a roaring fire and the smell of baking bread was just wonderful, but with all the drying clothes and nearly twenty people in the room, it did become very hot and steamy. The warden was disturbed from his task of preparing dinner when 'the man with the posh voice' poked his head round the door.

'Do you by any chance have a bunk available for the night? It is not imperative as I am more than happy to camp if you are full.'

The warden explained that there was still one bunk left and the man with the posh voice could have it, with pleasure.

'Are you sure it's no bother? I'm quite happy to camp.'

Who did he think he was kidding? Quite happy to camp? It was sluicing it down outside. Nobody in their right mind would be 'happy to camp'.

Reassured that it was no trouble, he made his way to the dormitory returning a few minutes later to add his wet clothes to the rack and his wet boots to the beam. He must be loony, I thought, to even consider camping in this weather but, he must be round the twist to stay in Black Sail Hut, particularly as he must have been six foot six and his feet would protrude well beyond the end of his bunk. We asked how far he had travelled and his ultimate destination.

'I'm doing the Coast to Coast Walk. I travelled down from London by rail to St. Bees yesterday, walked a few miles and camped last night and walked on from there today. I was hoping to stay here tonight as I have heard it is one of the best hostels, but I didn't have time to book in advance. You see, a window of opportunity arose unexpectedly and I decided to utilise it to fulfil an ambition of mine to do the C to C. I work in the City and have been given garden leave, so it is an ideal opportunity.'

Here was a man trying desperately to dispel the myth of the soft southern Jessie. But failing. Travelled 'down' from London? Who, but a posh southerner, would believe that travelling from south to north is 'down'?

'Window of opportunity'? 'Garden leave'? He'd been sacked!

'Could I have a word with you please, Rupert? You've been with us for twelve years now, haven't you, Rupie? Twelve good years, but this is a young man's business and things change, don't you know? We're in a new paradigm and we need young blood to carry the business forward. I'm sure you'll find a position better suited to the qualities that you bring to the party and, meanwhile, I'm going to suggest you take twelve months garden leave. We'll pay you of course, in accordance with your twelve month notice period and we're prepared to consider a 'bonus' payment of, shall we say, half a mill in recognition of your loyal service, subject to certain conditions that the legal boys will tie up later.'

Had he worked in the north, the parting of the ways may have been more blunt.

'Come into my office now, Rupert me old son. We pay you a lot of brass for doing what you do and, for the last year or two, you've not been earning it. In fact, you've been fucking useless. My cocker spaniel could've done better. Unfortunately, we made the mistake of giving you a twelve month notice period and we'll honour that, but I don't want you pissing about in the office for the next twelve months, so clear your desk and bugger off. Oh, and Head Office don't want you stirring the shit with a claim for wrongful dismissal, so they'll give you a shedload of cash to keep your mouth shut.'

Well, at least he'll be able to afford the shed to store the cash and keep an eye on it whilst he's doing all that gardening. Anyway, finding himself with nothing to do (other than garden), he had chosen to use some of his now less valuable time walking 'up north'.

Once we got to know him a little better, we found he was good company, although he was one of those who sounded as though he had swallowed the OS map.

'I found a super route along Little Mickle Bottom and then up High Bessie Beck, and then over Big Bore Pike and down Great Yawn Ghyll.' Yes, all very interesting.

It continued to rain so heavily that a wetsuit was needed even to venture out to the toilet. As we waited for dinner, the door opened to reveal a group of young men looking very sorry for themselves in the pouring rain. They were hoping for shelter, but the warden had to tell them that the hostel was full. Like the man with the posh voice, they were supposed to be camping but it was so cold and wet that they really would have preferred the 'comfort' of the hostel. It must have been grim outside then! The warden went out to show them where they could pitch their tents, returning a few minutes later to serve dinner. He was a bit of a weird character but served up a terrific meal. The home made soup was presented in large jugs and he left us in no doubt that we would not get our main course until all the soup was gone. The good food and the warmth generated by all those bodies in a confined space, together with the hubbub of conversation, made me forget I was at a youth hostel. For a moment anyway. As we finished our meal, the door opened and the warden came in with five bedraggled young men. This was the same group who had asked for bunks earlier and conditions outside had deteriorated so much that their tents had blown down and even their sleeping bags were now sodden. In these extreme circumstances, the hostel probably was marginally more comfortable. They were doing the Duke of Edinburgh Award so were supposed to camp, but they were so downhearted they had decided to give up and try again another time.

The warden had agreed to them sleeping on the floor of the

common room and we now had another five sets of wet clothes and boots to cope with, let alone the wet sleeping bags and enormous backpacks. But of most significance was the extra five bodies in the small room. Five seventeen year old youths take up a lot of space, particularly when they are all seven feet tall! Have you noticed that teenage boys these days are enormous? They seem to come in two varieties. Either they are built like poles so I half expect to see a belisha beacon on the top, or they are extremely broad with no necks. It's as though their bodies grow so quickly that they reach their heads before their necks have had time to react. Still, perhaps this is a good thing as, if they had necks as well, they could be nine feet tall.

With the room so packed, we decided to call it a day and went to our bunks. I confess that I made a decision to be a dirty pig and passed up on the opportunity to utilise the jug and ewer and, as I lay on my bunk watching the dim, flickering light from the gas lamp reflecting on the water jug, I wondered whether this was what it was like in the Victorian workhouses, described so often by Dickens.

The gentleman with the posh voice, who hereafter shall be known as Rupert Trumbleweed, stooped as he entered the room, his high domed forehead avoiding contact with the doorframe by the merest whisker.

'Felicitations to all' he boomed cheerily, the words resonating around the dimly-lit, incommodious room as his close-set eyes examined the occupants with whom he would be sharing the scant facilities in this remote establishment.

It was the best of tim ….. Oops, must have been dropping off to sleep.

The rain continued throughout the night which presented a problem for anyone wanting a pee. It was raining so heavily that just standing outside was not an option, but there was no light in the toilet so that running round there would not only result in another drenching, but also there was no guarantee of hitting the right spot, as it were. Why on earth do hostellers think this is such a wonderful place? Yet it is almost like the Bethlehem of the youth hostelling world, with the innkeeper (sorry, warden) turning travellers away. 'No room at the hostel' is the cry. I almost expected the warden to spread straw across the dormitory floor and allow another twenty or so weary wanderers to rest their heads.

Before morning, I needed a pee but could hear the rain continuing to pour down and could not bring myself to venture outside, so had to hold on until it was time to get up. As I lay in my bunk hoping I would be able to last until morning, drifting in and out of sleep, my mind wandered back to primary school days when, if taken short during a lesson, the afflicted boy (or girl) had to put up a hand to attract the teacher's attention and hope that it would not be long before the teacher decided to notice. With luck, if the teacher was in a good mood, relief would come quickly. On the other hand, if four classmates had already been excused during the same lesson, the teacher's gaze might never fall on the desperate, fidgeting child. Surely the teacher should realise that the later in a lesson a child wanted to go, the more pressing the need of the child was likely to be. If my childhood experiences are anything to go by, teachers minds do not work like that!

There was a set protocol at my school which involved using the prescribed words and any error resulted in permission being refused.

'Please may I go to the toilet?' were the passwords to blessed relief and any variation resulted in further discomfort for as long as teacher decided.

'Please may I go to the toilet, *with paper*?' was the open sesame for those who needed more than a wee. The magic words 'with paper' signified a more serious call of nature and evoked a speedier reaction from the teacher, who doubled as the keeper of the class toilet paper, and became a one-man rapid response unit as he fumbled with the key to the stronghold that was the toilet paper drawer, whilst the hapless child squirmed in front of his classmates. The drawer would be opened to reveal the precious material within, but still the protocol had to be followed with teacher counting out the mandatory five pieces of Izal toilet paper. The flustered pupil was then allowed to scurry off along the corridor, the fingers of one hand secured between clenched buttocks whilst clutching the five pieces of Izal in the other hand and hoping that the sanctuary of the toilet cubicle could be reached without mishap, all the time wishing that someone would invent something more effective than Izal. The youngsters of today don't know they're born, I say, they don't know they're born. Now they have a wide range of tissues from which to choose, including soft toilet tissue, super-soft toilet tissue, extra strength soft toilet tissue, super-soft toilet tissue with aloe vera, strawberry-flavoured soft toilet tissue and the top of the range luxury *moist* lightly-fragranced toilet tissue, whereas our choice was Izal and, if we were lucky, the tissue they used to wrap oranges in. The fruit tissues were a great luxury but didn't last long as you had to use about six at a time to make sure it was the tissues that did the wiping.

As I held up my hand in the hope teacher would let me go before I wet my pants, I awoke to find that there was a great deal of activity in the dormitory as the inmates were up and preparing for another day's walking. Everyone else had managed to obtain the warden's signature on their parole papers and were moving on after just one night of detention, but we faced another night in the Black Hole ... I mean Black Sail.

It seems to me that regular hostellers have an inexplicable need to suffer hardship, almost as though it takes them back to sufferings in the past. For the man with the posh voice, Black Sail probably reminded him of boarding school and the shared dormitories and cold showers. For people like Tom, it is a reminder of young days sharing with siblings and of national service. For me, it is purgatory and I had to face another night of it.

We rose to find that it was still raining, but only lightly. The big problem now was that the cloud base seemed to be within touching distance above our heads, so that visibility on the fells would be zilch. Paul's shin was no better and he decided to limp all the way to Great Langdale to collect his car and drive home. This was a long walk in appalling conditions and must have been murder for him in view of the pain. What a man! Still in competition in the discomfort stakes, Andy claimed that his back had seized up and that he was also in considerable pain.

'I need someone to put my socks on for me.'

'Piss off, Andy.'

There was no point in continuing our quest for peaks above 2,500 feet in those conditions and our only option was to walk to Ennerdale Bridge for a drink. Although this is a relatively flat walk, it is about ten miles and was pretty miserable on a day like that with so much water underfoot and with light rain or drizzle still coming down. After a couple of drinks, we made our way back – a round trip of twenty miles just for a couple of drinks, but then again there was nothing else for us to do (and Tom had been lying about his secret hoard in the wall).

That evening it started pouring down again, but we had another great meal with another full house. During the evening, a middle-aged camper arrived and asked the warden where he could pitch his tent. Clearly, he was a much more experienced and hardy individual than either the man with the posh voice or the burly teenagers, as he did not even bother to ask whether there were any bunks available. Either that or he had stayed at Black Sail before and preferred his tent. It continued to rain heavily throughout the night so that, by morning, all the paths were doing an imitation of the Mississippi in flood. My slumber had been disturbed briefly during the night by a rustling as someone moved about. At the time, I assumed it was nearly morning and that someone had decided to make a very early start, even though it was still dark. When it was lighter, I swung my legs out of the bunk and stood on the camper, asleep on the floor. Rather than someone leaving early, it was the camper I had heard, much earlier than I had assumed, as he moved all his belongings inside after his tent blew down!

With the footpaths little less than raging torrents and visibility poor, we decided to cut our visit short by one day and trudged over the soggy fells to Grasmere to collect the car and drive home. So, our eight day trek was reduced to seven and, during the final two days of the seven, we had failed to notch up any 2,500 foot peaks. No wonder I felt that the resolve of some of my colleagues would be tested over twelve days on the Coast to Coast route.

As an introduction to youth hostels, I don't think this trip could have been any worse, although I acknowledge that a major factor was the poor weather over the final two days. I have heard recently that there is a campaign to raise funds to revamp Black Sail Hut, with a target of £250,000. The mountaineer, Sir Chris Bonington, is leading the campaign and has been quoted as saying it is his favourite hostel. I imagine it is comparatively luxurious to someone like Sir Chris who is used to far worse conditions on his frequent Himalayan adventures, and the warden's food must be a feast to anyone more used to eating llama penis butties and yeti testicle stew. On a more serious note, Black Sail Hut is a welcome sight to the weary hosteller, being the most remote hostel in England, set in the heart of beautiful countryside. Although I joke about it, I can understand the popularity of the place and hope that it will remain in existence for many years to come (just as long as I don't have to stay there). Having said that, I'm sure that the traditionalists will not want the money to be spent on too many mod cons. A bigger septic tank and electricity in the dormitories – perish the thought!

CHAPTER TWELVE

HALF WAY TO PARADISE

Wednesday was the sixth day of our journey and had huge significance. Our destination was Keld in the Yorkshire Dales, which is not only the halfway point of the Coast to Coast Walk, but also the spot where the Pennine Way dissects the Coast to Coast route. The distance from Kirkby Stephen to Keld is comparatively short at only twelve and three quarter miles, so I was able to restrict my pasty intake at breakfast to just one. After five days of tough walking, a short day seemed appealing and I was looking forward to a relaxing afternoon sampling the pleasures on offer in Keld. The fact that this would be another day when we would not be able to spend any money during our journey didn't bother me as I knew we would reach Keld early in the afternoon and I would be able to choose between the range of eating houses and have a slap-up meal then.

We met outside the hostel and I soon discovered that there was trouble in the ranks:

'I don't care whether there's a spare bunk at every hostel now that Andy's dropped out,' said Joe, 'you can camp in future.'

'Yes,' Paul concurred, 'it's a bit unfair to keep the rest of us awake.'

'But I can't help snoring,' Don replied defensively.

I wondered why Tom had nothing to say on the matter and it dawned on me that he had kept out of the arguments about Don's snoring throughout the trip. Whatever Tom's reasons, I was able to give myself a pat on the back for avoiding the snorer's blight. Little did I know at the time that I was due a rude awakening, in more ways than one.

After leaving the town of Kirkby Stephen, the route climbed up a tarmacked road past quarries for a considerable distance before joining a bridleway which continued upwards to Nine Standards Rigg at almost 2,200 feet. The summit can be attained in about one and a half hours by a determined walker and no doubt Paul did, as he disappeared into the distance before I could say anaphi ... annafilla ... you know, that sting thing. Nine Standards Rigg is where the Pennine watershed is attained with all streams from then on making their way towards the North Sea.

'So it's downhill all the way now then, is it Tom?' Joe asked.

'Well, not quite. There are still a few climbs, but we won't be as high as this again.'

This was a day for significant achievements, with Keld being the halfway point, the watershed being passed and no more higher ground, and we soon achieved another as we passed into the Yorkshire Dales National Park soon after leaving Nine Standards Rigg.

After five days of almost perfect conditions, the weather was beginning to change and we walked on through the sort of light drizzle which leaves you undecided on whether or not to put on waterproofs, and this diminished our enjoyment of what should have been a beautiful walk in delightful countryside.

At lunchtime, we found shelter behind a wall and had a break. As usual, Don produced his Ryvita and cheese spread and, although we were now almost halfway through the journey, I could see that the Ryvitas were still plentiful and almost no impression had been made on the spread. As I watched, Don began to pull from his pack a string bag and ..... oh, no, it contained two complete onions.

'Bloody hell, Don, you didn't bring three bloody onions, did you?'

'Well, they sell them in these bags of three,' he explained.

'Yes, but you could've cut the bag open and just brought one or two. Even with Joe's help, you've only eaten one in six days.'

'You could be right.'

Tom raised his eyebrows, but couldn't bring himself to comment. He changed the subject:

'Now lads, Keld's a lovely place but I don't want you to expect too much.'

Klaxons sounded, alarm bells rang, sirens shrilled – this was classic Tomatalk for 'Keld might be all right if you like sitting looking at drystone walls but, otherwise, it's fuckin' crap and don't blame me if you haven't brought anything to read.'

'But don't worry lads, at least we'll be able to watch England play Northern Ireland in the World Cup qualifying match on the telly at the hostel tonight,' he added in a placatory way.

It was clear that we were going to reach Keld by early afternoon, despite taking our time and I gathered from Tom's comments that we would struggle to fill our time there but, although the result of the match was a foregone conclusion, England being the overwhelming favourites, at least we could look forward to an evening watching football.

Tom was still fiddling about with his pack as we set off again, and I found myself walking alongside Joe.

'How are things going, Joe?' I asked, in an attempt to open the conversation.

'Very well,' he replied, although I thought I detected a slight hesitancy, 'but I'll have to see how I feel when we reach Keld.'

Feeling that, perhaps, 'how are things going?' was a question to be added to the 'how are things at home?' bin, I continued:

'Why, is there a problem?'

'Just that I've been finding it tough going,' he replied, with a grimace. 'I had that cramp attack on the first day and I still get shooting pains in my calves every now and then, as though another attack isn't far away, but I noticed that Tom just walked at his own pace on that first day and wasn't bothered if everyone else left him behind, so I decided to walk with him, which was a good decision, I think. The poles are a big help as well. I'm sure I wouldn't have managed that descent near Grasmere on the third day, when we had to slide down on our backsides part of the way but, even with the poles, it knackered my knees and I haven't recovered yet.'

'Well, I think the toughest section is behind us now,' I said, trying to offer some encouragement.

'I'm hoping so. With this being a shorter day, I'm hoping I'll feel better. I'm not a quitter, but my knees are giving me real pain.'

'What would you be doing if you weren't doing this?' I asked, trying to lighten the mood.

'Oh, I'd be keeping myself busy with something,' he said, in a non-committal sort of way. 'Everything changed when my wife died six years ago,' he added, and I made a mental note to delete 'what would you be doing if you weren't doing this?' from my list of opening gambits.

'We were married for nearly forty years and had great plans for all the things we would do when we retired,' he continued, 'but then she fell ill and I had to retire a couple of years early to look after her.'

During our first few days together, I had realised that there was more to Joe than is evident at first sight and now I risked a glance sideways at this extraordinary man and could have sworn I glimpsed a moistness in his eyes. Fighting against the lump in my throat, we walked on, as he continued to reminisce.

'It was hard at first, but I lead a full life now even though money can be a bit tight at times as I didn't qualify for my full works pension, what with having retired early. I realised that I needed to keep busy and I've been very lucky because I've got the choir and I've always loved classical music and the opera. As well as that, I've always been interested in Roman history, so I enrolled for the Open University course, which I'm thoroughly enjoying and it fills a lot of time. In the winter, the site where I live closes for a few weeks, but I can go off to stay with my daughter and family in Spain and enjoy some winter sun.'

'That sounds good,' I said, marvelling at how he turned every-thing into a positive light. 'Do you have any family in this country?'

'No, but I do now have a lady friend to keep me company.'

'Oh, that's good,' I said, genuinely pleased, 'is she waiting at home now?'

'Oh, no,' he said quickly, 'we don't live together. I don't think I could ever live with anyone again. She comes round two or three times a week and I make a meal, or sometimes I go to hers. It suits me like that.'

'And does it suit her?' I asked.

'I think so,' he answered. 'I haven't really talked to her about it, but she's always given me the impression that's the way she wants it as well.'

'It's nothing to do with me, Joe,' I said, 'but women can be a bit strange, you know, and they sometimes say one thing when they mean another. She could be making out that she's happy the way things are because she doesn't want to push you into anything when, in reality, she's pissed off.'

'Do you think so?' he asked.

'Well, it's possible,' I said. 'How would you feel if she wasn't there when you got back?'

'I don't know,' he said, apparently deep in thought. 'I think I'd miss her,' he added, reflectively.

'It seems to me that you need to talk to her and find out what each of you expect out of the relationship,' I suggested.

'Thanks, Alan. That's good advice,' he said, which made me miss my footing and fall on my arse. 'I'll give it some thought,' he said, as he resumed his position one pace behind Tom, leaving me to pick myself up.

We walked on and, in spite of the annoying drizzle, we enjoyed our first taste of Dales walking. Grouse moors gave way to field enclosures, each with a smattering of moving white dots which transformed themselves into sheep as we came closer. The wonderful countryside prompted Tom and Don to become more and more animated as the abundance of abandoned barns and shelters sparked their creative talents into action. A shelter knee deep in sheep shit would make a wonderful artist's studio, apparently, and a medium sized barn could be converted into a five bedroom, five bathroom property which Prince Charles would be proud to ..... well .... visit if he is ever in the area and needs to use a bathroom. After all, you can't have the heir to the throne peeing in the heather; at least not if he's forgotten his crisp packet. They happily discussed building a wall here and knocking one down there and even considered where to place roof-lights in the non-existent roof. It was all very interesting (to them, anyway), but I was just glad that Paul wasn't with us to encourage them with his architect's knowledge. Mind you, if he could have told them there was no chance of getting planning permission, it might have shut them up. On second thoughts, that would simply start a discussion of their experiences with Planning Departments, which I have heard so often before I might have been driven to commit donslaughter.

The final approach to Keld is along the B6270 road and, for tired walkers, the sign post 'KELD ?' is a welcome relief. However, it is unwise to celebrate too soon and, as Wainwright said, this is the longest quarter of a mile in the north of England. In fact, it must be more than twice that distance. As we approached the youth hostel, I looked ahead in an attempt to spot the bustle of activity associated with village life, but all I could see was a cluster of five or six houses down a lane to the left.

'Where's the pub, Tom?' I asked.

'What pub?' he responded. He could be a little imp at times.

'The village pub,' I said. 'In fact, where's the village?'

'There's no pub and, can you see those houses down that lane?' I nodded in acknowledgement. 'Well, that's the village.'

This was a major shock. After all, this was the crossroads of two famous long distance walks, not to mention a popular attraction in Swaledale in the National Park. Even I had heard of Keld and yet there were no shops or pubs and precious few places to spend the night. This must be the best known cluster of houses (I hesitate to call it a village) in the whole of England. Swaledale may be very beautiful and Keld may be one of Swaledale's gems, but what were we going to do until next morning? To cap it all, and despite Joe and Paul's protestations, all five of us were booked in at the youth hostel that night, so we faced the prospect of sharing a dormitory with Don.

We checked in at the youth hostel and, in answer to our enquiries, the warden told us that there were no soundproofed dormitories in which snorers could be confined. Things were going from bad to worse and Tom was soon in trouble again when we discovered that there was no television.

'I'll have to remember that for next time,' he said, before quickly adding 'hush my mouth. What am I saying? This is the last time, but what a good thing Andy isn't here. He'd give me such a bollocking for this, even though he's not interested in football.'

With no football to anticipate, we had a lot of time on our hands but, at least we had a dormitory to ourselves. We expected Paul to be waiting for us but there was no sign of him at the YHA even though it would not have taken him much more than four hours to reach Keld. Eventually, he arrived late in the afternoon having walked beyond Keld to the Dales village of Muker where he had found a country fair taking place, the highlight of which was sheepdog trialling, and he had spent a pleasant hour or two watching. At least, that was what he told us, but I was beginning to suspect that there was another reason for his solitary walking. It was quite apparent that he was much fitter than the rest of us, so my suspicion was that he must have snaffled a copy of my Care training tips which he was using to good effect, walking on ahead to eat all the pasties he could lay his hands on. No wonder all the tea shops were out of pasties by the time we got there, so we had to make do with scones or toasted tea cakes.

In Andy's absence, Tom was not getting as much confrontation as he would have liked or expected but one of the wardens almost redressed the balance. Apparently, during the afternoon, Tom had been mooching about in the reception area trying to pass the time and, despite his age, he still has that little boy habit of touching everything he sees. This makes shopkeepers alert to the possibility of shoplifting and, when you add the Liverpool accent to the equation, alarm bells ring in their heads. As a respectable elderly gentleman, this attitude irritates Tom no end. Quite rightly, why should an accent single out a person as a potential thief? Anyway, the warden was keeping a very close eye on him. At first, Tom wondered whether the man was scrutinising him because he recognised him from somewhere, but then he began to wonder whether it was purely the suspicion that he might be a shoplifter that had aroused the hawk-like watchfulness. After a while, Tom's irritation got the better of him and he fixed the warden with a hard stare from which the warden refused to stand down.

'Are you looking at me?' Tom asked in his most aggressive tone, laying on the scouse accent in the hope of intimidating his antagonist.

'Actually, I was just wondering why you don't answer your phone. It's been ringing for ages.'

'Oh, I hadn't heard it. I'm a bit deaf,' Tom explained as he fumbled in his pocket to retrieve his mobile.

The youth hostel was full, with a mixture of Coast to Coast walkers and other visitors, but including a group of about fourteen older people (is that possible I hear you ask) who explained that they were a walking group who had enjoyed walking together for many years, and who were in the Yorkshire Dales not only to do some walking but also to celebrate the birthdays of a couple of the group. Whilst we had our meal served by the youth hostel staff in the conservatory, this group used the members' kitchen to prepare their own meal and had a little party in a room adjoining that kitchen. Unfortunately for them, our only access to the members' kitchen to make our own drinks was through their not so private room. They didn't seem to mind and they even insisted on doing our washing up for us.

'After all, what are a couple of mugs on top of all the washing up we are doing already?' one of them said. They were having a wonderful time but had made far too many puddings so we felt compelled to help them out by devouring some beautiful home-made rhubarb pie and custard (excellent for carbo-loading).

Joe had volunteered to sleep in the bunk below Don and had threatened to jab the bunk above with one of his walking poles at the first rumblings of a snore. I had yet to experience Don's nocturnal noisiness and was not sure what to expect, but had not been in my bunk long enough to fall into a deep sleep before I was shaken by an explosion; no, an earthquake measuring at least twenty-seven on the Richter scale. I waited for the roof to fall in, grateful that I had chosen a bottom bunk which I convinced myself would give me some protection from the falling debris. A second or two passed before I realised that the bunk had stopped shaking, but then I heard another, different, sequence of noises, starting with a rustling of bedclothes, followed by the clink of walking poles and the thud as one of them made firm contact with the bunk overhead, an 'ow', and more rustling bedclothes as Don rolled over. This pantomime was repeated at regular intervals throughout a disturbed night, except that one of the performances was extended. In the very middle of the night, an earthquake measuring only six on the Richter scale was followed by the now customary thud of the walking pole on bunk and the heartfelt 'ow', but this time additional dialogue was appended:

'It wasn't me. I'm not snoring.'

'Who do you think you're trying to kid,' said a voice that was unmistakeably Joe's.

'It wasn't me. Somebody else is snoring,' pleaded Don.

'Bollocks,' was Joe's response.

Eventually, and after a very disrupted night, dawn broke and I was glad to get up. Of course, Don's snoring was the only topic of conversation as we got dressed and during breakfast:

'How does your wife put up with it?' Paul asked.

'Oh, she copes,' Don said.

'How?' Joe queried, clearly not satisfied.

'We sleep in separate bedrooms,' Don muttered, almost inaudibly.

'What was that?' I asked, aware of our earlier conversation about his marital problems. 'Did you say you sleep in separate bedrooms?'

'Oh, all right,' he said, 'yes, we sleep in separate bedrooms.'

'For how long?' we asked.

'As long as I can remember now; she used ear plugs for years but, when we moved house, she decided we should have separate bedrooms.'

'I'm not surprised. In fact, the only surprise is that she didn't insist on separate houses,' Joe said. 'What do you think, Tom?'

'I don't know what you're all on about. I haven't heard a thing,' Tom said.

'What, even last night?' Joe asked, incredulously.

'No, once I'm asleep, nothing wakes me. Mind you, I am a bit deaf. And, anyway, it wouldn't be fair to criticise Don when Pam tells me that I snore sometimes.'

'There, I told you it wasn't me every time last night,' Don said to Joe, 'it must have been Tom. That wasn't fair.'

'Well, if it wasn't you, I apologise,' Joe said, doubtfully, 'but, you deserved everything you got,' he mumbled.

'I've had enough of this,' Don whinged, 'I get it in the neck at home and now you lot are getting at me all the time. Tom's the only person who never complains. As soon as I get home, I'm going to ask for a divorce.'

'Why?' Joe asked in astonishment.

'So I can ask Tom to marry me.'

Keld was not only the halfway point in terms of distance, but also in terms of time and it seemed appropriate to complete an appraisal of our performance so far. During the remaining six days, we would not encounter anything as strenuous as the terrain we had covered in the first half of the journey but there would be at least two long days in terms of distance to be covered. Were our bodies and minds equipped to cope with another six days of relentless pounding?

I considered each of my colleagues in turn. Paul seemed to be managing without any trouble and, although appearances can be deceptive and he is the type who would not tell the rest of us even if his leg was falling off, I had little doubt that he would reach Robin Hood's Bay. I believed I had discovered the secret of his success, the 'sold out' signs in all the pie shop windows giving the game away. Tom was being held together by bandages and sticking plaster and supported by poles and, although he had completed the course nine times before, it was clear that he was taking it very steadily and walking at his own speed. As long as his creaking body stood up to the strain, he would achieve his ambition to do it ten times, thereby creating a new record ..... for a sixty-nine year old living in his house! Following his cramp attack on the first day, Joe had come to his senses and walked at a less ambitious pace, forming an 'almost septuagenarian club' with Tom and adopting all of Tom's methods of keeping himself together. He had been awarded his Frequent Farters card which provides him the privilege of using a special lounge at any YHA establishment. As long as he continued to track Tom, aided by his regular turbo-boosts from the rear, he should reach the North Sea coast. That left Don, who seemed to be managing better as we went along. There could be a number of reasons for this. Firstly, his pack was getting lighter as he ate his way through the corner shop he was carrying. Also, it was possible that he was surreptitiously discarding unwanted items along the way, although I thought this extremely unlikely given his hoarding mentality. Secondly, six days of walking had made us all stronger so, barring accidents, Don should make it too. All the hard walking was now behind us and, although we still had some long days ahead, there were no more really steep sections. The only threat I could think of was Don's temperament. We didn't want any more tantrums and threats to go home.

CHAPTER THIRTEEN

SLIPPING AND SLIDING

The middle section of the Coast to Coast Walk incorporates three consecutive irritatingly short days, if Wainwright's description is followed to the letter. The twelve and three quarter miles from Kirkby Stephen to Keld is followed by an eleven and a quarter mile stretch to Reeth, and an even shorter ten and a half miles from Reeth to Richmond. As none of these sections are particularly taxing, at least compared to the tough walking in the Lake District, it would be easy to reach each destination in early afternoon.

Setting off on Thursday morning, we decided to take the low route alongside the Swale in view of the drizzly conditions. Paul had to make a phone call to his office (at least, that's what he said but I had my suspicions that he had arranged to pick up a pie order), so we left without him in the knowledge that he would soon catch up. When we entered the woods alongside the Swale, Tom ignored the footbridge which would have taken us to the north side of the river and, at that stage, Don was walking just ahead of me with Tom and Joe perhaps twenty yards further in front.

'I'm sure we should have crossed the river at that footbridge,' Don called but, if Tom heard him, he took no notice. If anything,

I thought I detected his head thrust forward a little and his pace quicken slightly. The footpath on our side of the river was very narrow, winding between the trees about twenty yards above the water, and the drizzle made the steep slope very slippery. Tom and Joe seemed to be managing this more comfortably than us, perhaps because they are shorter and did not have to do as much ducking and weaving to avoid the branches and tree roots. Don continued to grumble that he didn't think it was the right way and, as I had no idea, I kept quiet. Again, if Tom heard Don's grumbling, he did not respond but the gap between us seemed to be increasing.

'Fuck,' Don shouted suddenly as his unwieldy pack caught on a branch and he was yanked back. 'Tom, are you sure this is the right way?' he shouted. There was no response, but I sensed that Tom's head went down a fraction and his pace quickened.

We continued to make our precarious way along the slippery path, concentrating intensely so as not to lose our footing:

'Fucking hell,' Don shouted, louder than before, as he slipped on the mud and was just about able to stop himself slithering down the slope to the river but unable to prevent his new breathable, wickable, water-repellent, UV protected shorts being covered in mud. 'Tom, I'm sure this isn't the right way.' We were now only catching the occasional glimpse of the other two through the trees but again I sensed Tom's head drop another fraction and his pace quicken.

'Fucking bastard shit,' Don yelled at the top of his voice as his pack snagged on another branch and he was almost yanked off his feet. 'Tom, this is definitely not the right way.' They were so far ahead now that we could not see them at all, but I knew that he had moved up yet another gear. On we went, slithering forward.

'Ow. Fucking nettles. I've been stung,' Don thundered. 'Tom, we're going miles out of our way.'

Don is one of those blokes who is so nice that it is a surprise to hear him swear. In fact, it is so unexpected that it sounds unnatural and walking behind him now, watching him working himself up into such a paddy was quite a revelation. I realised that this must have been what he was like on the previous Saturday when Tom said he had 'thrown his rattle out of his pram.' Again I thought that Whinger Spice would have been appropriate but, now that I knew he was preoccupied with other troubles, I was prepared to make allowances.

His grumbling was making me wonder whether my appraisal of his physical and mental condition had been too optimistic and whether he was about to sit down and refuse to go any further but, before that happened, we emerged from the woods and followed the footpath close to the riverbank. Unlike us, Paul must have crossed the river at the footbridge because we could now see him on the other side. He crossed the river at the first opportunity and we walked together, and this was the first time that all five of us had walked together for any distance throughout the entire journey and it felt good. I don't know what had happened to change things, but Paul would walk with us for the rest of the trip. Either his pie order hadn't come through or he had broken his leg, I decided. The walking was pleasant and the weather improved and, by mid-morning, we reached the attractive Dales village of Gunnerside, which does not have much but does boast a pub, tea room and the cleanest public toilets I have seen in many a while. We were anxious to know how many goals England had scored against Northern Ireland and the few walkers we had encountered since leaving Keld had not been able to help us. As we stood outside the tea shop deciding who should go in with our order (we didn't think the proprietors would appreciate five pairs of muddy boots), two couples came out. They were clearly visitors to the area, but not walkers, and likely to be staying somewhere which had a television.

'Excuse me, can you tell us how England went on last night?'

'Lost one nil,' came the reply from one of the men.

'No, seriously, how did they go on?'

'It *was* one nil,' said the other man. 'He's not joking. England were awful. Most of them didn't seem to be trying.'

'What about Rooney?'

'At least he tried. He played like two men,' said one.

'Yeah, the only trouble was, they were both crap,' declared the other.

During our break, the conversation turned towards family matters and, of course, Tom's reasons for having no more than three children were known to us already, but Don was asked whether there was any particular reason why he had only the one daughter.

'My wife decided she didn't want any more and she persuaded me to have a vasectomy. Actually, I think her exact words were 'I'll cut your balls off myself if you don't get down to that clinic'. Anyway, she made the appointment for me and, on the appointed day, accompanied me in order to provide support.'

'Which you were certainly going to need, in the circumstances,' laughed Joe.

'We arrived at the clinic half an hour early, so we decided to have a cup of tea and a cake at the clinic café and I noticed a sign that really put the wind up me.'

'Why? What did it say?' we asked.

'*Please Note That the Cakes May Contain Nuts or Nut Extracts*. I said 'they're not making cakes out of extracts from my nuts' and headed for the door. Unfortunately, Jane dragged me back before I could make a break for it.'

'So, you went through with it and, since then, your activities have been recreational rather than procreational,' Paul said.

'Yes, but it was a very traumatic time, you know. Apart from the sign, I needed convincing that it was worth all the pain and discomfort and it didn't help when I got talking to a young bloke in the waiting room.'

'Why? Did he try to talk you out of having the snip?'

'He didn't have to. Just listening to him made me want to run a mile. He had five children under eight years old and he was in for his third vasectomy.'

'Get away. You mean the first two hadn't worked?' I asked in astonishment.

'That's right,' Don said, 'I didn't realise that it doesn't always work and, apparently, it is quite rare for the op to be unsuccessful. He must have been very unlucky.'

'Or very potent,' Tom said, almost enviously.

'But you'll never believe this,' Don added 'when the nurse came for him and called his name, I fell off my chair.'

'Why?' we demanded as Don burst into a fit of laughter, 'what was his name?'

'Andy Cocks,' he spluttered, as he collapsed with laughter, spilling his tea on the table.

Recovering from Don's hilarious tale, we asked Paul about his family, knowing that he had two sons.

'We couldn't have children, so our two boys are adopted.'

That was news to the rest of us and it was good that Paul felt comfortable enough to tell us, but the conversation soon moved on to the subject of children never believing that their parents have sex and, indeed, even though we were all in our sixties, the thought of our own parents ever having had sex seemed preposterous.

'I was working in the garden years ago,' Paul said, 'and overheard one of the boys, who was about eleven at the time, talking to one of his little mates, and they must have forgotten that I was weeding behind the bushes. Of course, they could not believe that their parents ever engaged in sex and they were both boasting that their own parents never 'did it'.

'Well, your Mum and Dad must have at least once, 'cos there's you' I heard my son say.

'Well your Mum and Dad must have twice, 'cos there's you and your brother,' his little pal responded, triumphantly.

'They haven't,' Philip said, defending his mum and dad, 'we're adopted.'

The weather was improving as we walked from Gunnerside through fields of pasture, until we emerged onto the road at Isles Bridge. Where we crossed the road there was a public footpath sign indicating REETH 3? MILES. At the pace we were walking, I reckoned we should be in Reeth in just over an hour. Exactly one hour later, we reached the village of Heelaugh where there was a road sign REETH 1?. Now, admittedly this was a road sign rather than a public footpath sign but, as the footpath runs parallel to the road all the way into Reeth, there was no doubt that we still had a long way to walk. In any event, we had walked far more than two miles in the last hour.

We were lucky because we were not walking a great distance that day and were not very tired but, in other circumstances, it would have been quite distressing to find that we still had so much farther to walk than we anticipated. Whoever is responsible for these signs should be punished.

As we walked, I imagined the scene in the local Highways Department in Richmond back in the 1950s with two young men lounging with their feet up on their desks.

'Arnold, is there owt for us today?'

'We've got to let t'signwriting department know how far it is from Isles Bridge to Reeth so they can put up a footpath sign.'

'Well how far is it?'

'No idea.'

'We'll have to measure it then, but I don't fancy going out in this rain.'

'We'll just have to guess then. T'signwriters won't know any better. Any road, I was along there last week and I reckon it's about two miles.'

'But that was in your Dad's car, Arnold.'

'You're reet there, Ern. It takes much longer on a bike tha knows.'

'Exactly, it must be at least three and a half miles by bike.'

'But don't forget this is a footpath sign and it takes even longer on foot. I reckon it must be at least five miles.'

'I don't think t'signwriting department will be very 'appy if we ask 'em to do a sign saying REETH 2 (BUT 3? BY BIKE AND 5 ON FOOT).'

'I think I'll just tell 'em to put REETH 3?.'

'That's reet sensible that is, Arnold.'

So it is Arnold and Ernie who are responsible for building up and dashing the hopes of tired walkers in the Swaledale area.

We reached Reeth in the early afternoon. It is a large village with a number of shops, pubs and small galleries and is a popular tourist destination, being the main centre of population in mid-Swaledale. As it was now warm and sunny, we were able to sit outside the Black Bull and relax with a drink. The Black Bull is set on one side of the large village green and, unusually, it is next door to another pub, the Kings Arms and only about forty yards away from yet another, the Buck.

Because we had reached Reeth so early, we were able to watch the world go by for an hour or so before moving on. We faced a dilemma over what to do over the next couple of days because we would have only ten or eleven miles to walk to Richmond the following day (and this after two short days already) but that would be followed by about twenty-five miles to Osmotherley the day after. Apart from being a long distance, the stretch from Richmond to Osmotherley is the least interesting of the entire journey. Don had already decided to even out the distances by walking on a few miles that afternoon, which he could do as he was camping. Indeed, he planned to walk on for each of the next two days and would not see us again until Sunday evening at Blakey. He was sorting out his rucksack and put some of the contents on the table while he reorganised his packing and, amongst the items was a boil-in-the-bag meal, which I picked up to read the label and was astonished at the weight of it. The advertising read *Not dehydrated, so heavy, and you wouldn't want to carry too many, but no bowl is needed and they'll cook in the water you boil for a brew.* The packaging also showed that this one was *Beef Stew & Dumplings in Gravy.*

'It's a bit heavy to be carrying around, but it sounds good,' I said.

'Yeah, but they all taste the same whatever it says on the label.'

'Why, how many did you bring?'

'Well, I worked out that I would need five for the time we're away, bearing in mind the nights I'm not camping and the nights we're all eating out together. I've eaten three already.'

'No wonder you were struggling with your pack, if you were carrying all those as well as all your other stuff, but at least you've only got two to carry now,' I commented.

'Well, actually, I've got three.'

'How come?'

'When I went to the camping shop, I selected five of them but, when I went to pay, the bloke said I could have another one free because there was a 'three for the price of two' offer on. I told him that I only needed five, but he insisted and put another in the bag.'

'But, Don, you didn't have to bring it with you, you daft bugger.'

'I suppose not.'

Having been away from our wives and partners for a week, we began to wonder how they were managing without us:

'Pam would have no idea how to change a fuse,' said Tom.

'And that time when my arm was in a sling and I asked my wife to wire a plug, she just stood there … like a woman … looking at me as though I was an imbecile,' Don added.

'Christine's pretty good but, if we had a leak, she'd have no idea where the stop tap is,' Paul asserted.

'Yes, they just can't manage without us. On the other hand, we cope very well when they're away,' I said, to nods of agreement.

'Well, men are very adaptable and although women are very good at things like washing…'

'…and enjoy doing it…'

'it's not at all difficult, is it?'

'No, it's not like the old days when it was done by hand. All they have to do is put it in the washing machine and take it out when it's finished.'

'Actually,' Don interrupted, 'when Jane was away for a couple of weeks, I did have a bit of a problem. By the end of the first week, I didn't have any clean shirts left and I didn't know how the washing machine worked.'

'It's easy; you just bung the shirts in the machine and turn it on.'

'You may be right but I wasn't sure. Anyway, I solved the problem by a bit of lateral thinking, which is another thing that women are no good at,' Don congratulated himself.

'Why, what did you do?'

'Went to Marks and Spencer's at the weekend and bought five new shirts for the next week,' he said smugly and awaited our admiring approbation.

'But Don, didn't you wash them before you wore them?'

'Why would I do that? They were brand new, so they must have been clean,' he said defensively.

'They may have been clean, but they would be stiff and uncomfortable, particularly around the collar.'

'They seemed all right to me,' he replied, perking up a bit thinking he had deflected what he clearly believed was an unnecessary implied criticism of his ability as a lateral thinker.

'Well, even if you were prepared to wear them without washing them, you would still have to iron them.'

'Why? You only iron a shirt after it's been washed.'

'Don, you didn't go to work in new shirts that still had all the creases from being folded in the box, did you?'

'Yes,' he said, reddening at what he saw as more aspersions about the effectiveness of his lateral thinking.

'When you get a new shirt normally, doesn't your wife wash it and iron it before you wear it?'

'I don't know. I just get it from the wardrobe.'

'I suppose women can be quite useful at times,' Paul concluded, to sceptical agreement.

CHAPTER FOURTEEN

TOM AND THE MISSING GPS

Tom and I had spent a couple of days in Reeth on a short visit to the Yorkshire Dales in 2000 and it's amazing how quickly change occurs. I don't necessarily mean the landscape; I'm thinking more of technological change and how we seem able to adapt. Nothing illustrates this better than the rapid acceptance of the GPS. Sitting outside the pub in the sunshine, I couldn't help thinking about that earlier visit and had to tell the others the astonishing story of Tom's GPS.

Tom is the Inspector Gadget of the older generation; the pioneer of technological gimmickry. He must have been one of the first to acquire a hand-held GPS (and learn how to use it) and I think that was one of the reasons for his suggestion that we should explore the Dales. In those days, hardly anyone had even heard of a GPS, let alone owned one. During a long day's walk to Reeth, Tom had been playing with his hand-held gadget, attracting curious glances from other walkers and having to explain to them what the initials GPS stood for and what it did. It seems astonishing now, only a few years later, that not only does everyone know about them but also a great many have them in their cars.

Inspector Gadget became tired of playing with his toy by the afternoon and tied it to the side of his rucksack. When we reached

Reeth, we had to stop while he checked the address of our B&B for the night and he had to remove his rucksack to find his notes. As it turned out, we were no more than a hundred yards from our digs. Next morning, we were ready to leave when Tom realised his GPS was missing and, after searching our room without success, the landlady and her husband were enlisted to check the house to make sure we had not put it down anywhere else. The only explanation was that it had fallen off the rucksack when Tom was searching for the address the previous evening. We went and searched the area and called in at a nearby Health Centre to see whether anyone had handed it in there, but again without success. Although disappointed, Tom consoled himself that he would be going to America shortly and would be able to buy another one (being cheaper in the States than here) and that it would be more up-to-date than the old one. As we left the village, we noticed a police car parked at the kerb outside a detached house which turned out to be the local Police Station, if that is the correct way of describing it. We went up the path to the front door, only to find that it was locked. This seemed very strange considering there was a police car parked outside, and we thought it even stranger when no one replied to our knocking on the door.

As we stood at the door, wondering what else we could do to attract the attention of the officer inside, we noticed one of those intercom systems on the wall to the right of the door but at about knee height (well, about my knee height but Tom's waist height). Tom pressed the buzzer and the most bizarre conversation ensued.

'Hello,' said a disembodied voice.

'I'd like to report the loss of a GPS.'

'A what?'

'A G ... P ... S,' Tom said slowly.

'What's one of them?'

'Look, why don't you let us in?' asked Tom.

'What do you mean?'

'Open the door and let us in.'

'I can't.'

'Why not?'

'I'm at police headquarters in Northallerton.'

Northallerton! Fucking Northallerton! What happens if there's an emergency in Reeth? Northallerton is bloody miles away.

All this time Tom was bent almost double, speaking into the intercom and, after he had recovered from the revelation about the disembodied voice, he tried another tack.

'I'm in Reeth and I've lost a GPS, which is a Global Positioning System.'

'What does it look like?'

'It looks a bit like a mobile phone but you can't make calls on it,' said Tom.

'Where did you lose it?'

'I think it must have dropped out of my rucksack last night when I arrived in Reeth.'

'I'd better take some details. Let me get an incident report form. What did you say it was called – a globe of positioning cistern?'

Tom answered endless questions for the ridiculously long form, stooping the whole time with his ear to the intercom.

'I'll give you an incident number. You'll need this for your insurance company,' the voice said at last.

'Just a minute. Let me find a pen and some paper.' When you are on a walking break and staying in B&Bs, you carry a great many things but pen and paper are not usually amongst them (unless your name's Don, of course. He has a complete office suite at the bottom of his pack). However, Tom did manage to find a pen and also managed to find a till receipt, the back of which he could use to write the number. He crouched down again.

'OK. I'm ready.'

Tom, bending down, now had his right leg raised and held his scrap of paper on his right knee with his right hand and, holding his pen in his left hand, tried to write as he wobbled about on one leg, struggling to keep his balance and each time he started to write, the pen pierced the paper.

'2 … 5 … 7 … 3 … 6 … 2 … 4 … 9.'

'Couldn't you make it any longer?' Tom asked sarcastically.

'3 … 5,' continued the voice.

'I didn't actually mean it.' At last, Tom had all the digits written down.

'I'd better give you this reference number as well.'

'Another number?'

'8 ... 7 ... 8 ... 1 ... 4 ... 6 ... 9 ... 9 ... 2.'

Tom struggled again but at last he had all the details and we were able to set off on our day's journey.

Tom hoped that he would hear nothing more about the GPS as he was keen to buy a more up-to-date model, so he was disappointed when he received a letter from police headquarters in Northallerton a few weeks later, informing him that the GPS had been handed in and asking how he wanted it to be returned to him. He replied to the effect that it should be sent in the post, but asking whether the police could give him the name and address of the honest person who had handed it in, as he would like to send a small reward. He had in mind sending £10. When he received the package, the accompanying letter gave the name of the honest person as Lavinia Pemberton-Smythe and the address was The Grange, Grinton. Tom visualised The Grange as being the residence of the local squire and Lavinia being the beautiful daughter who had been out riding on her white stallion when she spotted the GPS. How could he possibly send a £10 reward to someone like that? As always, he came up with what he thought was a brilliant solution. He has raised a great deal of money for a local charity by producing and selling books of short walks from pubs in his local area and these retail at £5.95. He decided to write to Lavinia thanking her very much for her honesty in handing in the GPS, for which he was most grateful, but his letter went on to say 'I had thought of sending a cash reward but when I saw your name and address, I did not want to insult you by offering cash. In the circumstances, I enclose a signed copy of my book *Walks Around Langley and Sutton.*'

'You bloody idiot,' I said when he told me, 'I remember walking past The Grange and it's an Old Peoples Home. Lavinia is probably a doddering ninety year old in a motorised wheelchair and she only spotted the GPS on her way to the Health Centre because she is closer to the ground than anyone else. The chances are she pocketed it, thinking it was a mobile phone and that she would be able to sell it and buy a bottle of gin. The reason that it took her a month to hand it in was because she couldn't work out how it worked and couldn't sell it to any of the other residents in the home because they couldn't make it work either. So don't be surprised if you get a letter back saying 'Keep your poxy book. Just send me the money.' And what would a ninety year old in a wheelchair, living in North Yorkshire, want with a book on walking in Cheshire anyway?'

CHAPTER FIFTEEN

IT'S A SIGN, IT'S A SIGN

After our hour's relaxation in Reeth, we decided to move on to Grinton, our destination for the day. Although Grinton is a mile or two beyond Reeth and is slightly off the Coast to Coast route, Tom had decided that, as there is no Youth Hostel in Reeth, we would have to go off route to find the nearest centre of discomfort, and that was the hostel at Grinton. Fortunately, following the disturbed night at the Keld Youth Hostel, I was to stay at a B&B.

We said our farewells to Don, who we would not now see for three days and it seemed a pity after spending most of that day with all five of us walking together. On the other hand, I knew that Don had some thinking to do and that could have been one of his reasons for choosing to walk on in solitude.

'How are things at home, Al?' Tom asked.

'Okay,' I answered, thinking this is my opportunity to dump on Tom for being careless with his choice of question. There was no point though. He knew already that things at home were not okay and hadn't been for several years. This was one of the reasons I was here and not away in the Canaries or some other sunny part of the world with Suzanne. The problem was that she has been suffering from one of those chronic fatigue illnesses for years; the sort of illness that doctors have little clue about. They can't pinpoint a cause and certainly can't suggest any treatment.

'Is Suzanne no better?' he asked, knowing the answer.

'No,' I said, 'I don't know how she copes. It's impossible to imagine feeling exhausted every hour of every day, week after week, year after year, getting no restorative sleep, waking up each morning feeling just as tired as when you went to bed the night before. Add to that the constant pain and discomfort of aching muscles and fibres, knowing that lifting your arms to hang out washing or fold a sheet or even wash your hair will hurt like hell. Then, if she has to carry shopping even a short distance, she'll be in pain for two or three days.'

'It must be awful,' he sympathised, 'and, yes, it is impossible to imagine.'

'One of the worst parts of it for her is that people don't seem to accept that she's ill. Even friends. I think the trouble is that she looks normal and people forget everything they've been told, so even friends will expect her to do things without help. When they visit, they'll let her make tea without offering help and they'll outstay their welcome so she's almost falling over with exhaustion by the time they go. They have no idea. Then they'll phone and suggest going out somewhere as though she can do everything they can do without it having any effect. The trouble is that she *can* do everything they can do – it's just that she suffers for it afterwards. They don't see the effect and it's this lack of understanding or acceptance that frustrates her most.'

'But what about you?' Tom asked, even though he had listened to most of this before.

'It's difficult for me as well,' I said, 'I try my best, but I don't think she thinks it's enough. And anyway, it's hard to strike a balance. She's determined not to give in and lie in bed feeling sorry for herself, so she keeps going however tired she feels. I want to do what I can but, at the same time, I know that she wants to do some things herself. The result is that if I leave something for her to do, she bollocks me for not doing it and, if I do it thinking I'm helping her, I get bollocked for doing it.'

'I sympathise,' he said, although the broad grin on his face told me otherwise.

'I can't do right for doing wrong,' I said, thinking I sound more like my grandmother every day.

'Have you done any rustling lately?' Tom chuckled.

'This is not funny, Tom,' I replied. 'How would you like it if Pam told you off for making too much noise every time you read the paper? The problem is that her illness has enhanced her senses, so she seems to react to the slightest noise. I tried on a new shirt the other night and left it on whilst we watched television, but she complained that it made too much noise every time I moved, so I had to take it off. And I got another bollocking for making too much noise taking it off.'

'The curse of the creaking shirt,' he laughed, with no pretence of sympathy. I had noticed before that he thought my tales of woe were hilarious, which I did not find supportive.

'It's not just her hearing either. She's sensitive to light as well, so we've had to have 'black-out' blinds fitted behind the curtains in the bedroom,' I continued, to Tom's obvious amusement. 'When I get up in the morning, I stumble about the bedroom in the dark, afraid to switch the light on, and being careful to make as little noise as possible. When I go in the bathroom, I close the door behind me, as quietly as I can, waiting until I'm inside before I put the light on, have the quietest shower and shave imaginable before creeping out. I sneak across the bedroom on tiptoe and as I reach the door, I hear a voice from under the bedcovers:

'It's like Piccadilly bloody Circus in here.'

'It's not funny, Tom,' I said again, as he doubled up in laughter.

'It's entertaining, though,' he said 'in fact, they could make a good television comedy out of it.'

'Maybe, but it's not funny when you have to live with it. What I have to remember is that it's much worse for her than for me. I think I'd be much more irritable than she is if I'd woken up every day for the last five years or more feeling as though I had a really bad dose of flu.'

'Is she coping while you're away?' he asked, more serious now.

'I think so,' I replied, 'I phone every night and she seems alright. In a way, it's good that we spend a bit of time apart. It's difficult for us to go away together very often because it's such a big effort for her to prepare herself for the journey, and I think she quite likes to have a bit of time on her own now and then.'

We crossed the Swale on the road bridge in Grinton and, passing up the opportunity to patronise the Bridge Inn until later, we went our separate ways, the other three plodding up the hill to the youth hostel after arranging to meet me at the Bridge that evening at six thirty. I set off up another road to my own digs which, inevitably, was uphill.

My landlady, Mrs Brown, welcomed me with a pot of tea and homemade cakes and I settled in the lounge to watch the final hour or so of the final Ashes Test match on Sky. I had to drag myself away from the cricket just before six o'clock to tidy myself up before meeting my pals but, whilst I was in the middle of shaving, Mrs Brown pushed the telephone round the bathroom door as there was a call for me. It was Tom letting me know that they had decided to eat at the youth hostel, firstly because it had started to rain, but mostly because it had been more of a struggle up the hill to the youth hostel than he remembered and they didn't want to face it again. I think that meant *he* didn't want to face it again. Well, thanks Tom. Not only could I have watched the cricket till close of play, but also I had to eat on my own now, not to mention that I faced an uphill struggle from the Bridge as well. To cap it all, the arrangement was that I would meet them at the hostel next morning, so I would be undertaking the climb up the hill that they were so anxious to avoid this evening!

On my walk back (uphill) to the B&B after my lonely dinner at the Bridge Inn on Thursday night, it was raining and it was still raining on Friday morning. In fact, this was a morning which, even if I had been a gratuitous walker, would have prompted me to stay indoors. As it was, I had to meet my chums and be in Richmond that evening. Mrs Brown provided a fantastic breakfast and I set off early as I had a twenty minute walk to the youth hostel. This entailed walking down the hill to Grinton and then climbing a longer hill to the youth hostel. By the time I reached there, I was already thoroughly wet. From the youth hostel, the obvious way to rejoin the Coast to Coast route would have been to walk back down the hill to Grinton and cross the Swale over the road bridge. This would have suited me as I could have met the others outside the Bridge Inn and avoided the stiff climb (in the rain) to the hostel, but Tom said he knew another way, which entailed following the road further uphill from the youth hostel before cutting across. He had warned us that this did involve fording the Swale which would necessitate taking off our boots and socks. I had not been at all keen on this idea from the moment it had been raised a few days earlier but, if everyone else thought it was all right, there was no point in arguing. So, we set off from the hostel in the pouring rain and walked up the road for half a mile or so and then turned left onto the moorland in poor visibility. We seemed to make reasonable progress, although I was a bit surprised when, after about forty minutes, we had seen no sign of the river, and even more surprised when we spotted the youth hostel through the mist no more than fifty yards to our left. We had come round in a complete circle!

'Thank God Andy isn't with us,' said Tom 'he'd give me hell. 'I thought you said you knew the way. We'd have been better off asking the village idiot for directions' he'd be saying. Anyway, I'll have to remember that for next year.'

'What's happening next year, Tom?'

'What am I saying? There won't be a next year.'

As the path we were following would bring us out on the road below the youth hostel, we had a lively and democratic discussion about which route we should take, the result of which was that Tom decided that we should carry on and walk through Grinton to rejoin the Coast to Coast route. In Grinton, we strode past the Bridge Inn, over an hour after I had passed it on my way to the youth hostel, and crossed the bridge over the Swale which was a raging torrent after the night's rain

'Bloody hell, Tom, and you said we were going to ford the river. We'd have been swept away if we'd tried it.'

'Yeah, but look on the bright side, we'd have reached the North Sea a damn sight quicker. Probably this afternoon by the look of that water.'

As we trudged through the rain on our way to Richmond, I was getting wetter and wetter despite the waterproof jacket and waterproof over-trousers. Although we were staying in Richmond that night, we had agreed during our strategy meeting in Reeth that we would walk on beyond Richmond and get the bus back and then, on Saturday morning, we would catch the bus back out to where we finished that day. If we could put in an extra seven miles or so, this would make the next day's walk to Osmotherley more manageable. In reaching this decision, we had not anticipated walking the extra couple of miles circumnavigating the youth hostel (or the pissing rain) and, by late morning, all I wanted to do was to get to the B&B, take off my wet clothes and dry out. Don't forget that I had been pissed on longer than the others. However, we agreed (or, to be completely accurate, Tom said) that we would defer our final decision until we reached Richmond.

My mood was not improved by an incident along the way. Although the walking was easy, the rain had made steep sections treacherous and, as we descended one such stretch, I took a tumble. As I fell, I put out my right arm to stop myself falling, only to knock Paul forward into Tom. Fortunately, they managed to stay on their feet but I went headlong down the path landing slightly on my left side with my left arm out in front of me and almost upside down with my head down the path and my feet up it.

'I can't get up,' I wailed, as the others rushed to me.

'Don't move. Where does it hurt?' Paul asked anxiously.

'I can't get up,' I shouted.

The others were all asking questions at once.

'Do you think you've broken anything?'

'Shall we call Mountain Rescue?'

'Are you in pain?'

'There's nothing wrong with me. I just can't bloody get up.'

Well, I was upside down on a rocky track wearing several layers of clothes, a heavy pair of boots and, to make matters worse, had a heavy pack on my back. I lay floundering around like an upside-down turtle for several moments before my colleagues decided to help me up and we walked on.

We arrived in Richmond in the early afternoon and took

refuge in a pub, where we had a drink and a sandwich whilst reviewing our situation. My view was that we should call it a day and hope for better weather on Saturday, even if it did mean a longer walk. However, I said nothing and the decision was made to walk on. Democracy at work. Those who keep quiet are governed by the vociferous. Not that I felt aggrieved or petulant in any way.

The route beyond Richmond is not at all attractive for walkers. The Vale of Mowbray is rich farmland at the northern end of the Vale of York, but it is flat and featureless and unattractive to walkers. On top of that, much of the route is on tarmac as there are no suitable public footpaths heading in the right direction. Indeed, there is one stretch of eight consecutive miles with tarmac underfoot. With this knowledge in mind, our decision was to forget footpaths and simply walk along the road, perhaps as far as Catterick Bridge, in order to complete as many miles as we could as quickly as we could. Tom had obtained a bus timetable whilst we were in Richmond so that we knew that there was a bus service from Catterick Bridge but, after giving it some thought as we walked along, I suggested that we would be better getting a taxi as the cost, split between four of us, would be cheaper than four bus fares and it would be more flexible as we would not need to worry about bus timetables. You see, petulance and grievances can lead to effective lateral thinking (even though I say again that I was not feeling petulant or aggrieved, of course).

We made rapid progress and, for the first time that day, the rain had stopped. To our surprise, Paul had stayed with us again rather than walking on ahead and, as we stretched our legs, I found that I was walking with him with Tom and Joe some way behind. When we reached Brompton-on-Swale, we stopped for the other two to catch up and, fortuitously, a taxi pulled up across the road and the driver went into a house. When he came out a few minutes later, I crossed to have a word with him about the possibility of being picked up in Bolton-on-Swale in an hour's time. He agreed, although he said that it might be another driver. By walking the additional distance, we knocked seven and a half miles off Saturday's walk. We were dropped off outside the B&B soon after five and arranged to be collected by the taxi at eight thirty next morning. As we stood at the side of the road, I wondered why Tom was faffing around with his pack when all I wanted to do was get inside and have a nice hot bath or shower. Eventually, he produced his notes listing the places he had booked and studied them carefully for a moment.

'Now, I couldn't get us all in at one B&B,' he announced and, dispensing with his customary sham of a democratic discussion, he continued, 'me and Joe will stay here and Paul and Al can stay at the Castle Guesthouse, which is a much nicer place than this.'

Bells, sirens and alarms went off. This was more Tomatalk which I translated as 'I couldn't give a shit what either of these two places are like, but the other could be bloody miles away for all I know, so I'm bagging this one.'

Accepting our leader's decision, we arranged to meet later for our evening meal and went our separate ways. Fortunately, our digs were only a short hike away and we arrived before dark.

We were welcomed by the landlady and, as we walked down the tiled hall, I could see a newspaper spread out on the floor below a sign on the wall which said PLEASE LEAVE YOUR BOOTS HERE. However, it was not necessary to read the sign as the landlady stopped next to the newspaper and said 'leave your boots here please' pointing to the newspaper. There was another sign higher up on the wall THANK YOU FOR NOT SMOKING. That's alright, thank you for noticing.

This was definitely more of a guest house than a B&B and our landlady ushered us through a door (with a THANK YOU FOR NOT SMOKING sign on it), up some stairs, through another door (with a THANK YOU FOR NOT SMOKING sign on it), along a corridor (with a THANK YOU FOR NOT SMOKING sign on the wall) to a bedroom. It was a pleasant room (with a THANK YOU FOR NOT SMOKING sign in it) with twin beds and a washbasin in the corner. After allowing us to pop our heads round the door to inspect the bedroom, she took us along the landing to another door marked BATHROOM. She explained that this bathroom would be for our exclusive use, as the other bedroom on that landing would be vacant that night, and that the key to the bathroom door was in our bedroom. After settling in, I took the key and toddled off to use the bathroom. As I washed my hands, I read the sign above the washbasin saying *AS WE HAVE RECENTLY HAD A WATER METER INSTALLED, IT WOULD BE HELPFUL IF GUESTS COULD REFRAIN FROM USING MORE WATER THAN NECESSARY*. I duly flushed the toilet again. Having washed my hands, I turned to leave and as I gripped the door handle, a sign on the door instructed me

NOW
WASH YOUR HANDS

I turned obediently back to the washbasin before thinking 'hang on a minute, I already have'.

Paul is the clean-cut sort and one of the few people who somehow manages to look almost smart even in his walking gear. He is average height but has an enormous stride-length and moves deceptively quickly when out walking. As a part-time National Park ranger in the Peak District, he keeps fit by walking in the National Park most weekends. He is always pleasant and never seems to complain about anything. In fact, he is so uncomplaining that you do not even know he is there most of the time. In short, he is the ideal bloke with whom to share a room.

I had noticed that he had been even quieter than usual during the last couple of days and wondered whether there was any particular reason. The fact that he had phoned his office the morning before could suggest a problem at work, I thought. When I got back to the bedroom, he was just putting away his phone and had what I interpreted as a troubled look on his face.

'Is everything alright?' I asked.

'Yes, fine,' he said, distractedly. 'Actually, no. Everything isn't alright,' he added, after a moment's thought. Oh, no, add *is everything alright* to the questions which should never be asked under any circumstances even if you can't think of anything else to say and you feel stupid just standing there saying nothing list.

'The thing is,' he continued, as I wondered whether there was any polite way I could resign from my unelected office of group counsellor, 'I've got a potential health problem. I had some tests a day or two before we came away and the results should be through by now, but they seem to have gone astray.'

'What sort of tests?' I asked, in some alarm, despite Paul's obvious fitness. For him to even mention it suggested that he was very concerned.

'Well,' he continued, hesitantly, 'to be honest, I've got a lump which could be cancerous.'

'Bloody hell!' I couldn't think of anything else to say.

'The results should have been through by yesterday and the Consultant told me to phone his secretary, so that was the call I made yesterday morning,' he explained.

'So, what was the result?' I asked, knowing that I would not like the answer.

'They didn't have the results through, so I was told to phone again this morning.'

'This is not on,' I said, 'they must know how important it is to you and should make sure they have the results when they say.'

'It's much worse than that,' he gulped, as I prepared myself for the worst, 'when I phoned this morning, the secretary told me that the lab claimed to have sent the results a couple of days ago, but they haven't arrived.'

'What?' I exclaimed.

'She said she was organising a search and would ask the lab to send a copy of their report, and asked me to phone later. Now, she tells me that she hasn't been able to track down the report and, when she spoke to the lab, it was too late for them to get a copy across today, so I've got to wait until Monday now.'

'That's disgraceful,' I said. 'They can't really expect you to wait all that time. There must be something someone can do.'

'She says not. She was very apologetic and I believe her when she says she has tried everything, but there's nothing more she can do.'

Poor Paul. There was nothing I could do or say that could possibly help. He had come away with us, burdened by this anxiety about his entire future, and knowing that he would have to wait until Thursday before he would know any more. During those days of waiting, he had thrown himself into his walking, stretching himself to the limits of physical endurance, not caring about the consequences, believing that this could be his final opportunity to enjoy walking in the beautiful English countryside. The solitary walking had, in a strange way, brought a certain peace. He had been able to consider his life to date, remembering the good times, and had convinced himself that his time had not yet come. By Thursday morning, he was ready to make the most important call of his life; the call that would determine his future. Instead of clarifying his prospects, the last two days had renewed the nightmare and, after the latest call, he now knew it would last for another three days, at the very least.

He faced up to it well that evening and the others wouldn't have guessed there was a problem, but I think he was glad to get back to the guest house.

Inevitably, in the middle of the night I awoke and needed to go to the bathroom. I crept out of my bed as quietly as I could so as not to disturb Paul, but why do doorknobs in guest houses always make so much noise? Stealthily, I moved on to the landing and started to pull the door shut behind me to ensure it didn't bang as it closed but it was one of those doors with a spring-loaded mechanism which seems to resist any pressure to close it faster than it wants to go. I stopped pulling when it had only an inch further to travel, ready to close it gently. BANG! Oh shit, it was one of those doors that deceives you by not wanting to close, but then travels the last half inch at a hundred miles an hour.

As I padded along the landing, I could only hope that Paul's slumber had not been disturbed. Bloody hell. What's wrong with this door? Oh bugger, it's locked and the key's on my bedside cabinet. I retraced my steps to the door and tried to re-enter as noiselessly as possible but, once again, the doorknob creaked. However, I managed to open the door without further incident. The problem now was that I couldn't risk the door slamming shut again whilst I was retrieving the key, only to have to open it again. Fortunately, I found that, by holding the door with the toes of my left foot, I could just about reach the bedside cabinet with my right hand. My fingertips reached the key and dragged it across the cabinet. Success. Oh, sod it. The key tumbled to the floor and in stretching to retrieve it, my foot released the door. Now it was a race against time, as I groped around on the carpet trying to find the key in the dim light from the landing as the door made its slow, relentless progress. There was only one thing for it. I lay flat on my stomach on the carpet (hoping that the landlady had done a thorough hoovering that day), with my legs out of the doorway and my hands out in front of me trying to find the key. The towel protecting my modesty came loose and there I was, completely naked, stretched out on the floor with my feet sticking out on the landing. At that moment, I hoped that Paul was still fast asleep and that he did not raise his head to see me scrabbling about on the floor. At least, there was no one in the other bedroom, was there?

Eventually, I found the key and the door only banged twice more before I was back in bed. Paul did not mention it the next morning so I have no idea whether he slept through it all or whether, in his usual uncomplaining way, he was hoping that he would not have to share a room with such a noisy pillock again.

Readers may be wondering about two matters arising from this tale. Firstly, why was I naked and, secondly, why did we bother to lock the bathroom door when we were supposed to have exclusivity rights and were the only guests on that landing? My answer to the first is that I did not pack pyjamas as that would have meant more to carry, although I do now accept that I could have helped Don out by borrowing one of the five pairs he was carrying. As far as locking the bathroom door is concerned – good question. The answer is that we didn't think about that at the time, and there's no need for you to feel so bloody clever.

CHAPTER SIXTEEN

EGGS CAN FLY

Richmond is a busy little town nestling in a kink in the river Swale. It has a large cobbled square with pleasant cobbled streets and a castle poised on a hill above. It is the largest town visited on the Coast to Coast route and has plenty of hotels, pubs and guest houses and, with a small Woolworths and Boots the Chemists, it is a shopper's paradise after what has passed before. However, the unpleasant weather meant that we did not see it in its best light and we were glad to be on our way next morning.

We had left the Yorkshire Dales National Park on our approach to Richmond and would not enter the North York Moors National Park until later in the day on our final approach to Osmotherley.

The taxi drew up outside the guest house at exactly eight thirty on the Saturday morning and, bugger, it was the same driver who had picked us up from Bolton-on-Swale at five o'clock the day before. We could not ask him to drop us off a couple of miles further along the road then. Not that the thought ever crossed our minds, you understand. He left us at the village green at Bolton-on-Swale, exactly where he had collected us the evening before.

Although it was not raining, we agreed (or, Tom decided) not to change our resolution to do this section to Osmotherley on the road although, after a couple of miles, we did have to follow a footpath across three or four fields to reach the eight mile section of road walking described by Wainwright. This short section was the only non-road walking we would do that day but it was to prove rather exciting.

We reached a gate to a field where the map showed the footpath going from the gate down the left side of the field. What the map didn't show us was the herd of excited heifers milling about in the corner of the field on the other side of the gate. They showed little sign of wanting to move to the other side of the field to let us through but, being four strong, brave men, unperturbed by the threat posed by several tons of agitated beefsteak, we opened the gate and strode through, waving our arms around to find a passage between them and the hedge marking the limit of the field. Didn't they know that this was a public footpath and that we were the public? I was leading the way and had gone only a few yards when I heard Tom's voice behind me:

'There's a bull,' he whispered, hoarsely.

'You don't expect me to fall for ..... oh, shit.'

Only a few yards away and surrounded by the rest of the herd, a bull was pawing the ground, with hot breath steaming from his nostrils exactly as depicted in the comic strips in the Dandy or Beano, except that this one didn't make me laugh. Despite my panic, I did not fail to notice just how fast the over-sixties can move when death or serious injury is the alternative. I was particularly impressed by my own athleticism in setting a new world record for the combined high and long jumps, clearing two heifers and the field gate in one stupendous leap.

Safely outside the field, we leant on the gate wondering what to do next as the restless animals gave no indication that they had any intention of moving from this corner of the field. The farmyard was not far away and our athletic activities had alerted a farm dog who was barking incessantly, prompting the farmer to come out and investigate and he joined us in our sojourn at the gate.

'There's a bull in the field,' I said.

'Arr.'

'The public footpath goes through the field.'

'Arrr.'

'Well, isn't it going to be dangerous to go through a field with a bull in it?'

'Arrrr.'

All five of us leant on the gate, surveying the scene and, as we watched, the bull de-heifcrised one of the herd.

'What are we going to do?'

The farmer suddenly became more talkative and explained that he had only just put the bull in the field, so he was likely to be very aroused and, therefore, he could not give any assurance of safe passage across the field. Whilst he was telling us this, the randy bull de-heifericated another one of the herd. Several minutes passed, during which he had his evil way with two more virgins, but this gave me a ray of hope. If he continued at this rate, he could tire himself out and we could race down the field and out-pace him. The problem was that he showed no sign of flagging yet. Eventually, the farmer decided that he would have to try to help us and entered the field, waved his arms around and ushered the herd away from the gate sufficiently to allow us to make our way down the field, looking over our shoulders at frequent intervals.

We soon reached the road where the eight miles of road walking described by Wainwright began. This 'road' walking was mainly along country lanes with virtually no traffic and, at times, we walked for half an hour or more without being disturbed by a passing car, so it was not quite as bad as it sounds and we made rapid progress towards Danby Wiske, a name which has a special ring to it. I can imagine Terry Wogan now, saying 'Danby Wiske. Ah, the old Shakespearian actor.' Unfortunately, the reality is a major disappointment. There is a pub, the White Swan, but it does not open until lunchtime and we were there soon after eleven. It seemed odd at first that the pub did not see the advantage of catering for Coast to Coast walkers but, thinking about it, we had set off from Bolton-on-Swale whilst most walkers travel from Richmond and will not arrive in Danby Wiske until much later.

However, we thought we were in luck as we had seen a sign advertising teas at Ashfield House, which was only a hundred yards or so further on. As we approached, there were no signs of activity and when we went to the door, we were told that they did not open until two o'clock. Disappointed again, Paul and I decided that we would wait here for Tom and Joe to catch up but, as we sat on the wall, the owner, Mrs Norris, came out and said that she would be happy to serve us. Ashfield House is a private house and Mrs Norris had only started the tea shop business, serving teas and home-made cakes, three or four months before. She opens from eleven on Mondays to Fridays but not until two on Saturdays. She looked after us extremely well, particularly considering that she was not supposed to be open and also had a constant stream of visitors delivering cards and presents, as there had been a birth in the family. Mrs Norris also does bed and breakfast for Coast to Coast walkers but, unfortunately, there is little else to recommend about Danby Wiske, which is only 110 feet above sea level and is the lowest point on the journey (other than at the coasts, of course). The altitude (or, rather, the lack of it) gives an indication of the featureless nature of the landscape in the area although, on a positive note, it does make for easy walking.

The road walking continued for several more miles until we reached the point where the Wainwright route reverts to public footpaths. The footpath route is easier underfoot, but continues across the flat plain and is hardly exciting. After the rain of the previous day, we just wanted to cover the miles as quickly as possible, so we turned south, making our way towards the A684. Paul and I reached the village of Brompton and stopped to let Tom and Joe catch up again and, fortuitously, found that we were waiting outside a pub, so forced ourselves to help the landlord meet his overheads by having a drink. The barmaid happened to mention that we were only half a mile from Northallerton. Northallerton! It had taken us two whole days to walk here from Reeth, and I could not help thinking about Tom's conversation with police headquarters a few years earlier. If we had been reporting an emergency, the entire population of Reeth could have been murdered by the time the police arrived. In fact, the situation is even worse now as the police house in Reeth is no longer there. Well, the house is still there but it is no longer a police house. I can only hope they have a helicopter for emergencies.

It was not long before Joe and Tom joined us and, after our period of refreshment, we walked on to join the main road for the last few miles to Osmotherley. The main A684 is a busy road, particularly on this Saturday afternoon in September, and we kept a close watch on the traffic as we made rapid progress.

As in all spheres of life, walkers respond to encouragement and there is one small group of people who take great delight in providing that encouragement and I must take the opportunity to acknowledge that here. These are youths who always seem to drive either a Volkswagen Golf or a little Peugeot something or other. This was evident now as we trudged along the busy main road and a youth's head appeared from the window of just such a car and shouted something unintelligible. It's a great pity that these youths are unable to grasp that their words are lost on the wind and that, perhaps, their encouragement would be better received if they were to slow down but, undaunted, they take great satisfaction from their good deed. A minority of them must have realised that shouting from a vehicle moving at sixty miles per hour may not get their message of goodwill across, so they add a shaking of the hand as though they are holding a snake. Unfortunately, I don't know what this means but it is nonetheless encouraging.

No doubt, that evening they would brag to their pals about the excitement of their day:

'You'll never guess what we did this afternoon. We drove along the A684 and shouted out of the window at some old farts out walking. Silly old buggers didn't seem to hear us, but it was dead exciting. You should have come.'

'I wish I had. It sounds great. Certainly more exciting than my afternoon.'

'Why, what did you do?'

'Went to Old Trafford to watch Manchester United play Chelsea.'

'You poor sod.'

Not all of these youths are as friendly as those who encouraged us with their cheery calls and supportive gestures, as Andy discovered on one of his earlier Coast to Coast expeditions. He and Tom were walking along the same stretch of road when, in addition to shouting, a youth hurled an egg which struck Andy on his left calf. No doubt the youth found this funny and would argue that he was only trying to 'egg on' the old farts, but an egg thrown from a vehicle moving at sixty miles an hour hits its target with enormous power. Fortunately, the egg was not hard-boiled and broke on impact, leaving Andy with a yolk-soaked sock and boot, as well as a nasty bruise.

Andy is a big, tough man and, like the Incredible Hulk, you won't like him when he's angry. He was still fuming when they walked into Osmotherley an hour later and kept his eyes peeled for Volkswagen Golfs and little Peugeot something or others. He peered into every parked car, looking for the tell-tale egg carton on the back seat. If he had found the give-away clue, I can imagine a furious Andy lying in wait for the owner's return, shirt buttons popping open from the strain of his tense muscles, only to frighten to death the innocent old lady who had the misfortune of buying eggs that morning.

For the first six days of our journey we had been scattered, rarely walking as a group, but this was the third day running that we had kept together, apart from the missing Don. Admittedly, Joe and Tom fell behind at times but Paul and I would stop to let them catch up, so that we really did seem to be a group. Whether it was Paul's renewed anxiety that had caused the change, I didn't know, but it was good to feel part of a group of friends undertaking a major challenge together and supporting each other.

Arriving in Osmotherley in mid-afternoon, we made our way to the Queen Catherine for a drink and to catch up with the cricket, having heard nothing for the last two days. We learned that Friday's appalling weather in Yorkshire had not extended to London where they had enjoyed almost a full day's play, finishing early only because of bad light. However, the poor weather had travelled south on Saturday and, whilst we were enjoying a reasonable day, frequent showers were interrupting play in London throughout the day. As England only needed to draw to regain the Ashes for the first time in many years, the poor weather was to our advantage. After our forced march along the roads of the Vale of Mowbray, we were enjoying our Saturday afternoon relaxation with a drink and the cricket when the light seemed to dim and we wondered whether there had been a power failure, but that wasn't possible as the television was still showing replays of Friday's play. Then we realised that there was a familiar figure standing in front of us, blocking out the light and we heard that unmistakeable voice:

Oh, and there we were, all in one place
A generation lost in space

'Andy, how the devil are you?'

Being weekend, he had decided to drive up and take us by surprise and spend the night with us. We were staying at the youth hostel in Osmotherley that night and, of course, Andy's bunk was already booked. We were delighted to see him and pleased to learn that his blisters were healing well, although not well enough for him to do the rest of the walk with us. Also, there was a sense of relief that the disappointment of going home early had not caused him to fall into one of his dark periods. His presence encouraged us to have another drink or two before finding our way to the hostel and, by way of celebration, Tom told us that he was going to treat us all to a Duckfart. In fact, he had promised Duckfarts to us a few nights earlier in Kirkby Stephen but, by now, we were convinced that they were a figment of his elderly imagination. There was a story behind this:

'When I visited my brother, George, in Oregon a few months ago,' he said, 'we went in a bar one day to sample the beer. George recommended the local brew, which is Weinhard's, and he went to the bar for the first round but brought back two cocktails.

'What are they?' I asked.

'Duckfarts,' George said, 'they're cocktails.'

'I thought we were having beers,' I said, 'I don't normally drink cocktails. Why did you ask for them?'

'I didn't. I asked for two Weinhards but the barman must have thought I said two Duckfarts.'

Unlike me, George is a very quiet, diffident sort of bloke and, rather than cause a fuss, he just paid for them and said nothing.

'Well, I'm going to tell him,' I said, and picked up the glasses but George called me back.

'Now then, our Tom,' he said, 'don't go causing a fuss. I live here and I don't want to get a reputation as a bolshie Englishman. We can drink these and then have a beer.'

Surprisingly, I took a liking to them and had a few more before I came home.'

At the pub in Kirkby Stephen, he had gone to the bar and asked:

'Can you do five Duckfarts for me?'

I watched and noticed the barman's broad smile change to a wary half-smile:

'Are you looking for trouble?' he asked in a slightly threatening way.

'No, no,' Tom said, 'I'm not asking you to fart like a duck ..... it's a cocktail. It's called a Duckfart.'

'I don't do cocktails; I've only been here a few weeks and wouldn't know what to do,' he said. 'I'll ask the landlady.' He called to a rather large woman at the other end of the bar, who was wearing a dress of which my grandmother would have said 'it fits where it touches', which was just about everywhere (and even where it shouldn't), and she made her inelegant way towards Tom and the barman.

'The gentleman here wants to know whether we can do Duckfarts,' he said. He had his back to Tom but, from my vantage point, I noticed one eyebrow flicker slightly upwards and an almost imperceptible movement of his head back over his shoulder, as if to say 'careful, the bloke's a nutter.'

'Now, what is it that you want?' she asked, in a manner which suggested she would call the police if the answer was not to her liking.

'I asked for a cocktail called a Duckfart,' Tom said, in what he clearly thought was a patient tone, although I knew him well enough to know trouble was brewing.

'Never heard of it,' she said, almost triumphantly it seemed. 'Mind you, there's not much demand for cocktails here,' which, looking round the bar, I could understand. Tom just stared at her and I waited for the cutting remark but she must have sensed that he was not going to give up that easily, so she offered 'tell me what's in it and I'll see if I can make it for you.'

'Bailey's Irish Cream, Kahlua and Crown Royal, in that order,' Tom said.

'We've got the Bailey's,' she said, hopefully.

'What about the rest?' Tom asked, clearly not impressed.

'I think I've heard of Crown Royal,' she said, 'but can't remember what it is.'

'It's a bourbon, but you could use Scotch if you haven't got any,' Tom suggested.

'And what's this Carl Lewis?'

'I didn't say Carl Lewis, I said Kahlua. It's a coffee liqueur,' he replied, now beginning to wish he'd never asked for a bloody cocktail.

'Never heard of it,' she said.

'Give me five pints,' Tom said, in desperation.

Looking round the bar in Osmotherley, Tom had assessed that the Queen Catherine attracted a better class of customer. Indeed, he was convinced that cocktails were part of the staple diet in this corner of Yorkshire, so he disappeared to the bar. We were about to send a search party to look for him, but he returned before we set off, carrying a single glass, which he placed in the middle of the table, a satisfied, not to say smug, grin on his face.

'There,' he said, 'one Duckfart. The barman hadn't done one before but he was determined to learn how to do a new cocktail. The only trouble was that it cost an arm and a leg. You can have a sip each and, if you like it, you can buy your own.'

We sat round the table, gaping at the concoction in front of us, wondering who was going to be the first to sample this renowned beverage (renowned, that is, among Tom's friends).

'Tell us, Tom,' Joe said, 'why is it called a Duckfart?'

'Just look at it. Doesn't it remind you of anything? You know when you go to the park and walk by the lake and all those

Canada ducks waddle around, shitting on the path; doesn't it look like one of those sort of layered shits?'

There was silence for a moment as we all continued to stare at the glass and it was Andy who broke the reverie:

'So why is it called a Duck**fart** if it's supposed to look like a shit?' he asked, quite reasonably in my opinion.

'And anyway,' Paul added, 'they're actually Canada Geese, not ducks.'

'Yeah,' I said 'if it's a goose, not a duck and a shit, not a fart, why isn't it called a Gooseshit?'

'I don't know,' said a beleaguered Tom, 'because it's American.'

We took turns to have a sip and I noticed there was no rush to the bar for full measures of the transatlantic brew.

As we enjoyed the relaxed Saturday afternoon atmosphere, we watched the customers coming and going and Andy could hardly contain himself when two very attractive young women walked in to the bar. One of them in particular took his fancy and I have to admit that she was spectacularly beautiful:

'Just look at that figure … and those legs … and that face … she's absolutely gorgeous,' he enthused 'and so sexy. She's sex on legs. In fact, she exhumes sex.'

'I think you mean she exudes sex,' said Paul patiently.

'That as well,' Andy mumbled 'she reminds me of that lass who used to go to the gym. You know, the one that made all the lads go cross-eyed. What was her name?'

'I think you mean Suzy Jones.'

'That's right,' acknowledged Andy, 'but we used to call her Erogenous Jones.'

The Queen Catherine is a pleasant and popular place, although I did notice a rather unusual announcement on a chalk board, which read:

LIVE JAZZ EVENINGS
EVERY ALTERNATIVE SUNDAY EVENING

I was left wondering what is an alternative to a Sunday evening? Is it a Friday evening or a Saturday evening, and how would anyone know when to attend in order to enjoy the jazz? Being more charitable, even if the notice should have read: *EVERY ALTERNATE SUNDAY EVENING,* how would anyone know whether it was a week or a fortnight since the last jazz evening? Perhaps the people of Osmotherley are brighter than we think.

The confusion about which is the next jazz evening is similar to the bewilderment created by those signs so often stuck to shop doors – *BACK IN HALF AN HOUR.* When did the half hour start, you moron?

After a while, we decided to move on to the youth hostel and, as Andy made his way to his car, I noticed that he seemed to be checking the back seats of all the parked cars along the way. Old habits die hard!

During the short walk from the village to the youth hostel, we passed a guest house which prompted Tom to tell us about one of his previous walks with Andy. They had endured a long day in poor weather and, by the time they reached Osmotherley, they were wet, bedraggled and tired and just wanted to relax with a pot of tea before having a nice bath and going out for a meal. It was already about six o'clock and they expected the B&B to be in the village centre but could not find it. The address they had was simply the house name and, search as they might, they could not see it anywhere. After several minutes of fruitless searching, Tom spotted a man he recognised as the proprietor of the aforementioned guest house (where he had stayed once before) and approached him and asked for directions to the B&B. Unfortunately, the property was about half a mile outside the village, inevitably in the direction from which they had come but he did point out that he had vacancies that night, if they didn't feel like walking the extra distance. Although they certainly did not feel like walking a further yard, let alone half a mile (plus another half mile back for their meal), they had already booked their accommodation and it would be unfair not to turn up. As they made their weary way to the B&B, they thought it odd that he should have tried to poach guests from their landlady in such a blatant way.

They arrived at the B&B expecting it to be really nice as the nightly rate was higher than it had been at any of their previous B&Bs on that trip. However, they were disappointed. The landlady was kind enough to offer a pot of tea and a scone but, immediately, she proceeded to tell them about two Coast to Coast walkers who had stayed with her a few weeks before. Apparently, she had just baked a fresh supply of scones and had put them on a plate to cool and when she gave them their pot of tea, she told them they could take a scone from the plate but, when she returned, they had eaten the lot. Relating this story to Tom and Andy was her way of telling them not to be greedy pigs and she made a point of giving them just one scone each and only enough milk for two cups of tea each.

Although slightly disappointed with the quality of their accommodation, at least they were able to have a hot bath and relax after their difficult day. As they prepared to walk back up the hill to the village for their dinner, Tom said he felt certain that the landlord at the guest house who had directed them to the B&B had the same surname as their landlady and he proceeded to look up the names and found that this was, indeed, the case. On their way out, Tom mentioned to the landlady that they had had to ask for directions and had asked the proprietor of the guest house and commented that it was a coincidence that he had the same name as her.

'Oh, him,' she spat, in the sort of tone that only ex-wives are capable of achieving. They thought it best not to tell her about his guest-poaching activities although, by that time, they were wishing they had taken him up on his offer.

The hostel is about half a mile outside the village (uphill, of course) and we were fortunate enough to have a dormitory just for the five of us and this one even had its own toilet cubicle. Luxury indeed. Unlike Keld, this hostel not only had a television but also had its own television lounge so we would be able to catch up with the football on Match of the Day later that evening.

After dinner at the hostel, we settled down in the television lounge where Andy was already talking to a female guest and, as their conversation progressed, gradually the rest of us joined in. I became a little concerned when it became apparent that she knew a lot about us and wondered whether she could be some sort of mind reader. How else would she know so much? Could she be a stalker who would follow us for the rest of our journey? When she mentioned that she was at the hostel for the weekend, having arrived the day before, the penny dropped. Don must have stayed here on Friday night and she had been chatting to him! That being the case, he had walked about thirty-five miles between leaving us on Thursday afternoon and arriving in Osmotherley on Friday, walking in the rain for most of the time. Adding the distance from Keld to Reeth, he had covered about forty-six miles in two days. As we were due to meet up again on Sunday night at Blakey, that meant that we would cover the same distance in one day that he had given himself two days to do. So much for his idea of evening out the distances. He had left himself two very short but, nevertheless, exciting days. As we cursed him for giving personal information about us to this serial man-eater, little did we know that he faced greater danger himself at that very moment!

CHAPTER SEVENTEEN

NOWT SO QUEER AS FOLK

Just before reaching Osmotherley on the Saturday afternoon, we had entered the third National Park of our journey, the North York Moors National Park, through which we would now walk to the end of our odyssey in three days time. Sunday's trek would take us to the Lion Inn at Blakey, although Wainwright split this into two sections of about twelve miles to Clay Bank Top, followed by a further nine and a quarter miles to Blakey. Our journey that day would be about twenty-one and a half miles, coinciding with the Cleveland Way for much of the day.

Andy was nowhere to be seen when we got up but, when we went down for breakfast, we found him watching television again and it was fortunate for us that there was no TV in the dormitory or, no doubt, we would have had a disturbed night. He was watching one of those Sunday morning political programmes and Tony Blair was on screen surrounded by a group of new Labour MPs.

'Just look at the puffed up nancy boy with his gang of aconites,' he blustered.

'Aconites are a type of plant,' Paul pointed out, in his customary quiet way. 'I think the word you're looking for is acolytes.'

'Well, look at them all sucking up to him. Bunch of bloody psychopaths.'

'I think you mean sycophants,' Paul corrected.

'I know what I mean.'

Having driven all the way up from Derbyshire, Andy was not going to miss out on walking altogether, so he walked with us for the first three quarters of an hour or so, before leaving us to follow a circular route back to the youth hostel and his car. The weather was good and the morning's walk over the Cleveland hills was just wonderful. These hills may not be particularly high but provide great walking with good views on a clear day such as we enjoyed that Sunday. The highest point on the first section of the day's walk is the summit of Carlton Moor at 1,338 feet and there are great views of the agricultural plain to the north and to industrial Teesside. After Carlton Moor, there is a descent to a depression in the hills, known as Carlton Bank Top. This proved to be a busy area on this pleasant Sunday morning as there is a minor road through the depression which allows car trippers access, and the area is popular with kite fliers and hang gliders. It is also a popular spot for cyclists.

However, one of the main attractions and *the* main attraction for us was the presence of the Lord Stones Café, which is built into the hillside. A pot of tea and a homemade currant scone (with jam and butter) was good value at £2. Paul and I had established a lead over Tom and Joe, but they arrived just as we were leaving the Lord Stones and we would not see them again until they reached our destination later that day.

The only problem with a depression is that you have to gain height again and we were faced with a short, stiff climb to Cringle End where there is a wonderful view point. From Cringle End the path led on to the summit of Cringle Moor at 1,427 feet.

Along this stretch, we passed two young men and a young woman who were on the Coast to Coast but travelling east to west and camping, so they had the customary heavy packs although, strangely, we never met anyone with a pack the size of Don's. I wonder why? They also had a little dog who was carrying his own equipment in panniers strapped to both sides of his body, and he seemed very pleased with himself. My first thought was that I could have brought Robbie, Bryn and Maddie, our three border collies who could have eased my own load considerably if I attached panniers to all three of them. But when I thought about it a bit more carefully, I decided that it was not such a good idea as Suzanne would have insisted that I take enough dog food for twelve days, water, bedding, leads, poo bags, dog first aid kits, food bowls, treats and no end of other doggy things. The thought of my own burden being eased was quickly erased as I realised I would need to employ at least two Sherpas to share the load.

The path continued with two or three more ascents and descents over the hills until the B1257 road was reached at Clay Bank Top. This is the end of the day's walk for those who are following Wainwright's recommendations, but the problem here is that Clay Bank Top is simply a spot on a map where a road happens to pass. This may be all right for campers who can simply pitch their tents, but anyone else has to arrange transport to the nearest B&B which is likely to be several miles away.

Crossing the road at Clay Bank Top, we were faced with another climb onto Urra Moor, which is the highest ground within the National Park, rising to 1,491 feet. Once on the top, the walking was easy for the rest of the day. Four or five miles beyond Clay Bank Top, the route of an old railway line was joined which is where the Coast to Coast route leaves the Cleveland Way, although the route is still coincident with the Lyke Wake Walk. The walk continued along the old railway track for six miles to Blakey, following the contours of the moors so that the walking was very easy, but soon became rather tedious and this was a section which needed to be covered at speed.

The red grouse were abundant and unconcerned at our presence, allowing us to approach to within a few feet before scuttling away. Perhaps they had become blasé about having survived for a month since August the twelfth.

The Lion Inn sits on Blakey Ridge and is situated on a road which runs along the ridge. Apart from the Lion, there is one house directly opposite and no other habitation in view. Towards five o'clock, we left the old railway line to climb the last few yards to the Lion and, as we approached, Don was waiting for us. He seemed very pleased to see us and quickly told us that, rather than camping that night, he had gone to the expense of booking a room in the pub, even though he was having to pay for a twin-bedded room.

Of course, we were eager to learn what he had been doing for the last three days, but we were totally unprepared for what we were to hear and, as Don related his frightening story, we began to understand why he was so pleased to see us and why he had booked a room in the pub that night.

Apparently, he had decided to follow Wainwright's original itinerary, which covered the distance from Osmotherley to Blakey in two days, staying overnight at Clay Bank Top, leaving him just eleven miles to walk on Sunday. The absence of any accommodation in the vicinity meant that he had to camp but some of his gear was still damp as a result of Friday's heavy rain. Fortunately, he had not had to walk too far that day and the late afternoon sun encouraged him to stop and try to dry it out before pitching his tent. He had left the footpath and walked about twenty yards up the hillside to spread his tent out on the heather, hoping that the weak sun would have some effect, and was making himself a mug of tea when he noticed three men on the path below.

'I was feeling quite relaxed and shouted 'good afternoon' to them and raised my hand in acknowledgement in exactly the same way I have to hundreds of other walkers in the last ten days,' Don explained.

"Lovely day now,' the one who appeared to be the leader of the three said and, surprisingly, he started walking up from the path towards me. I thought it was a bit unusual because most people are happy enough just to say hello and keep walking.

'Couldn't be better,' I replied, thinking of the contrast with Friday's torrential rain.

'Have you walked far today?' he asked in a Geordie accent. Well, I would call it Geordie but he could be a local because we're not far from Middlesbrough, are we? So, I told him I'd walked about twelve miles, and then he said something that made me realise how vulnerable I was on my own:

'Are you camping here tonight?' he asked me, which made me very apprehensive, even though there was nothing threatening in the way he asked. I wasn't sure exactly what troubled me, but why had he left the path to come and talk to me and why had he asked whether I was camping there?'

'What was he like?' we asked Don.

'He looked about thirty years old, with short black hair and a black moustache and I would describe him as looking like someone from the SAS, although I don't think I've ever met anyone from the SAS,' Don said. 'He was wearing army type boots rather than walking boots, and camouflage trousers that made his hips look enormous so that he looked immensely strong. He was wearing a dark blue teeshirt and the short sleeves seemed to bite into his biceps. It's funny what goes through your mind at times like that because, even though I was starting to get a bit worried, I couldn't help wondering whether you can buy teeshirts with very narrow armholes these days, or whether he was just excessively muscular.

He seemed pleasant enough but I thought it was odd that his two mates stayed on the footpath. They were younger, probably about twenty, and both of them had shaven heads. Again I found myself wondering the strangest thing – why do young men want to look prematurely bald when they might not have a choice in a few years time? Maybe it's to make them look 'hard' and, if so, it worked. They both had earrings and tattoos which added to the effect, but what bothered me more was that neither of them made eye contact with me or said a word. I really did feel uneasy, but tried to stay calm. I couldn't admit that I planned to camp there, so I told a white lie and said I was just trying to dry some of my things and would be moving on. I'd spread my wet socks on a rock and pointed to them and said I needed to dry them in particular because I had only two pairs and I'd been wearing the other pair for two days.

What happened next really got me worried,' Don continued.

'Why? What happened?' we asked, wondering what terrible event could have made him so obviously agitated.

'He went across and picked up the socks and felt them, as

though he was checking that I was telling the truth, and then he said the most perturbing thing so far:

'I can do you a favour,' he said, 'I'll take these home and dry them for you and bring them back later.'

Well, the thought of them coming back later, possibly when it was dark, scared the shit out of me. I tried to tell myself that it was all innocent and the bloke was really trying to be helpful, but what sort of person goes to so much trouble without an ulterior motive? It seemed to me that it was a ruse to find out exactly where I'd be. It was very hard not to panic, but I managed to stammer;

'No, it's alright, I'll be moving on and, anyway, I'll be meeting my mates soon.'

As soon as I said it, I knew it sounded weak and that they wouldn't believe me. Daft as it sounds, I had this feeling that they knew I wouldn't be meeting you for another twenty-four hours, and I was thinking I could have been robbed or tortured or even murdered by then.

Fortunately, they decided to move on and I began to think that my fears were irrational and made myself something to eat. When I'd finished, I decided to pitch my tent, but still moved on a couple of hundred yards to be on the safe side.'

'It all sounds very strange, Don. It must have been quite a relief when they went,' I said, assuming that was the end of his story. 'Should we go and have a drink?'

'That's not all,' he said, hurriedly.

'Why? Did they come back?'

'There was no sign of them during the evening and I began to think I'd blown it up out of proportion and I had never been in any danger. I settled into my sleeping bag soon after half past nine – well, there isn't much to do when it goes dark – and I must have fallen asleep straight away, but woke in the middle of the night. At least I thought it was the middle of the night because it was pitch black and I felt as though I'd been asleep for hours but, when I checked my watch, I found it was only just after eleven. Anyway, having woken up, I decided I might as well go outside and water the heather but, as I went to unzip the tent, there was a flash of light which made me hesitate. There were several more flashes of light, and then my whole life seemed to flash before me.'

'Why, for God's sake?' we asked, imagining that some wild animal must have slashed through the side of his tent with razor sharp claws and run off with his remaining boil-in-the-bag meal. But no, this was no laughing matter.

'I heard his voice. The Geordie. And he was saying:

'He was somewhere round here.'

My stomach felt as though it had leapt up inside my chest, my mouth went dry and my legs felt as though they belonged to someone else. My heart was pounding so much, I felt sure they'd be able to hear it. I don't mind admitting I was absolutely petrified. Why had they come back? What did they want from me?'

'They might have had some dry socks for you,' I suggested, helpfully.

'I could see the lights through the side of the tent, moving up and down and across the hillside as the torches sought me out,' he continued, reliving the experience and recalling his terror. 'If there were three of them, they were bound to find me, but then what? It's amazing what thoughts go through your mind in a situation like that.'

'What? Like 'I wonder how Liverpool went on today?' I suggested, trying to ease the tension.

'I was figuring out my options. I could make a run for it, leaving all my gear behind but they'd be bound to hear me unzipping the tent and stumbling about in the dark and, anyway, they had torches and would soon spot me.

Alternatively, I could sit in the tent and hope they wouldn't find it, but that was wishful thinking. There were three of them with torches, so it was only a matter of time.

The only other option was to go outside and confront them. There could be an innocent explanation although, for the life of me, I couldn't think of one, so I decided I'd have to be prepared to defend myself. I had my Swiss army knife and I started to search for it in my pack but then I thought better of it. I'm sixty-two years old and haven't fought anyone since I was at school and even then I lost and that was one against one, not one against three. In the end, I decided to sit tight and hope for the best, although I realised it was only a matter of time till they found me.

I sat there, my mind racing. What did they want? Surely they didn't believe a single camper was worth robbing. Did they get their kicks (literally) from beating someone senseless? Or was it possible that they wanted to kill someone, just to see what it's like? I started thinking what it would be like to be beaten to a pulp. It's really scary what goes through your mind, you know.

I sat there for what seemed like hours but might have been only a few minutes and then I realised that I hadn't heard the voice again and hadn't seen the torches for a while. Everything seemed to be in complete darkness again and I started to believe that they might have moved on although I still couldn't relax. I didn't get much sleep I can tell you and I was up as soon as it was light. I just wanted to get as far away as possible in case they came back.'

'Hell, Don, I don't know how you coped,' I sympathised. 'Shall we go and get a drink?'

'That's still not the end of the story,' he said. 'I told you that after they left yesterday, I moved on a couple of hundred yards to set up camp but, a little later on, I realised I'd left my socks on the rock and decided to go back for them. When I got there, they weren't on the rock and I assumed they must have blown off and had a little search around but couldn't find them. I thought that was odd, but it was going dark so it wasn't easy to see and I didn't think it was worth wasting too much time on a pair of socks and gave up.

This morning, as soon as I'd packed all my stuff, I set off down towards the track and, as I was walking down the hill, I could see a big rock alongside the track and I thought I could see something on it. At first I couldn't make out what it was but, when I got close, I could see that it was a clear polythene bag and you'll never believe what was in it, and this was the really scary thing, it was …. a pair of socks.'

'Were they yours?' I asked, wondering where this story could lead now.

'I think so, but I didn't stop to check. It scared the shit out of me just seeing them there. I can only think that they had taken the socks yesterday afternoon and brought them back last night and, when they couldn't find me, just left them there. The other spooky thing about it was that, even though I didn't touch the bag, I could see that the socks were clean as well as dry, and had been folded very neatly before being put in the bag, almost as though someone was really trying to impress me.'

'Now that is spooky.'

As a consequence of his early start, he had arrived at the Lion well before lunchtime. There had been little for him to do during the day but at least he felt safe. We commiserated with him and pondered whether he should report the incident to the police, but I think he just wanted to try and forget about it so we didn't ask him any more about it.

After catching up with Don's news, we finally went inside for a drink and to find out how England were doing in the Test. We had not heard anything all day and the television in the bar was simply showing re-runs of earlier play. Bad light had stopped play in London and there had been hardly any play during the afternoon. This was good news for England who just needed a draw. After a while, play was abandoned for the day with England, batting for the second time, holding a small lead but the final day's play was going to be crucial. If Australia could bowl England out cheaply, they still had a chance of winning the match and keeping the Ashes.

Tom and Joe arrived and were astonished to hear Don's story but pleased that he was safe and seemingly in good spirits now. After another drink, we made our way to our rooms and I was again sharing with Paul. We took it in turns to make use of the en-suite facilities and I went down to the bar whilst Paul took his turn. I was soon joined by Don, who looked far less anxious than earlier.

'I'm glad I've caught you on your own. I wanted to talk to you,' he said ominously, as I mentally dusted off my counselling manual once again.

'Last night's trauma made me realise exactly what I've got and I don't think I could cope without Jane. I didn't get much sleep and spent a lot of time thinking about what you said the other day and you were right. We needed to talk, so I phoned as soon as I got here,' he said.

'And?' I prompted.

'Well, I told her all about what happened last night first and she seemed genuinely concerned about me, so I took the plunge and told her I love her, just like you told me.'

'And?' I prompted again, not sure I wanted to know any more. If this had gone wrong, I would be in serious shit.

'She said she loves me too; more than I could ever know. All this time I've believed she was thinking I'm a failure and blaming me for the fact that she had to go back to work, when she's been reproaching herself,' he said.

'How come?' I asked.

'She's always been in charge of our joint finances and she thought I blamed her for not saving more when we were both working.'

'So,' I said, putting on my most sage expression, 'you've been reproaching yourself and, because you blamed yourself, you believed that Jane blamed you as well, which made you very defensive and prickly about any criticism, which was why you could never hold a sensible conversation about it.'

'Something like that,' he replied, with a regretful smirk.

'And,' I continued, exuding wisdom, now getting into this deep and thoughtful counselling stuff, 'at the same time, Jane was reproaching herself and, because she blamed herself, she believed that you blamed her as well, which made her defensive and prickly about any criticism, which was why she could never hold a sensible conversation about it.'

'I think so,' he said.

'Not much maturity in your house, is there?' I concluded.

Just then, the others appeared, forcing us to abandon our therapeutic session, with Don whispering his thanks to me as we made our way to our dinner table. It had turned out to be a good day for Don, I thought. He looked like a man who has had a great weight lifted from his shoulders (and not just because he had left his pack in his room).

We had an enjoyable meal and, as the evening wore on, the

relaxed atmosphere and the company of his pals, as well as his telephone call home, eased Don's tension. Fortunately, Tom didn't offer to treat us to Duckfarts in celebration of Don's narrow escape.

The Lion Inn is remarkable in that it always seems to be extremely busy, despite being so remote. People drive from miles around to have a meal there. They seem to like the drive out onto the moors and enjoy eating in a rural pub. It is not a small establishment by any means, but it was absolutely heaving with people on that Sunday evening. Later on, Don excused himself for a few minutes but, when he returned, he was as white as a sheet and extremely agitated.

'What on earth's the matter, Don? You look as though you've seen a ghost.'

'They're sitting at the bar.'

'Who?'

'The three men who were searching for me last night.'

'Did they see you?'

'Oh yes. The two younger ones didn't look at me but I know they saw me.'

'What about the other one?'

'He leered at me as though he knew I'd be crapping my pants. Do you think they've followed me here? What do you think they want?'

Don was shaking as he spoke and we tried to tell him there must be an innocent explanation, even though none of us really believed it. We had become such a close-knit group that we regarded a threat to Don as a threat to all of us. It might be all right for us to insult or threaten each other, but we couldn't have strangers upsetting one of our number.

'Let's go and confront the bastards,' Tom said, and began to rise from his chair.

'Yeah, where are the creepy sock-abducting slimy bloody pillocks?' we said as we rose to follow Tom, but Don called us back. He pointed out that confrontation may not be the wisest move as, in his opinion, they were three potentially violent men. Although there were five of us and only three of them, we were all over sixty and would be no match for three hard men if the situation turned nasty.

'It's a pity Andy isn't with us,' said Paul.

'Why?' asked Don, 'is he used to dealing with thugs?'

'He's not afraid of anything and is very public-spirited,' Paul replied. 'A few months ago, he was in Macclesfield town centre when a shoplifter ran out of an exclusive outfitter's with an armful of expensive designer shirts, chased by the owner who was in no condition to keep up with him, but Andy joined the pursuit.'

'I didn't know about this,' Tom said, 'he's been keeping this quiet.'

'Andy's pretty fit,' Paul continued, 'and that fitness and his determination kept him going long after the shopkeeper had given up. They ran right across the town centre and, eventually, the thief must have been knackered and turned to face Andy.'

'And what did Andy do?' Don demanded, eager to know the outcome.

'Thought 'shit, what do I do now?' if I know Andy,' Tom interjected.

'Come on, Paul' urged Don, 'what did he say really?'

'Have you got a collar size seventeen there?' suggested Joe.

'Belt up, you two,' Don instructed. 'What happened next?'

'Andy grappled with him and held him until the police came,' Paul explained.

'Bloody hell. I see what you mean about wishing he was here now.'

After long deliberation, we decided that we would have to approach them, in the gentlest way, and see how they reacted. We rose from our seats, took a deep breath, and made for the bar, all of us intent on leading from the rear. Alas, there was no sign of them (phew).

'There were three men here a few minutes ago,' Don said to one of the barmaids 'do you know where they are?'

'Oh, you mean the three gays – you've just missed them.'

'Gays!'

'Yes, they come in here every Sunday. They're lovely, they are. The two younger ones, Derek and Geoffrey, are partners but

Jonathan, that's the older one, he's been on his own for a year or two now, which is a real pity because he's such a kind bloke, the sort who will do anything for anyone. I think he comes in here hoping he'll meet someone but the problem is that he tries too hard and I'm sure he must give people the impression that he's desperate. Why, he hasn't tried to chat you up, has he?'

'No … er, I don't think so,' stammered Don.

CHAPTER EIGHTEEN

A BAD DAY FOR AUSSIES

Monday morning broke and, although Don was still very shaken, at least he knew that he had not been in danger after all. It was hard for the rest of us not to laugh, but we knew how badly he had been affected and how embarrassment would now be increasing his discomfort. With only two days and twenty-nine miles to journey's end, all five of us set off on the walk to Grosmont. This was an easy walk of twelve and a half miles heading north for about a mile along the road before crossing the moors. The next couple of hours provided wonderful walking along the high moors with a view of the peak of Roseberry Topping, ten miles to the north west, and with magnificent views into Great Fryup Dale (yes really) down to our left.

Our old friends, Arnold and Ernie, must have had a period of secondment at the local Highways Department.

'What have they got for us today, Ernie?'

'T'Ordnance Survey want some names to put on t'ordnance survey maps. Some of th'ills and dales on th'old maps don't have names on 'em.'

'Let's have a look.'

'There's this dale 'ere,' Ernie said, pointing at the map.

'Well, does it 'ave a name?' asked Arnold.

'I don't know, but we can make one up. No-one will know any better.'

'Aye, except folk what live there, but they'll never find out 'cos they don't need to look at t'map. In't that where we went camping that time and it poured down all neet and all our gear got drenched?'

'That's reet. An' t'farmers wife made us breakfast. It were a great fryup. There was bacon, egg, beans and potatoes.'

'That's it. That's what we'll call it.'

'Don't be daft. No one will believe it's called Bacon, Egg, Beans and Potato Dale.'

'No, stupid. We'll call it Great Fryup Dale.'

'Good idea. What's next then?'

'There's this 'ill up 'ere, you know the one what's a funny shape.'

'You mean the one what looks like those cakes in Mrs Sidebottom's cake shop? You know, she calls them Strawberry Toppings. That's a thought — we could call it Strawberry Topping.'

'That doesn't sound reet. You can't have a 'ill named after a cake.'

'Why not, if you're naming a dale after a breakfast?'

'I know. Why don't we name it after Rose Berry, you've always fancied her? If we name it Roseberry Topping, it'll put her name on t'map forever and you might stand a chance.'

'Sounds good to me.'

We had left the Lion at half past eight, which meant Paul had not been able to make his important phone call before we set off. He had decided to leave the call until ten, hoping that the results would be available and that he would be able to speak to the Consultant. Once again, we had established a lead on the others and I gave him some space when he made the call, standing perhaps fifty yards away. The call seemed to take an age and, as he had his back to me, I had no indication of how he was taking the news. Eventually, I saw him fold his phone away and he turned slowly towards me. His face gave nothing away and I feared the worst as he meandered in my direction. As he approached, I detected tears in his eyes; were they tears of devastation or of relief? Could they be tears of frustration, if the results were still unavailable? At last, a broad grin spread across his face – the lump was benign. Thank God. We hugged each other, but only for a moment, as befits grown men. A great surge of relief passed through me, and it wasn't me who had the lump! We walked on with a spring in our steps.

After walking on the high moors all Sunday afternoon and again on Monday morning, the path eventually took us down to the village of Glaisdale, where we hoped to stop for a drink. Unfortunately, the main pub in the village had closed and was being redeveloped for housing but there was a little general store and a butcher's shop. We went into the store where I bought a packet of Eccles cakes but when I looked round there was no sign of Paul. I emerged from the store just in time to see him coming out of the butcher's with two pork pies. I knew it! Now I had the evidence. He must have had a copy of Care's Nutritional Advice all along.

I find that I don't eat much when I'm out walking. If we pass a tea shop, I'm more than happy to stop and have a scone or a flapjack but, if not, I can keep going as long as I have some energy drinks to provide my body fuel (I still like that). Otherwise, I find Eccles cakes are ideal for keeping up energy levels. Paul clearly takes his walking nutrition more seriously. On this occasion, he may have been influenced by the sign in the shop window – *Hand-reared Pork Pies*. This was an interesting concept. I imagined a clutch of pork pies hatching and being deserted by the parent pies, leaving the defenceless pielings to fend for themselves and the butcher's wife staying up all night to feed them. Watching Paul wolf them down, I was not sure that he noticed the difference.

After our fuel stop, I remembered Tom had mentioned another pub about a mile further on so we walked on in anticipation. We'd be able to have a pint before the others caught up but, and there's always a 'but' and you've guessed it, the bloody place does not open at lunchtimes. Thwarted again, we decided to sit at the picnic tables opposite the pub and wait for the others but, after a minute or two, a man emerged from the pub, the Arncliffe Arms, and for a moment, we thought we were in luck, assuming he was the landlord coming to offer us refreshments. He chatted to us but made no mention of opening up the pub for us, and I thought it odd that he had a strong Australian accent and began to wonder whether he had come out to gloat about the cricket. Surely, England hadn't thrown it all away on the final morning of the final Test. It transpired that he was, indeed, an Australian and he had been doing the Coast to Coast Walk himself but, when he reached Glaisdale, he fell in love with the place and decided to settle there. Well, that was what I thought he was going to say but, in fact, he was in the middle of a two month visit to Europe and he had left his wife sightseeing in London whilst he undertook the walk. Not for the first time, I wondered how so many visitors had heard of the Coast to Coast. He went on to explain that, unfortunately, he had been forced to give up the walk the day before because he was having knee trouble. We could not imagine anything worse as he had completed ninety per cent of the distance and then had to give up and, being Australian, he was unlikely to have another opportunity to complete the walk. He had stayed at the Arncliffe Arms the night before and was waiting for a bus to take him to the nearest mainline rail station.

Whilst we had great sympathy for our new friend, the fact that he had dropped out even though he still had one good leg was not in accord with our vision of the tough Australian male. After all, Joe was suffering considerable pain and discomfort from a leg injury but, even at sixty-nine, the thought of dropping out had not even occurred to him.

At least he was able to tell us the cricket score and the outcome was still very much in the balance. Australia had taken five wickets and England were only one hundred and thirty ahead. If Australia could take the other five wickets quickly, they had a chance of winning the match and retaining the Ashes. Our Australian friend had been watching the match on television but admitted that he was not really interested in cricket and could not even tell us which English batsmen were at the crease. We couldn't believe it. An Australian who wasn't interested in cricket?

Apparently, he had set off to do the Coast to Coast on his own but, on the very first day, he met a group of young Englishmen and tagged on to them for several days, even though they covered the ground rather faster than he would have wanted. Perhaps this was why he suffered later. Our illusions about Australians were completely shattered when he told us about his young English friends:

'Boy, could they drink. They drank me under the table every night.'

An Australian who gave up whilst he could still walk, who was not interested in cricket and admitted to being unable to keep up with a group of Englishmen in the bar. We decided he must be of Italian or French extraction. Nevertheless, he was a good sort and we wished him well for the rest of his European tour.

We were now in Eskdale and followed the course of the River Esk for the two miles to Egton Bridge, which is no more than a cluster of houses, but in a very pleasant setting. It also has the advantage of having a pub, the Horse Shoe Hotel, and on a nice day such as this, people were taking advantage of the tables set out in the garden in front of the pub. This is a place that has pretensions to being something better than it is and sells what must be the most expensive sandwiches on the whole Coast to Coast route. They did not have a TV in the bar but the young barman was happy to go through to the back and return with the latest score. England were now two hundred ahead but had lost seven wickets, so Australia still had an outside chance if they could take the remaining three wickets quickly. Kevin Pietersen was the hero for England and was approaching his century. As long as he stayed there, England must still be just about favourites.

Soon after Egton Bridge, the path took us along a lane through the Egton Estate and, although vehicles are now barred, this used to be a toll road and the toll charges are still displayed on a sign prepared by the Egton Estates Office in August 1948.

BARNARDS ROAD TOLL

1	HORSE	2 WHEELS		4d
2	"	"	"	8d
1	"	4	"	8d
2	"	"	"	1/-
3	"	"	"	1/-
MOTOR CAR	4			1/-
	"	3		1/-
MOTOR CYCLE SIDE CAR				1/-
MOTOR LORRY				2/-
MOTOR BUS				3/-
TRACTOR				1/-
HEARSE				6d

THIS GATE IS CLOSED AND LOCKED
AT 10 PM DAILY

Fortunately, there is no charge for pedestrians and none of us needed a hearse just yet so we passed safely through the estate and soon reached our destination for our final night, in Grosmont. This is a village which is, to me at least, more popular than it deserves. The major contributor to the popularity of Grosmont is the railway station as, not only is this on the line from Middlesbrough to Whitby, but also steam trains run from Grosmont to Pickering, via Goathland which has been popularised by the Heartbeat television series.

There is a souvenir shop in the station itself and a small Co-op store across the road from the station, both of which burst at the seams whenever a steam train arrives and disgorges its passengers. The village also boasts a pub, the Station Tavern, and tea rooms. We were booked in at the B&B above the tea rooms and we made our way there. Unsurprisingly, Don had decided that he did not want to camp so we hoped that an additional room would be available. It had been noticeable all day that he didn't want to be far from the rest of us, so the incident two nights earlier had really affected him. As we arrived, the landlady was showing two young women to their room, so it was left to her husband to show us our rooms. There was one small single room and a larger room in which three single beds had been made up. There was a shower cubicle in the corner of this room which took up unnecessary space and, if this was supposed to be a family room, the family members would have to have no inhibitions about having a shower in full view of the rest of the family.

Tom allocated the single room to me, I think out of habit rather than deliberation, but there was still the problem of where Don would sleep. The landlord said that there were no other rooms available but Don indicated that he would be happy to sleep on the floor of the larger bedroom. It was obvious that he needed to be close to the rest of us and I wondered whether one of us would have to seek alternative digs. However, he insisted that he would be happy to sleep on the floor but, rather than allow that, the landlord said that his wife could put up a camp bed, even though I couldn't see how a camp bed would fit in such a confined space, as three beds were crammed in already. It may surprise readers to learn that I do have a cynical side to my personality and this surfaced now as I wondered whether his concern was more about complying with any health and safety rules which may not permit guests to sleep on the floor but, whatever, the camp bed was provided and Tom was adamant that he would sleep in that, allowing Don to have a bed. This was typical of Tom's compassion for his companions although, if challenged, he would claim that he did it only because he enjoys sleeping in camp beds. The others showed their compassion by not mentioning Don's snoring tendencies, although they may have been influenced by the fact that the beds were so close that they could elbow him in the ribs without moving.

The bed was installed between two of the single beds and Paul was allocated the bed against the far wall on the basis that he was the least likely to have to get up during the night and have to clamber over Tom in the camp bed and Don in the other bed.

Don might have been happy to sleep anywhere but it seemed to me that the landlord was even happier, raking in another £25 in return for shoving a camp bed in the room. The landlady returned from showing the young ladies their room just as her husband was leaving:

'When would you like breakfast in the morning? We serve at eight and eight thirty,' she asked, but added hastily 'the two young ladies are having theirs at eight thirty.'

'OK, eight thirty will be fine,' Tom answered for all of us, not bothering with the customary sham of consulting the rest of us. A relieved smile appeared on her face and I thought that Tom had fallen for that one. The latest we had been served breakfast throughout the trip had been eight o'clock. Tomorrow would be our last day and I was beginning to think of home and would have liked to have set off earlier, rather than later.

After a quick wash, we set off to explore Grosmont or, more precisely, the Station Tavern, and found that a big screen was set up in the bar and that the Test was in its final throes. Pietersen had been magnificent and had scored 158 to make the game safe for England, bringing the Ashes home for the first time since 1987.

It was nearly six o'clock and the sun was still shining, so we sat outside feeling thoroughly relaxed, our spirits uplifted by England's victory and by the knowledge that we had only a few miles to walk to our destination the following day. Suddenly, Grosmont wasn't such a bad old place after all.

Across the road was a gallery selling what I would call 'expensive crap' but perhaps this was just my cynical side again as both Don and Tom had seen ceramic vases which they were considering buying for their wives. The difficulty was that they would have to carry them the next day, along with all their other gear. They were bemoaning the fact that they could not justify carrying any extra weight, but consoling themselves on the monetary saving, when Tom had one of his brainwaves.

'We could get Trevor to drive us back through Grosmont tomorrow and pick them up. We could pay for them now and ask the shop to parcel them up so that we can collect them tomorrow afternoon.'

So, off they trotted to the gallery to do the deals, coming back ten minutes later looking very pleased with themselves. By now, they had decided it would be a good idea to leave their packs at the B&B and carry only what was necessary for the day, which did make some sense if we were going to have to come back to Grosmont the following afternoon anyway. All I wanted was to be home as quickly as possible so coming back to Grosmont was not on my agenda at all.

CHAPTER NINETEEN

ON OUR LAST LEG

Tuesday morning came and another fine day was in prospect as we made our way downstairs to the tea rooms for breakfast. It was twenty past eight and the landlady's husband made the point of reminding us that breakfast was not until eight thirty, which was unnecessary as we were not exactly chomping at the bit. If we had been sitting at the tables, knives and forks in hand, singing 'why are we waiting?' I would have understood his irritation. As it was, we were just looking around, checking the weather outside, throwing stones at the ducks on the stream, and generally behaving in a patient manner as befits a group of mature gentlemen.

After breakfast, Tom had a word with the landlady about our packs and the parcels from the gallery and suggested that they could be left in the garage and she happily agreed to this. However, when we were ready to leave, we came downstairs and only her husband was around. We explained that we had agreed with his wife that we should leave our bags and collect them later and that she had agreed that they could be left in the garage. Clearly, he was unhappy about his wife having the temerity to make such an important decision without consultation, and dismissively pointed to an undercover area just outside the tea rooms, alongside the outside seating area, where he said the bags should be deposited. His whole attitude suggested that he was afraid he might catch something unmentionable if he allowed our bags to be in his premises a moment longer than the overnight rate covered. This seemed to be unusually uncharitable to me, so I decided to carry my pack rather than leave it where anyone could walk off with it. After all, I had been carrying it for the last eleven days and one more was not going to break my back. I soon regretted this decision as all my companions took advantage of the fact that there was a backpack available which they assumed was now the team pack. Individually, the few items that each of them felt they needed were not heavy but, in total, they weighed a ton, particularly as one of them was determined to apply the final straw to break the camel's back!

'Bloody hell, Don,' I said, as he gave me a small bag containing his essentials for the day 'have you been collecting rock samples along the way?'

Ah well, at least we didn't have a long day ahead.

'I'll be glad when it's Saturday,' the landlord said to me as I was waiting for the others to store their packs in the designated place.

'Why is that, then?' I asked, thinking that something special must be happening on the Saturday and hoping that it might be his funeral.

'Because we close for the winter.'

If ever there was an observation to make a customer feel unwanted, this gratuitous remark was it but at least it confirmed the view I had formed of him already, namely that he was a complete and utter pillock. I vowed never to stay there or, indeed, in Grosmont, again.

After eleven days walking, the final section from Grosmont to Robin Hood's Bay seemed little more than a hop, skip and jump but the day started with a long and steep climb along the road out of Grosmont before, eventually, the path turned across moorland making for the Whitby to Pickering road (A169). This is a busy road and, as we waited for the opportunity to cross, a VW Golf or little Peugeot something or other passed at speed with a youth hanging from the window shouting something which, as usual, we could not hear. Once again, I wondered why these youths do this. Can they possibly enjoy any satisfaction from shouting at a few old gimmers who can't hear what they are saying anyway?

We walked on and soon came to the lovely little hamlet of Littlebeck from where the path climbed to the waterfall known as Falling Foss. I couldn't help thinking that whoever gave the waterfall its name didn't give the matter too much thought. To call a water*fall Falling* anything is not very original in my view. *Cascading Canopy* or *Plunging Pleasance* would sound more romantic, but perhaps they didn't appeal to Mr Foss when he named the falls after himself. After visiting the waterfall, we followed the path through the woods and, after emerging, we continued through disappointingly bland countryside for several miles to the village of Hawsker where, fortuitously, we found a pub, where we had the final break of our twelve day adventure.

'Nearly there, Tom,' Paul said as we quenched our thirsts, 'but why did you want to do it so many times?'

'I don't know really,' Tom replied, 'I didn't set out with the intention of doing it more than once. I walked by myself the first time and followed Wainwright's route to the letter and took fourteen days over it, but then other people started saying they wanted to do it and asked whether I'd do it with them, so it became a habit. Strangely enough, I enjoyed it more the second time. It's as though you are more relaxed the second time and notice more. Then it's even better the third time .... and the fourth time .... and so it goes on. After three or four times, it became sort of addictive and I wanted to do it each year and there was always someone who wanted to come with me. When I got to eight times, I just had to get up to ten. It was a big disappointment when the foot and mouth outbreak stopped me and I thought that was it; I'd never do it a tenth time, but it's nagged at me ever since, so I had to do it again one more, definitely final, time.'

'What made you decide to arrange it over twelve days this time?'

'Well, after the first time, I decided that fourteen days was too long and that twelve was about ideal. The problem always is fitting it in to the time available, so I've done it in eleven days a few times.'

'But didn't you do it in less than that with Andy?'

'Oh, yes, and there's a story behind that,' Tom said. 'The first time, we did it in ten days because I had to get back for something, but that was all right because Andy's very fit and I was younger and fitter then.'

Tom was being rather modest here as this was something of an achievement. After all, we were taking twelve days which works out at an average of about sixteen miles a day, which is a manageable distance each day for a reasonably fit walker, despite the rough terrain. Over ten days, the average increases to nineteen miles each day, which is pushing it a bit even for a good walker. When they reached Robin Hood's Bay, they were justifiably proud of their achievement and were in good spirits after their celebratory drink, but understandably hungry after their epic journey.

'Anyway,' Tom continued, 'Andy decided to visit the fish and chip shop and the proprietor, realising he was a Coast to Coast walker chatted to him and asked how long it had taken. Of course, Andy had to brag that this outstanding feat had been achieved in an awe-inspiring ten days. There was a young girl immediately ahead of Andy in the queue, with her boyfriend, and she turned and said:

'Well done. We've just done it in nine!'

When he came out of the chippy a few minutes later, he came stomping over to me, almost foaming at the mouth:

'You'll never guess,' he said, 'there was a young lass in the chippy and she's just done the Coast to Coast in nine days.'

'Right,' I said in a stupidly determined way.

'Right,' Andy said, even more resolutely and stupidly.

'Next year, we'll do it in eight.'

Anyone else would have told me not to be so bloody daft, but not Andy:

'Right,' he said.

For the next twelve months, I hoped he would come to his

senses and back down and I'm sure he was thinking the same about me, but neither of us would give in. You know what he's like – I'd never have heard the last of it if I'd admitted I couldn't care less about some young girl having done it in nine days and called the thing off.'

'What you mean is you'd rather suffer the pain of walking a hundred and ninety miles in eight days than have to put up with Andy's niggling for the rest of your life.'

'Precisely. At least I'd only have to put up with the pain for eight days.'

So, twelve months on, they undertook their eight day journey, a challenge of walking almost twenty-four miles a day on average which, in practice, meant that one or two days must have been in excess of thirty miles. They were determined to prove that if a young girl could cross from Coast to Coast in nine days, two alpha males (well, possibly beta) could do it in eight. They strained every sinew and, eight days later, they arrived in Robin Hood's Bay, well and truly shattered, but they had proved their point!

Unfortunately, neither of them has ever been able to explain to me how they think their female antagonist would learn of their achievement. In any event, she could have been lying.

Following the short break at the pub, we set off for the final four and a quarter miles of the Coast to Coast Walk and within a few minutes we were on the cliff path looking out over the North Sea, our epic journey nearing its end. We had set off twelve days earlier from the west coast to travel to the east, but the first part of the walk had taken us west and then north around St Bees Head before finally settling for the correct easterly direction, and this final section was almost a mirror image taking us round another headland, travelling south eastwards at first before turning to the south west and then entering Robin Hood's Bay.

We were hoping that Trevor had not forgotten that he was due to pick us up and it was a relief to see him sitting on the wall outside the Victoria Hotel waiting for us.

CHAPTER TWENTY

JOURNEY'S END

It would be easy to understand why Wainwright chose to conclude the Coast to Coast Walk at Robin Hood's Bay. A small town, hanging on the hillside, with tightly-knit cobbled streets leading down to the beach, it is a quaint and picturesque spot with plenty of shops, cafes, pubs and guest houses. It's an ideal journey's end, on the face of it, at least. Yes, it would be easy to understand, but he didn't choose it. Well, not exactly. It was a fortuitous circumstance. After walking the Pennine Way in 1967, he concluded '*I cannot truthfully say that I enjoyed the Pennine Way.*' Anyone else would have simply put it down to experience and moved on, but good old Alf was not 'anyone else'. He decided he would devise his own long distance walk! His route '*would have to be in the northern counties of England*' which he '*personally preferred to other parts of the country*'. That decision made, he '*wanted the starting point and finishing point to be exactly defined and not a source of doubt*' which made the coasts the obvious choices. '*By laying a ruler across the map, the route almost chose itself: the most spectacular point on the western seaboard was St Bees Head, and in the same latitude on the east coast was the quaint and attractive resort of Robin Hood's Bay.*' In fact, St Bees Head is the westernmost point in the north of England, so his ruler would have been drawn there like a magnet. It was pure good fortune that Robin Hood's Bay was almost exactly due east on the North Sea coast. I think he may have been unduly modest about his choice as I am sure it was not just a coincidence that the route passed through three National Parks and *'nowhere along this line was there an industrial blemish.'*

There are, however, a couple of drawbacks to finishing the walk at Robin Hood's Bay. The first is that vehicular access to the lower town is prohibited so, having made it down to the beach and officially ended his journey, the weary walker then has to climb all the way back up the steep street to the lift home. Not exactly the celebration most have in mind after almost two weeks of arduous marching.

The other problem with Robin Hood's Bay is that it is a popular place for holidaymakers and daytrippers too. During the summer months in particular, the narrow streets are crammed with visitors dressed in their smart, brightly coloured summer clothes, making the scruffy walker feel extremely conspicuous, particularly those wearing knee bandages which have not been washed for twelve days. Wainwright knew how we were feeling and described the scene perfectly – *'the cramped streets and alleyways are invariably congested with visitors, today unaware that a great feat is about to be accomplished and in any case not caring a damn that a hero has joined their ranks.'* (A great feat! A hero! I like it. Not so sure about them not giving a damn though.) He went on to say *'a man with a pack on his back feels uncomfortable and rather lonely'* and *'his travel-stained outfit and heavy boots seem out of place among the smart clothes and sandals of those around him.'* However, *'clothes don't make a man, and a Coast to Coast walker arriving here has every right to consider himself a man above other men; after all, few of these happy holidaymakers could do or would have the initiative and courage to do what he has just done – 190 miles on foot.'* (A man above other men! Precisely. Initiative and courage! I'm warming to the man at last.)

Neither of these drawbacks crossed our minds as Trevor joined us and we marched triumphantly together down the steep cobbled street, through the bustling crowds and past the souvenir shops, ice cream parlours and cafés towards the beach. The selection of knee bandages on display may have been among the grubbiest and least attractive ever seen on the streets of Robin

Hood's Bay, but nothing could dent the sense of euphoria we were feeling. It must have been the euphoria that brought out the poet in me:

'You know, the way the houses cling to the cliff face as if to cascade into the waters below, it's very reminiscent of Positano on the Amalfi coast in southern Italy.'

'Yes, but most of the houses in Positano are painted white to reflect the sun,' Paul commented in his know it all about property architect's way.

'Well, they don't need to worry about reflecting the sun here. They only have about five sunny days a year,' Don piped up, unnecessarily.

'And when you walk down the street in Positano, you gaze into the deep turquoise blue of the Mediterranean below, which is a bit different to the shitty grey of the North Sea,' Tom added.

At this, Joe decided to come to my rescue in the face of this unjustified verbal assault:

'But look on the bright side lads, we've got North Sea oil. The Italians haven't got Mediterranean Sea oil now, have they?'

Grateful for Joe's intervention, I was relieved when Don appeared to change his allegiance:

'I think Alan's right; there is a similarity between Positano and Robin Hood's Bay.'

'What's that then?' asked doubting Thomas.

'They're both in Europe,' he said to great hilarity.

'Very funny,' I mumbled sulkily.

The street became the slipway on to the shingly beach, where the incoming tide had driven the sunbathers to the small remaining patch of dry land. As we took the final steps on to the beach, we hugged each other and entertained the astonished crowd by performing a little jig on the sand. Well, actually we shook hands and exchanged 'well dones' in a restrained, manly way before taking the final few strides to the lapping waves to dip our toes in the water, just as we had done at St Bees twelve days earlier.

As we looked out over the seemingly endless sea, I couldn't help reflecting how different everything seemed to the last time I had stood, gazing out to sea, just twelve days ago. Then, I had looked westward over the open sea to the horizon, with St Bees Head to our right, waiting patiently for our ancient feet to start our initial ascent, and with the sandy beach to our left stretching as far as the eye could see. Behind us lay the promenade and gardens and the extravagantly large car park. Open space was everywhere, as if inviting us to enjoy England's green and pleasant land and willing us to accept the challenge of walking from one coast to the other. In contrast, Robin Hood's Bay closed in on us, as though telling us this was the end of the line. Just behind our backs stood the town, forming an effective barrier with only the one narrow means of access. Yes, the sea stretched out endlessly in front of us, but the cliffs around the bay seemed to wrap themselves around us in a protective hug whilst we reflected on a job well done.

There was a contrast in our emotions too. As we tumbled out of the minibus at St Bees, glad to be in the open air, our feelings were of excitement and anticipation. After months of preparation, we were at last embarking on our great adventure, raring to get started, not knowing exactly what faced us or whether we would complete the journey. Now, we had proved to ourselves that we were capable of not only taking on a formidable test of our powers of endurance but also that we could enjoy ourselves at the same time. Strangely, although we were elated by our success, we felt vaguely deflated at the same time. For the last twelve days, we had risen from our beds knowing that a major challenge lay ahead, each one different to the day before, the excitement of not knowing what faced us beckoning us to make haste. Standing on the beach now, we knew that the sense of anticipation was in the past and that, tomorrow morning, we would be back to our normal routine.

The origin of the name Robin Hood's Bay is a mystery and there is no known connection to the semi-mythical Robin Hood. The first recorded reference to Robin Hood's Bay dates back to 1536 and even then fishing was important to the community. The fishing industry reached its zenith in the mid-nineteenth century, but smuggling was another thriving occupation. Indeed, Robin Hood's Bay was reputedly the busiest smuggling community on the Yorkshire coast in the eighteenth century and, with a network of passageways and tunnels, it was said that a bale of silk could pass from the bottom of the village to the top without leaving the houses.

We had followed the traditions of what the locals sometimes call Baytown by smuggling our own contraband across the country and, having completed one of Wainwright's rituals by dipping our toes in the sea, we now had to perform the second by throwing the pebbles which we had carried all the way from the west coast into the waves of the North Sea. Not wishing to carry any unnecessary weight, I had chosen a small flat stone which I now retrieved from the pocket of my shorts, gave it a little rub on the groin of my shorts in the manner of that great Yorkshire fast bowler, Fred Trueman, before sending it skimming, effortlessly across the grey-green expanse of water. I was watching Tom, Joe and Paul carrying out the same ritual when I felt a hand on my shoulder. It was Don, asking for the bag he'd given me to carry that morning. Throughout the journey there had been something strangely fascinating about watching Don rummaging around in his mysterious bags. We never quite knew what was going to emerge. I took off my pack and struggled to extract the weighty Tesco bag, which I handed to him, once again wondering what on earth it contained. Don's last surprise was soon revealing itself from the deepest recesses of the bag. It was a pebble, or more accurately, a rock the size of a grapefruit.

'I don't bloody believe it,' I said, 'look lads. Don enjoyed Grike so much, he's brought most of it with him. And the cheeky sod's had me carrying it for him all day.'

Undeterred by the incredulous shaking of heads, he simply shrugged his shoulders:

'It's a symbolic moment,' he said. 'There's no point in fannying about. Got to have something that makes a splash.'

'Well it will certainly make one of those Don,' I said. 'Go on then.'

With what seemed an enormous effort, he hurled the missile seaward and I wondered whether Air Traffic Control should have been notified so that they could have warned aircraft in the area of the danger. Its flight path was unusual. If anything it went upwards rather than forwards, then seemed to hang in the air, as if debating what direction to take next, before plummeting earthwards and landing no more than two yards in front of him! It did make an almighty splash though.

'Fuckin' hell, Don. I'm soaked,' spluttered Tom, who was nearest the point of splashdown. As always, Don was oblivious to Tom's discomfort.

'There,' he said, a satisfied smile on his face. 'Job done.'

Wainwright's rituals completed, we now had a third and final formality to perform and made our way back up the slipway to the first building on dry land, the Bay Hotel, where we were determined to become, if not Robin Hood's merry men, then Robin Hood's Bay's very merry men. Wainwright referred to the Baytown Hotel in his book, but it appears it has never been called that. It was an easy mistake for him to make. Perhaps he celebrated too much.

The final ritual was the signing of the Coast to Coast book. This is something of which Wainwright was unaware, as the landlord of the Bay Hotel introduced the book in 1991, the very year that the great man passed away. At the time, the landlord clearly saw an opportunity to cash in on the Coast to Coast phenomenon and, by giving walkers the chance to record their feat for posterity, he could entice them inside where, undoubtedly, they would not be able to resist the opportunity to have a celebratory drink – or two. So many people are doing the walk now that it takes less than a year to fill each volume, even though the existence of the book is not known by all who complete the walk. The current landlady keeps all the completed volumes, although a couple have been mislaid. For those who completed the trek in 1993 and 1994, the evidence is no longer available.

This written record has no official title and the bar staff know it only as 'The Book'. Somehow, this seems to emphasise the importance and mystery of the tome.

'I'd like to sign The Book please' prompts a frantic search of the premises to trace the spot where the last signatory left it. Anywhere else, the question would be met with a 'what book?', but not here.

The current landlady reinforced the Coast to Coast connection by renaming the public bar 'Wainwright's Bar' when she took over a few years ago. Before signing the book, there is a compulsion to read the recent entries and, once again, it is astonishing to see how many Americans and Australians do this walk. The comments range between the pithy *that Wainwright is a bad man*, the brief *wonderful*, the long-winded *weather disappointing but enjoyed the scenery and the company although my feet ache and I'm not sure I would do it again*, the glass half full *had a wonderful time despite the awful weather*, the glass half empty *the weather spoilt it*, the moaning *doesn't it ever stop raining up here?*, the comic *doesn't Wainwright know I've only got short legs?* – there's enough material here for me to write a book!

By the time I got hold of the book, the others had made their entries. Tom's terse *tenth and last* was followed by super-fit Paul's *here's to the next time*. Don had decided that potential Coast to Coast walkers might appreciate his advice on achieving a successful outcome: *the secret is to travel light*, but Joe was typically straightforward: *great walk with great company*. It was hard to think of anything original, so I wrote what I really thought – *the best bit was all of it*.

As part of my training, I had abstained from drinking alcohol for a few weeks before, and during, the walk (with only the occasional lapse), but I was looking forward to a very large gin as the start of my warming down programme. Tom and Joe ordered large whiskies, and Don and Paul had pints. Trevor looked on enviously as we reminded him it was a long drive home. It was another moment to savour. Aside from us, the bar was empty and, for a moment the only sound we could hear was the screeching of gulls outside. For once it was Paul who broke the silence:

'Well, I have to say that was wonderful,' he smiled. 'I thoroughly enjoyed every minute. Thanks for organising it, Tom.'

'Yes, well done Tom,' Joe and I said, raising our glasses in our leader's direction. Don had been distracted by a map on the wall and was the last to join the toastmaking.

'Yes, thanks, Tom, I enjoyed it too,' he said, taking a slow, contemplative sip of his beer before adding, 'but I still think you should do it East to West next time.' Barely a day had passed without Don raising this subject at least once. And barely a day had passed without us bracing ourselves for Tom to explode. It was like waiting for Vesuvius to erupt. To his credit, however, he had steadfastly refused to rise to the bait. Why he had done this I really didn't know. But whatever heroic reserves of restraint he had been drawing on, it was soon clear that they had now finally run dry. Tom quietly placed his glass on the bar, signalled to the barman for a refill, straightened himself up and fixed Don with a glare.

'Look Don, first off, there isn't going to be a next time. This was the tenth and last time for me. That's it. Finished. No more Coast to Coasts.' The rest of us tried very hard to keep straight faces, which became impossible when Trevor chirped:

'Ding ding, end of round one.'

'Second ... ' Tom continued

'Oops, just a minute, round two, ding ding,' Trevor interrupted.

' ... even if I was going to do it another ten times, I still wouldn't do it East to West,' he said, picking up his glass and gulping down his whisky in one and nodding to the barman for another. 'I might do it with my legs tied together or I might try it walking on my hands or I might even give it a go dressed as a butler or stark bollock naked, but I am NEVER going to do it East to West.'

Tom had never explained his aversion to the alternative route (although I had established that they seemed to have different recollections of their first crossings), but I had a feeling that at least part of it was bloody-mindedness in the face of Don's relentless exhortations. Most people would have thought Tom had made his position quite clear and that would have ended the conversation, but Don's tendency to continue to fight a losing battle was never more evident.

'How do you know if you haven't tried it?' he countered 'you might enjoy it, you never know.' But this time Tom was having none of it.

'I do know Don, I do know,' Tom said, his scouse accent growing stronger by the second, 'and I know something else as well. You're starting to give me RSI.'

The grins were wiped from our faces as we all looked perplexed.

'RSI?' said Don, half mockingly. 'What do you mean? RSI. Repetitive Strain Injury? How do you work that out?' Tom once more drained his glass.

'I would have thought it was obvious,' he said, leaning closer to Don, 'you're being repetitive. I'm feeling the strain. And you're going to suffer an injury if you mention it again.'

As the laughter died away, I changed the subject before Don could say any more.

'Who fancies fish and chips?'

'Good idea Alan,' Tom said, placing his glass on the bar, pleased to get away from Don's persistent needling.

Joe joined us as we left the bar, leaving Don and Paul to finish their pints. We headed for a brightly painted cafe across the street, from where the irresistible smell of fish and chips was wafting in the sea breeze. Seagulls were wheeling overhead, waiting for the opportunity to swoop on any scraps dropped by the milling throng who wandered aimlessly from shop to shop, trying to decide whether to have ice cream before or after the candy floss.

'This place has a lot to answer for,' Tom commented as we approached the door, 'this is the chippy Andy went in and it caused us to do the Coast to Coast again in eight days. It nearly killed me. Still, there can't be any harm going in now – at least Andy isn't here.'

As we entered the shop, the proprietor, a ruddy-faced chap who looked like he enjoyed his fish and chips as much as the next man, astutely recognised his new bedraggled, bandaged customers as Coast to Coast walkers:

'Just finished the walk, have we?'

'Well, we have. I don't know about you,' I muttered under my breath.

'How long did it take you?'

'Twelve days this time,' Tom replied, his face now once more wreathed in a look of quiet, and justified, pride.

'This time? Do you mean you've done it before then?' the man asked, clearly impressed.

'Yes,' said Tom, pleased that the man had taken the bait and given him the opportunity to boast about his record breaking achievement, 'this was my tenth time.'

'That's incredible,' he said, clearly astonished that anyone would be daft enough to walk the breadth of the country once, let alone ten times, 'I've never heard of anyone doing it ten times before.' Tom seemed to grow a couple of inches, but still couldn't see over the counter to trace the source of a disembodied female voice which suddenly piped up from somewhere behind it:

'I have. There was a man in here the other day and he'd done it eleven times.' A young girl's head appeared over the counter and she smiled sweetly. Although Tom's head can still be turned by a pretty face, he was not best pleased with the bearer of this news. She could not have known that the real cause of Tom's wrath was the thought of having to do the walk twice more in order to beat the record set by this mystery chip-eating marathon man. Seeing the look on his face, she thought she should placate him and said the first thing that came into her head:

'Mind you, he was much younger than you.'

'That makes it worse,' he sighed, resigning himself to the fact that a younger man would be able to keep setting new, and impossible, targets.

'I didn't mean to upset you,' she said, now trying to boost Tom's spirits again. Ever the opportunist, he saw this as a chance to chat up an attractive young girl who was set on appeasing him:

'It's all right, you haven't really upset me,' he said.

'Oh, good,' she replied, 'because I think what you've done is inspirational to others .... I can't wait to tell my granddad.'

Tom's hopes and dreams were dashed and he seemed to shrink as the sparkle that had kindled in his eyes a few moments before was extinguished, but the final blow was about to be delivered, albeit unwittingly:

'To do it ten times is just amazing. But, why don't you do it again? I hear it's even better if you do it East to West.'

A few moments later we stepped out into the street and found an empty bench with a rather pleasing view of the beach below us, where we could sit and eat, but Tom seemed to have lost his appetite, which was good news for the gulls as they feasted on the chips he threw to them with distracted regularity.

'Why did she have to go and spoil it all?' Tom mumbled, 'She seemed such a nice ....'

It was the sight of Don emerging from the pub and walking towards us that cut him short. Don had his pack strapped to his back once more and seemed ready to make his way back up the hill to the car park.

'What are you three talking about?' he asked, 'you look as though you're plotting something.'

'Oh, nothing,' Tom said. 'We're just enjoying our fish and chips.'

'They look good. I might get some.'

'They're not that good,' Tom said, a little desperately, thinking that the girl in the chippy might repeat her thoughtless remark and give Don fresh ammunition for his long-running guerrilla campaign, 'you might be better going to that pizza place up the street.'

'No, I fancy fish and chips,' Don persisted.

'I think he was just closing after he served us,' Tom tried.

'It looks as though he's still serving. I'll go and see.' It was clear that Don was not going to give up, so Tom had to explain more plainly.

'Listen Don, I'm telling you, whatever you do, don't go in that fucking chippy.'

CHAPTER TWENTY-ONE

HOME AGAIN

Having one fewer passengers to carry home, Trevor had hired a people carrier which was splendid compared to the minibus in which we had travelled to St Bees twelve days earlier. Following the unwanted detour to Grosmont to collect parcels and belongings, we were soon on our way home and, although Trevor seemed eager to complete the journey in record time, we all nodded off on the journey (with the exception of Trevor, I hasten to add) or, as Trevor impolitely told us when we woke up, 'you've all been catching flies.'

I reflected on the events of the last twelve days as we sped along and it dawned on me that I had completed a major walk without too much difficulty and without sustaining any injury. I realised that doing the Coast to Coast Walk successfully is as much about mental strength as physical ability. It is about believing that you can do it and this is why it seems to become easier as the days go by. Once you have walked for seven or eight hours a day for five or six consecutive days, your brain knows you can do it and tells your body there's nothing to it. Oh, how I wished I had done something like this thirty or forty years sooner. It would have given me so much more confidence.

As the car drew up at Tom's and we began to gather our things together, Don had a proposition for me:

'I'm thinking of crossing the Pyrenees by elephant next year – are you interested in coming?'

'I don't think so, Don,' I said, trying to let him down gently.

'They have de luxe models now, you know. Heated seats, extra padding, anti-roll bars, satellite navigation, the lot,' he persisted.

'Sounds good, Don, but I don't think it's for me,' I replied, and I'm sure I heard my Grandma's voice coming from somewhere up above:

'He's not as daft as he looks, you know.'

'Thanks for the advice, Alan,' Joe said, as we shook hands, 'I'm going to have a long chat to my lady friend when I get home. I can see that I've been very selfish and haven't given her feelings a thought. Thanks again.'

After a terrific twelve days together, it was apparent that we had grown very close and it seemed very strange that, after the briefest of goodbyes, each of us jumped into our cars to make our separate ways home. Although the three of us who had not reached retirement had to be back at work next morning, it still seemed odd to part in such a way. We had enjoyed a great time together in wonderful weather, apart from the one day of rain, and now all we had to look forward to was the next time. Oh, I'm forgetting. There won't be a next time, will there Tom?

CHAPTER TWENTY-TWO

ENGLAND'S GREEN AND PLEASANT LAND

Since Alfred Wainwright devised the Coast to Coast Walk over thirty years ago, many thousands have followed in his footsteps across this beautiful country of ours. What is truly amazing is that, on this small, over-populated island, here is a walk which avoids crowds and main centres of population. On several days, walkers do not pass through any towns, villages or even hamlets, and it is possible to walk for hours on end without seeing another human being. If you like the countryside and enjoy walking, this walk is a must for your 'things to do before I die' list.

The great thing about walking is that almost anyone can do it. It is not restricted by class or age or anything else really. This is apparent from Country Walking magazine which features regular columns from such diverse characters as Lord (Chris) Smith and Stuart Maconie, the latter being a Radio 2 disc jockey, or do they call them radio 'presenters' these days? Whatever, neither DJ nor presenter adequately describes the job. A non-English speaker translating from a dictionary might deduce that a disc jockey is someone who rides a horse round a flat thin circular object and a presenter is someone who donates gifts.

'I play records and CDs on the radio and, in between, I talk about anything that comes into my head really, although sometimes I have to interview celebrities, usually because they want to publicise their latest record or film or whatever and I have to pretend I'm interested.' Well, I can see why it is easier to say 'I'm a DJ'.

Interestingly (for me at least), Mr Maconie's column in early 2005 described his New Year resolutions which included doing the Coast to Coast Walk and climbing Jack's Rake. Although I know very little about Mr Maconie, I know that we have a number of things in common, the main one being a love of the Lake District. Being a native of Wigan, only twenty miles from my own home town of Southport, he is a fellow Lancastrian. Perhaps his love of the Lakes is influenced ever so slightly by the fact that the southern part of the Lake District was in our home county of Lancashire until 1974, when Cumbria was formed from the old counties of Cumberland and Westmorland, the northern bit of Lancashire and a bit of Yorkshire. The photograph accompanying his column suggests that he may not be old enough to remember that but the relevant point is that he loves the Lakes and the walking.

His resolutions aroused my attention because one of them had already been crossed off my own 'to do' list, although only fairly recently. Jack's Rake is a route to the summit of Pavey Ark, one of the well-known Langdale Pikes in the Lake District, and is very definitely a climb, rather than a walk. Walkers ascending from New Dungeon Ghyll view the sheer rock face of Pavey Ark across the waters of Stickle Tarn, and an impressive sight it is. It is a fearsome precipice and one which only a madman would attempt to scale. As young Stuart wrote in 2005, 'this really is the year that I will climb Jack's Rake. Every time I find myself at Stickle Tarn, it leers down at me condescendingly with its jagged scar of a smile. I've spent many a happy afternoon … gazing up at the tiny figures ascending the rake, moving at an agonisingly slow pace along the defile, clearly in the grips of paroxysms of anxiety and self-doubt. While I find this as hugely enjoyable as the next man, I am nagged by the fact that it really should be me up there proving my alpha male credentials.'

Like young Stuart, I had often gazed across at the precipice and thought I should attempt the ascent of Jack's Rake, but had always opted for one of the easier routes. That is until the day I walked up to Stickle Tarn with my old pal, Tom. He would have been sixty-five or sixty-six at the time, so I would have been about fifty-six.

'Now, we've got three options here,' I said, as we took in the view across the tarn, 'we can take the path up to the left to the saddle between Harrison Stickle and Pavey Ark, or we can go to the right and work our way round and come up Pavey Ark from the other side, or we can take Jack's Rake up the cliff face.'

I should have known better!

'Yeah, yeah,' he replied almost before I had 'rake' out of my mouth. Like me, this would be a first for him as well. We made our way round the tarn and, ten minutes later, stood at the foot of the rake peering up the rock face. Rock climbers will scoff at Jack's Rake, being the easiest of climbs and not even requiring ropes, but Wainwright's description pointed out that 'as a WALK it is both *difficult* and *awkward*: in fact, for much of the way the body is propelled forwards by a series of convulsions unrelated to normal walking, the knees and elbows contributing as much to progress as hands and feet. Walkers who can still put their toes in their mouths and bring their knees up to their chins may embark upon the ascent confidently; others, unable to perform these tests, will find the route arduous.' I think I can say with some confidence that it had been many a year since either of us had put our toes in our mouths, but do you think we were going to turn back now?

It was at this point that I remembered reading an old guide book which cautioned walkers that Jack's Rake was for climbers only and should be avoided by walkers at all costs. I seemed to recall that the warning concluded with the words 'especially by two old farts on a wintry February day' but this could have been just my imagination.

Just before we reached the foot of the cliff, a young couple set off up the rake with climbing ropes slung over their shoulders and, as we stood awaiting the right moment to begin our own ascent, were surprised to see them come down again after ascending only about thirty feet. They explained that they had already completed one climb that day and had decided against tackling another. Perhaps this was their very oblique way of avoiding discouraging us, thinking that saying 'it looks too tough for us' would have caused us to abort. As if!

Eventually, we set off and enjoyed an exhilarating forty-five minute climb to the summit, with wonderful views as we stopped from time to time to look down. Despite the warnings, it proved to be far less difficult than the guide books had led us to believe, although there were one or two tricky bits. In fact, I enjoyed it so much, I did it again the following year!

I cannot recall any of Mr Maconie's subsequent articles confirming that he kept his 2005 resolutions but, if you haven't yet been up Jack's Rake, Mr M, I urge you to do it soon. After the first time, you'll be up and down there on a regular basis, I'm sure.

As for the Coast to Coast Walk, I will be very disappointed if I learn that this resolution was not kept. It is an absolute must for any walker.

Strangely, perhaps, although the Lake District is the most rugged section and where no human habitation is passed on most days, this is also the busiest in terms of the number of people out walking. Paradoxically, it is also where walkers are most likely to go astray, as a result of the plethora of paths within the National Park and the absence of signs within its boundaries. Certainly, this is where map and compass and, possibly, GPS have to be carried. There is a strange phenomenon on the fells of the Lake District. In reasonable weather, it is unusual to walk for more than an hour or so without seeing other walkers but, if the weather changes and the rain starts to fall, all other walkers seem to disappear. Where do they go?

Once through the Lake District, most walkers should find that they can manage with a good guide book, even though other walkers will be few and far between. Indeed, in my experience, it is rare to see anyone other than fellow Coast to Coasters and, as most of those are travelling in the same direction, the only time you see them is when either they or you stop for a break.

It is clear that this great adventure is becoming more and

more popular, not only with British people, but also with foreign visitors. There seem to be a great many American, Australian and Dutch walkers undertaking the trek, and we met one German couple on our recent exploit. So, the word is travelling far and wide. Most of the visitors have told me that they learned about the Coast to Coast by word of mouth, but I have heard that it is on a website somewhere which lists the ten best walks in the world. I know that readers of Country Walking magazine voted it the second best walk in the world (behind New Zealand's Milford Track), but this may not be representative, being a British magazine. Whatever, it is now an extremely popular walk.

Popularity brings its own problems though and, in this case, accommodation is going to prove more and more difficult to find. Camping is one answer and provides plenty of flexibility, but the big downside is having to carry so much weight on the back, particularly in very hot or in very poor weather. With the recent warm summers, almost all the campers I met were struggling in the extreme heat and, I imagine, it would be just as hard in wet and windy weather.

Youth hostellers will find it increasingly difficult to take advantage of their membership with the closure of the hostels at Kirkby Stephen and Keld and this will put even more pressure on the B&Bs along the route. What we are likely to see are more B&Bs away from the route either offering to pick up guests and return them the following day, or arranging taxis at guests expense. Foreign visitors will, no doubt, book early and the agents, such as the Coast to Coast Packhorse, will take many of the beds available, so there will be increasing difficulty booking suitable accommodation.

The Coast to Coast Walk is a wonderful experience, so my advice is *don't delay, do it now,* before Tom decides to do it again with a gang of over-seventies, taking up all the available beds. Oh, and don't forget to eat plenty of pasties.